the growing business handbook

We may be in the
business of numbers...

Institute of Customer Service

be the best!

be a customer service leader

join us to:
- improve your service delivery
- gain competitive advantage

ICS is the professional body for customer service

- helping people achieve customer service
  professionalism
- supporting CPD in customer service
- developing organisations through key
  assessment tools
- defining the National Occupational Standards
  for Customer Service

**our community of members is drawn from across
the private, public and voluntary sectors.**

to join us:
visit: **instituteofcustomerservice.com**
email: **enquiries@icsmail.co.uk**
or call: **+44 (0) 1206 571716**

ICS | Institute of
Customer Servic

the growing business handbook

9th edition

inspiration & advice from successful
entrepreneurs & fast growing uk companies

consultant editor: adam jolly

RECOMMENDED BY
INSTITUTE OF DIRECTORS

KOGAN
PAGE

London and Philadelphia

This book has been endorsed by the Institute of Directors.

The endorsement is given to selected Kogan Page books which the IoD recognises as being of specific interest to its members and providing them with up-to-date, informative and practical resources for creating business success. Kogan Page books endorsed by the IoD represent the most authoritative guidance available on a wide range of subjects including management, finance, marketing, training and HR.

The views expressed in this book are those of the author and are not necessarily the same as those of the Institute of Directors.

Publisher's note

Every possible effort has been made to ensure that the information contained in this book is accurate at the time of going to press, and the publishers and authors cannot accept responsibility for any errors or omissions, however caused. No responsibility for loss or damage occasioned to any person acting, or refraining from action, as a result of the material in this publication can be accepted by the editor, the publisher or any of the authors.

First published by Kogan Page in 1997 as *CBI Growing Business Handbook*
Second edition 1999
Third edition 2000
Fourth edition published in 2001 as *IOD Growing Business Handbook*
Fifth edition 2002
Sixth edition 2003
Seventh edition published in 2004 as *The Growing Business Handbook*
Eighth edition 2006
Ninth edition 2007

120 Pentonville Road
London N1 9JN
United Kingdom
www.kogan-page.co.uk

525 South 4th Street, #241
Philadelphia PA 19147
USA

ISBN-10   0 7494 4807 5
ISBN-13   978 0 7494 4807 3

British Library Cataloguing-in-Publication Data

A CIP record for this book is available from the British Library.

Library of Congress Cataloging-in-Publication Data

The growing business handbook / [editor] Adam Jolly.
       p. cm.
  ISBN 0-7494-4807-5
  1. Success in business. 2. Management. I. Jolly, Adam.
  HF5386.G787 2006b
  658–dc22
                                    2006026475

Typeset by JS Typesetting Ltd, Porthcawl, Mid Glamorgan
Printed and bound in Great Britain by Cambridge University Press

Software...

are you managing the risk?

27%* of software in the UK is being used illegally.

Do you know what software is installed in your organisation?

Do you have sufficient software licences? - if not, your organisation is at risk.

If anyone in your organisation is caught using under licensed or pirated software your company Directors are liable and they could face unlimited fines or prison sentences.
FAST Corporate Services can help you manage that risk.
Our software compliance programme educates and advises you on how to achieve excellence in software and IT management.

The FAST Standard for Software Compliance FSSC-1:2004, a private standard developed in collaboration with BSI, is the essential first step on the path to a legal IT environment. Registration to the FAST Standard helps:

- identify and eliminate the risks relating to software management
- maximise your software and hardware investment
- set up purchasing and installation procedures and educate staff

Find out how many organisations have benefited from the FAST Programme by visiting the case studies section on www.fastcorporateservices.com. Alternatively for more information call 01628 622121

Corporate Services

Conference Link – An Imperial Solution to Affordable Conferencing

It is acknowledged that Imperial College London is a world-class university, leading in the fields of science, technology and medicine. It is, perhaps, less well known that it is **London's premier academic venue** for conferences and events.

In order to uphold this reputation, Imperial continually invests in its infrastructure to ensure that its students have the best possible environment in which to live and learn. Imperial is able to offer the use of these amenities for conferences, training days and seminars, when they are not being used for academic purposes. More importantly, the College is able to provide a professional service, thanks to its Conference Office – Conference Link – at a fraction of the cost associated with purpose-built commercial venues in London.

Imperial's main South Kensington campus offers over 200 meeting and seminar rooms, 40 lecture theatres and extensive exhibition areas at evenings and weekends during term time. These are also available during business hours throughout the summer vacation period, providing a range of affordable options in which to hold your event. Imperial's offering is made all the more appealing with attractions such as the Royal Albert Hall, Harrods and the Science, Natural History and Victoria & Albert Museums on its doorstep, enabling your delegates to explore some of London's famous landmarks during their visit.

Strategy meetings and staff training days are easily arranged through Imperial's range of Day Delegate and Evening Meeting Room Rates. These packages include room hire, writing materials, bottled water, servings of coffee and tea, a variety of catering options, and in-situ audio-visual equipment – all at very reasonable rates.

Imperial can also accommodate residential conferences or workshops during the summer vacation.

Beit Hall, one of Imperial's most historic buildings, boasts 3 VisitBritain campus stars and offers 210 twin/single en-suite bedrooms and 52 single bedrooms with shared bathroom facilities.

Conference Link's 24 Hour Delegate Rate includes the same features as their Day Delegate Rate together with bed, Full English Breakfast and dinner. Residential Delegates are welcome to use on-site amenities such as Imperial's brand new Sports Centre, Ethos, re-landscaped Prince's Gardens, plus other facilities such as the College's concierge service, bank, bureau de change, restaurants and bars.

Alternatively, if you are looking for affordable accommodation that is of a slightly superior standard to student style accommodation Conference Link's Hotel Booking Service can provide you with discounted rates of up to 35% at a selection of 3,4 and 5 star hotels in the capital.

Furthermore, Conference Link offers a variety of services that distinguish it from many other university conference providers. These include taxi transfers to and from Central London, private tours of the Victoria & Albert museum, private flights on the London Eye, dinner-dance cruises along the Thames plus West End theatre and restaurant bookings – all at economical prices.

To make an enquiry, and to obtain a 5% discount on our Day Delegate Package, please call **020 7594 9494** quoting reference **IOD07** or email **conferencelink@imperial.ac.uk**

Alternatively, please visit **www.imperial-conferencelink.com** for further information

Contents

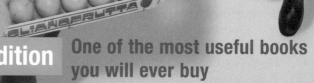

HONG KONG INTERNATIONAL AIRPORT

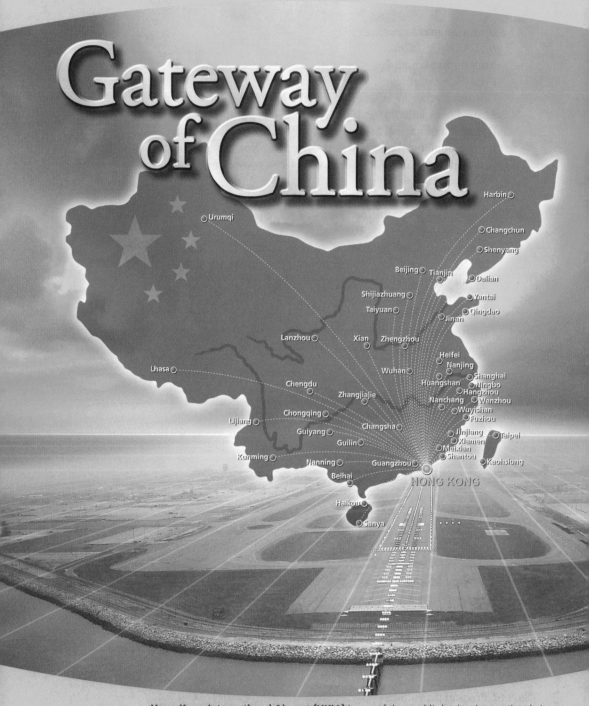

Gateway of China

Hong Kong International Airport (HKIA) is one of the world's busiest international airports - some 80 airlines operate more than 5,200 flights every week to over 145 destinations worldwide, including 45 cities in the Mainland of China. With half of the world's population within 5 hours' flying time from Hong Kong, HKIA is indeed a prominent aviation hub for the region and the gateway of China.

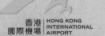

香港 HONG KONG
國際機場 INTERNATIONAL AIRPORT

AIRPORT AUTHORITY HONG KONG
1 CHEONG YIP ROAD, HONG KONG INTERNATIONAL AIRPORT, LANTAU, HONG KONG
TELEPHONE (852) 2188 7111 FACSIMILE (852) 2824 0717 WEBSITE WWW.HONGKONGAIRPORT.COM

daydream believer?

What should you expect from your accountants?

When looking for the firm that's right for you, you may start with the basics. But someone to look after your essential accountancy and audit work doesn't narrow the field too much. You'll want to dig deeper.

Business planning and advice, tax efficient strategies for you and your business, guidance on corporate finance issues – Menzies is trusted by hundreds of businesses right across the South East to provide all this and much more besides.

Wherever your ambitions lie, friendly expertise and a knack of turning dreams into reality is just a phone call away.

To find out more, call Mike Grayer,
Head of Corporate Finance, on:

01784 497100

or visit www.menzies.co.uk

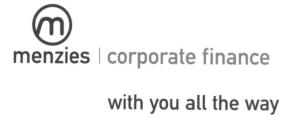

menzies | corporate finance

with you all the way

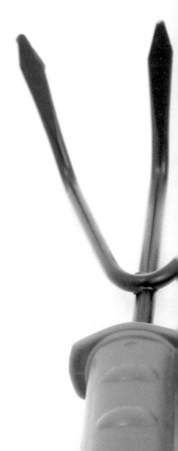

The Business Transition Specialists

How much is your business worth?

What are the components of your business that drive value? Is it assets that you can touch and feel or is it the systems, processes, people and activities of the business that provide real value. We'll help you unlock the value you've created. You will see the buyer's side clearly in order to gain an appreciation of how to position your business for its sale.

What is the 6 step process?

1. What do you want to achieve from the exit? What are your objectives?
2. What is the personal and family situation and what are the transition planning issues?
3. Where is the business at today and what does it take to reach its potential?
4. What is the desired transition plan to meet your objectives
5. What is the plan for transitioning the business?
6. How do we manage the sale or transfer of the business?

ROCG MOHAN CONSULTING specializes in working with privately owned businesses to improve their performance by replacing assumptions and gut-feelings with fact-based research, and expert analysis. We bring you the advantage of our local knowledge and expertise combined with the experience of hundreds of qualified consultants in our offices around the world, and the benefits of their expertise in every type of industry or engagement.

Transition planning is part of our commitment to providing our clients with complete business solutions. Your personal and business needs are intertwined, so your transition plan requires an integrated approach.

We can help simplify a complex process by providing a structured business transition process. And, while the process is methodical, the application is personal. Your plan will be fully customized to meet your unique circumstances and objectives.

1st Floor,Suite 5
The Avenue ,Beacon Ct .
Sandyford, Dublin 18

Telephone: (01) 2135910
Fax: (01) 2135911
Email: cormac.mohan@rocg.com

Time enough
Traa-dy-lioor...

The Isle of Man
Freedom to *flourish*

Isle of Man
Government
Reiltys Ellan Vannin

For further information:

[t] +44(0) 1624 687179
[e] development@gov.im
[w] www.gov.im/dti

With clean air, beautiful scenery and small, friendly communities, residents on the Isle of Man enjoy an enviable quality of life.

The crime rate is low and the schools are first rate (one private school offers the International Baccalaureate). Commuting is also trouble free because traffic jams are a novelty.

Locally produced food is of the highest standard - Manx meat and cheeses consistently win international awards - and the shopping is diverse, with a mix of local and UK high street names.

The Island lifestyle gives you time enough to get out and enjoy a lively arts and cultural scene, or a range of sporting activities on land and sea. If walking is your thing, there is plenty to enjoy - from moors to coastlines to glens.

All in all the Isle of Man provides everything you need to give you, and your loved ones, the freedom to flourish.

Dti   Department of Trade & Industry

Energy and Environmental Technologies

Middle of the UK? Absolutely.
Middle of the Road? Definitely not.

Wind power | Fuel cell technology | Tyre recycling | Sustainable construction | Water treatment
Centrifugal technology for waste treatment | PCB waste management | Rainwater harvesting
Biomass power | Anaerobic and biogas technology | Renewable energy growers
Resources monitoring | Methane energy generation

Here in North Nottinghamshire and North Derbyshire we are anything but middle of the road. The North Midlands is becoming recognised as one of the leading areas of the UK for the energy and environmental technology sectors.

If you are looking for bespoke property options, a quality of life, a central location and a large employee base, why not come and see what the area has to offer. We are already home to some of the UK's best businesss performers – we'd like you to join them.

If you are looking to relocate, set up a new operation or expand your business, please contact us and let us welcome you to the North Midlands.

Tel: **01623 811223**
Email: enquiries@alliancenorthmidlands.co.uk
www.alliancenorthmidlands.co.uk

Alliance
NORTH MIDLANDS
energy industry connectivity

CACTUS
EVENT SERVICES LTD

Event branding

Design & print

Project management

Consultancy

Equipment sales & hire

Exhibitor services

tel: 020 7924 3002
www.cactusevents.com

One day you will want to sell of your business – how will you succeed?

Some of us pass our businesses to our children, some are bought out by our partners or staff and some of us receive offers we cannot refuse from unexpected quarters. But most of us will sell our businesses to a third party. How do we ensure that our businesses will be attractive to prospective purchasers? SPS Director Mike Robson explains:

Prospective purchasers will critically assess your business, paying particular attention to their ability to successfully operate and develop the business without you and, in many cases, the ease with which they can integrate your business with their existing operations. Amongst other things they will assess the extent to which your business can respond quickly and effectively to your market and the strength of second tier management.

In preparing your business for sale you should be able to identify the attributes of your business that will be appealing to external investors and those that will be unappealing. You can then develop the positive and mitigate the negative attributes so as to create a business that is attractive to investors, leading to a quicker sale and a higher transaction price. This takes time. The earlier you start the more likely you are to succeed.

How can SPS help? We are a nationwide partnership of experienced business mentors actively helping business owners to build value in their companies. Many of us have owned and successfully sold our own businesses. We can help you do two things:

- Build value in your business prior to sale.
- Help you to make your business more attractive to potential investors.

Contact Mike Robson for a checklist of the areas you should consider
when developing your business for sale on **08456 581185**
or at **mike.robson@strategicplanningsolutions.co.uk**

I want my business to be a success

Business Link for London can help you make it happen

Successful businesses don't happen by chance. That's why Business Link for London does all it can to help small and medium sized businesses succeed. Whether you're just starting up or are already an established business, we'll give you instant access to the largest resource network around – plus ongoing advice and support from experienced Business Link advisers.

And because we're not out to make a profit, our help is affordable and impartial.

To find out more, call 0845 6000 787

www.businesslink4london.com

Then you're talking to the right people

Business Link

Business Link

About Business Link for London

If you're running your own business, or thinking about starting one, getting the right business advice at the right time can give you a real edge. That's where Business Link for London can help.

Every year we help thousands of businesses in London by delivering practical and tailored business support services face-to-face, over the phone, at events and via the web. We can help you on every aspect of running a business from cash flow and IT to staff development and finding new customers.

Our services include:
A Free Business Review offering a free independent and comprehensive overview of your business designed to help you talk through your issues, stimulate business change and improvement and point you to the right solutions for your business.

Business Support 24/7 through **www.businesslink4london.com** offering a rich source of expert and impartial information on a wide range of business issues and also register to our fortnightly email newsletter featuring the latest news, information, advice and events for businesses in London.

Events including interactive workshops and monthly networking events to assist you in developing your own skills and to help you build your business.

Whatever, your business needs, Business Link for London has the answers. And with access to the largest network of business contacts in the Capital, you'll have the right people helping you every time. Simply call 0845 6000 787 or visit www.businesslink4london.com

advertisement feature

A SMART PLAYER

...at the core

of your business

NIIT SmartServe... Your Indian Partner for Business Process Outsourcing (BPO)...

- → Back Office Administration
- → Life and Pensions Processing
- → Market Surveys and Database Updating
- → Customer Service
- → Call Centre – Inbound and Outbound
- → Technical Helpdesk
- → Compliance Services
- → Airline Ticketing and Change Requests
- → Telesales and Response Handling

BEST CONTACT CENTER-2006 IN APAC*

We deliver

- → Highly skilled manpower and quick ramp ups ensured by the training heritage of NIIT

- → Improved service levels and turnaround times, high quality and productivity

- → Customised solutions

- → Great pricing

*Awarded by Contactcenterworld.com during the BEST of BEST APAC Awards 2006

For more details, visit www.niitsmartserve.com or www.niit.com
Contact Rajiv Dey at rajiv.dey@niit.co.uk Tel: 01494 539 333

UK: NIIT Technologies Ltd, Westfields, London Road, High Wycombe Bucks, HP11 1HP, UK. Tel: +44 (0) 1494 539 333, Fax: +44 (0) 1494 539 444
USA: NIIT Technologies Ltd, 1050 Crown Pointe Parkway, Floor 5, Atlanta, GA 30338, Tel: +1(770) 551 9494, Toll Free: +1(888) 454 NIIT, Fax: +1(770) 551 9229
India: 223-224, Udyog Vihar, Ph-I, Gurgaon (Haryana)-122002, India. Tel: +91 124 4002702, Fax: +91 124 4002701

niit smart serve
—trust us to find the way—

MWIPL/09/06

SUCCESSION OR TRANSITION PLANNING – POSITIONING YOUR BUSINESS FOR SALE

Fundamentals of Selling A Business – Preparation

Business owners invest much time and effort into their businesses, and most arrive at the hard decision to sell their businesses at some point in time. There are various reasons for selling a business, and although each circumstance is unique as we have most owners have similar incentives and concerns.

It is an emotional and difficult process, and the most advantageous deal is achieved by understanding the steps and factors that determine the optimum time to sell in a structured and clinical fashion.ROCG'S unique methodology covers this in its planning phase in great depth.

However I would like to share with you some key pointers in positioning your business for Sale after the decision has been reached to let go.

Introduction:

After the decision to sell has been made, there are a number of preparatory measures that make a company more appealing to potential buyers, and they may take from one to three years to implement as outlined on our ROCG methodology.

The sale memorandum is likely to be the most important piece of advertising in the sales process. It will often be the first information on the company to be reviewed by potential purchasers. The Sales information memorandum should be tailored to meet the circumstances of the transaction, making it attractive for a potential buyer.

The key to successful presentation of a business for sale is to convince the acquirer to assess its full value. Without spelling out the valuation calculations themselves in the memorandum, we as ROCG consultants ensure our clients will provide sufficient information, in a clear and organised manner, for the reader to draw the intended conclusion with minimum effort. Above all, a sales memorandum must be consistent and must not beg questions.

Sales memorandum should be addressed only to those parties who are to complete/have completed the confidentiality agreement.Confidentiality agreements should always be executed with potential purchasers.The key is to have as short a sale process as possible in order to limit the inevitable leaks.

Strategic Positioning:

A bidder's 'gut feeling' for the business is a crucially important piece in the valuation jigsaw. Potential acquirers will always be sceptics and almost nothing influences a gut feeling in a more negative way than concerns that the information provided is not the complete picture.

Against this, however, the key for our clients as vendors is not to let out any more commercially sensitive information than necessary. The balance between providing sufficient information to value fully and as little sensitive information as possible to anybody other than the eventual purchaser will dictate how much information is contained in the sale memorandum and how much will be selectively released later in the process. This is a key ingredient and we as ROCG consultants do not underestimate the skillet required at this stage of the process.

Pre cursor to the Valuation:

The core of the valuation will be past and projected financial performance highlighted in the memorandum. These figures must be supported by a description of the company's commercial performance and future .

This is a key input for ROCG Consultants both as facilitators and preparers to ensure each step is properly monitored and that the appropriate quality checks are in place in order to give the whole process integrity and credibility.

The Sales **information memorandum should** be prepared which highlights the Key attractions of the business to potential buyers. Once identified, these attractions should be enhanced and the value proposition articulated.

Consistency and transparency are also the watchwords in addressing the reasons for the sale. The paradox of valuing highly something which you plan to sell must be addressed.

The mechanics of the expected transaction process should not be shrouded in any mystery.

***ROCG* MOHAN CONSULTING** specializes in working with privately owned businesses to improve their performance by replacing assumptions and gut-feelings with fact-based research, and expert analysis. We bring you the advantage of our local knowledge and expertise combined with the experience of hundreds of qualified consultants in our offices around the world, and the benefits of their expertise in every type of industry or engagement.

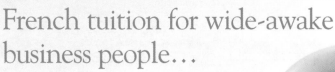

Active Vehicle Consultants Ltd (AVC) started trading early in 1998. The economic climate was not great at the time but the founder and Managing Director Mike Nevett thought that if he could start a company and maintain sales and growth during this period, the experience gained would prove extremely helpful in later years.

Mike's background was finance based, having worked for two major banks in the asset finance division. This sound grounding was to prove invaluable as Mike explains

"our client's needs have changed during the last few years. The competition is fierce, the growth of the internet has meant an abundance of choice which has meant that we have to become more sophisticated with the information and systems and how we deliver this to the market place. Running fleets of cars and vans is an expensive business and our clients need the right information on not only their existing fleet but moving forward with replacement etc. It is important, for example, to have sustainable prices with sustainable models coupled with the right funding methods."

AVC are able to offer independent advice on a range of vehicle funding options, such as contract hire, contract purchase, hire purchase and leasing. In addition, they are also able to offer fleet management services on behalf of larger clients. Their current client portfolio ranges from blue chip clients to smaller companies who run between 5-10 vehicles.

As Garry Evans, Sales Manager at AVC says "It is important for our clients to know that they can contact us and get a response straight away, not a remote call centre". As Garry explains "speed stuns! It is important, in an era where there is so much pressure on time, to build relationships and confidence and to offer consistent levels of service."

AVC also work closely with the accountancy profession "we find that accountants are often looking (on behalf of their clients) for ways to improve their client''s profitability and the running of their fleet is one obvious area where savings can often be made. By using a reputable company and not the first one from the internet, the accountant and their client know the type of service and response they will get from us".

Mike's philosophy on business matters is surprising "we are very loyal to our suppliers and tend to find that our clients are loyal to us. It is possibly a little old fashioned but I would rather use someone who was recommended or who we had previous experience with. We find our clients stay and grow with us."

AVC believe that business growth is a result of partnership, confidence and sustainability. AVC continue to grow based on the simple business ethics of offering sound advice and a level of competitiveness that only experience brings!

SPECIALISTS IN INSURANCE FOR GROWING BUSINESSES

Alexander Forbes Business Risk Solutions

For specialist advice call 0845 050 1450 or email afbrs@aforbes.co.uk

A partner in

eosrisq.com

Alexander For
INTERNATIONAL RISK SE
alexanderforbes.

The Royal Bank of Scotland

The Royal Bank of Scotland Group ("RBS Group") is one of the world's leading financial services companies. For the past four years RBS has consistently ranked in the top 10 global banks and within the top 3 in Europe. Operating in Europe, the US and Asia Pacific, RBS serves more than 36 million customers worldwide and employs more than 140,000 people.

Our local relationship managers provide access to the full range of financial solutions, supported by our teams of sector, regional and international specialists. So what ever your needs, the solution is always close at hand.

Our global capability and comprehensive product range allows us to offer considerable benefits to customers, however we believe our main strength to be our approach to structuring solutions.

We take time to fully understand a customer's business, to deliver comprehensive banking solutions, to assist businesses to develop and reach their true growth potential.

RBS can offer support through our comprehensive coverage of the UK and international relationships.

Through our network of partner and correspondent banks we can transact customer business with leading overseas banks, strongly established in their own countries that can deliver quality local banking services to our customers. This network also enables us to understand better the markets in which our customers operate; something we regard as fundamental.

In addition to the provision of a full range of banking services under The Royal Bank of Scotland and NatWest brands, RBS Group also includes Citizens Financial Group, Ulster Bank, Coutts Group, Direct Line and Churchill.

Bringing international solutions closer to home

Foreword

Taking a venture through a complete cycle of growth is a highly charged activity. The way in which each challenge is met and resolved holds the potential for creating or losing significant value.

No single formula for growth exists, but rigorous planning has to be combined with an acceptance that markets and organizations are highly exposed to change. Flexibility and adaptability must become the norm in anticipating the demands of customers whose expectations are being shaped by converging technologies and transparent global pricing.

Drawing on a wide range of professional expertise and commercial experience, this book gives a comprehensive insight into techniques and solutions for maximizing growth and controlling risks. With sections on marketing, funding, people, business technology, innovation, international expansion and property, it highlights potential new sources of value for enterprises to exploit. It also stresses that achieving high performance is inherently complex and elusive.

Costs can spiral out of control, cash can run short, customer service can flag, people can lose their way and innovative ideas can be copied. Many enterprises discover too late that the skills that served them well as start-ups are different from those required to capitalize fully on their potential. This edition of the *Growing Business Handbook* is designed as a practical guide for entrepreneurs and managers as they confront decisive points in the growth cycle in 2006 and 2007. All told there are over 60 expert contributions: the IoD and Kogan Page are grateful to them all for sharing their experience and knowledge so freely.

Miles Templeman
Director General
Institute of Directors

1

Planning for growth

Those that say starting up or growing a business is easy have never navigated through the quagmire of running a successful business. Last year 319,000 new businesses were set up in the UK. Recent research has shown that 18% of new businesses have failed in their first year, 40% in their second moving up to 50% in their third. However accessing good quality business support can significantly increase the chances of a business becoming a success.

Clients approach Prevista at various stages of development, as their businesses evolve and they need to confront decisive points in their growth cycle. Our business advisers draw upon years of direct, frontline experience across a wide range of industry sectors to support our client base of sole traders to companies of over two hundred employees. The majority are business owners or have managed businesses and therefore have an acute understanding of the issues which all businesses face when striving to increase profits, maintain their longevity and the evaluation of expansion, whether you are a sole-trader, limited company, a charity, social enterprise or a not for profit organisation.

Prevista is an independent London based consultancy which has been delivering quality business support and advice for over 10 years. During this time we have worked with over 14,000 small and medium sized businesses across London, in addition to providing over 500 mentoring agreements for early stage to high growth businesses. We employ a culturally diverse team of 50 employees and over 50 specialist associates from the public, private and community sectors.

The majority of our work is subsidised, as it is funded by the European Union, the London Development Agency and the Learning and Skills Council. As a result of this we offer a wide range of structured support programmes from business plan development, finance and money, marketing and sales, to improving business performance, human resource management and training courses for business owners and their staff.

Prevista so far has helped 4,808 individuals who were looking to start up their own businesses. Our experience tells us that the vital areas which need addressing at this stage in developing a business idea and turning it into a reality are:

- Researching the Product Offering and its Viability
- Product and Service Development
- Developing Marketing Strategies
- Developing Business Plans
- Accessing Sources of Funding
- Finding Suitable Premises

Our business advisers are adept at listening and responding accurately to our client's unique requirements and tailor their advice to our clients needs.

Once the business has started trading and become a start-up business, understanding and ensuring that the next level of business knowledge is imperative to its survival and financial longevity.

4,792 start-up businesses have been advised by Prevista in keeping them on route to economic development. Typical areas of support offered to arm our clients with the best tools in order to succeed are:

- Deciding the right Legal Status of the Company
- Finance and Money
- Record keeping and Accountancy relationships
- VAT and Taxation
- Promotion, Publicity and E-commerce
- Selling Skills
- Operational Plans, Tactics and Service Delivery
- Legal Obligations

One of Prevista's clients Quantum Metta (a school for those wanting to be practitioners of Thai Yoga, Hoslistic, Aromatherapy and Sports massage) found our support invaluable as they progress from a pre-start to a start-up business: "We were allocated a series of meetings with a business adviser from Prevista. At the start of our business we were guided to be very specific regarding our Business Plan and Marketing Strategy to ensure that we got off on the right foot. This got us to focus on exactly what our business was about and who our market was" explains Dympna O'Brien, the co-founder of Quantum Metta. "Since the start, we have looked at everything from legal requirements, financial considerations and marketing to website optimisation, publicity materials, database advice, networking and day-to-day procedures. From a promising start we have been able to expand our business to incorporate a much wider range of services. This happened more quickly and effectively because of the help we were given." Doreen Uzice, the other founder of Quantum Metta, continues. "As a business we have found that these meetings and the advice given have been invaluable. It was helpful to know that we would always get a very 'real' approach, which was practical, down-to-earth and tailor-made to our needs."

Like Quantum Metta, as a business continues on its growth cycle as a start-up business and looks towards its future longevity, it becomes apparent that the natural progression point has been reached. It is therefore necessary to evaluate your business position within your industry's market place. Whether you want to consolidate your business position or find avenues in which to allow your business to grow, in order to take your business onto the next stage planning is the priority to succeeding.

Prevista to date has worked with over 4,737 established businesses from small (2-9 employees) to the medium sized (10-249 employees) helping them look at moving towards further growth and development. Whether it be taking on staff or routes to further developing products and services.

Prevista has accumulated the know-how that enables us to offer the following types of advice and support to small businesses:

- Cash Flow and Debtor Control
- Access to Finance
- Customer Care Skills
- Management and Leadership Structure
- Line Management Mentoring as a Substitute for Non Executive Directors
- Owner/Managers as Employers
- Recruitment
- Legislation
- Equal Opportunities
- Health and Safety Responsibilities
- Quality Management

Prevista's business advisers are experienced at assisting the business owner in assessing the current strengths, weaknesses, threats and opportunities to the business and decide how well it is equipped to proceed onto its path of growth.

Medicspro is an example of a small business who wished to grow and utilise our business advice and support. It is one of only 40 NHS (PASA) approved businesses in the UK permitted to recruit and place GPs, doctors and locums in NHS hospitals. The business was started by Rajar Nathan who attended our next stage programme and has found our support extremely beneficial and profitable. Rajar stated: "Through the Gateway to Growth programme, we have been introduced to sources of finance that I was not aware of. We have also been introduced to other Prevista clients for networking purposes and received support on tendering including the key documentation needed. This programme has really addressed our key needs and helped us to grow and develop in our early stages.

As a part of the course we developed a Growth strategy that will take our business to a £4.5m turnover by 2007 and we have increased our staff. In addition we have started offering training support to their staff we place in the NHS and we are looking to start working towards Investor in People recognition!"

A successful business, throughout its development, needs to keep an eye on its bottom line. At the same time the owner/managing director needs to ensure that investment into the business itself is continuous. For example: a business with 10 employees looking to expand further will need to consider the best options for meeting these needs. This often includes whether to outsource, train up existing staff or alternatively take on new staff. This is a very important investment issue and a decision which cannot be taken lightly. People are the business' greatest asset, and the key to business success. To achieve this, people need the right knowledge, skills and motivation to work efficiently and productively. Our business advisers assist business owners/managing directors by taking an independent look at their workforce and are able to analyse the business as required, by reviewing, assessing our offering:

- Organisation Structure
- Appraisal
- Financial Forecasts and Budgets
- Investors in People Standard
- Project Management
- Innovation Strategy
- Change Management
- Training
- Training Brokerage

It is a well known fact that ensuring employees have the right skills to do the best job gives your businesses the competitive edge in the market place. Working closely with our experienced business advisers, we can provide quality, and often subsidised training for yourself and your employees. There are different types of training which you are able to access. Our business advisers gain a clear understanding of your business goals by working with you in carrying out a free review and analysis of your business to assess what skills your business has right now, and what it might need in the future. Our business advisers are specialists in training and have a proven track record of providing effective advice to businesses.

- Training BrokeraTogether you can:
- Identify the skills your business needs
- Pinpoint the right training
- Agree a tailored training package
- Find available funding

- Review the progress you are making

Examples of training courses available are:

- **Leadership Programmes**

  For the owners and directors of the company: Business planning and sales growth, managing risk and change, improving financial performance, getting best from your team.

- **Management Training**

  Supervisors/first line managers

  How to ensure effective processes, develop team motivation, how to handle resources effectively, how to deliver quality results.

- **Investors in People Standard**

  Getting ready for Investors in People recognition. A must for businesses wishing to be assessed this programme. This programme makes sure that you know what you need to do to be recognised.

- **Project Management**

  Beneficial for anyone includes: building a business case, developing project strategy, planning and estimating, scheduling and resourcing, health and safety, managing people, evaluation.

- **Customer Service**

  Different courses for front line staff and supervisors/managers.

  Includes everything from solving customer problems, creating positive impressions, how to effectively oversee a customer service team, how to spot weaknesses in current processes and improve them.

By investing in the development of your employees, your business is on the way to achieving a quality standard which is fast becoming highly regarded nationally and internationally. It could assist in making your company stand out from the rest and secure public contracts. Like all our training, Investors in People will improve the productivity and efficiency of your organisation. It can also help with staff retention, communication and greater marketing and sales opportunities. Prevista has a strong track record this area, having assisted more that 500 small to medium sized businesses.

Wherever your business is within the growth cycle; "about to start, just started or established", there is always an opportunity for growth. Successful businesses are those with owner/managing directors who are continually looking for ways to second guess the market trends, gain profit and invest in their commitment to the business. If you are interested in any of our services which we provide, please do not hesitate to contact us at **enquiries@prevista.co.uk** or telephone **020 7619 8300**.

Change the market

Karan Bilimoria, founder and chief executive of Cobra Beer, is always looking to turn threats into opportunities

Sixteen years ago, Cobra Beer was being trundled up and down London's Fulham Road by two graduates in the back of a £295 Citroën 2CV. Today it is on the way to becoming a global brand and has retail sales of £80m a year in 42 different countries.

Karan Bilimoria was one of those two graduates. In 1990 he had just completed a law degree at Cambridge, but to the consternation of his father, a general in the Indian army, he decided against a professional career to pursue an ambition to brew the best ever Indian beer.

His tastes had been moulded in the officer's mess of the Gurkhas and when he came to the United Kingdom as a 19-year-old student he went to Indian restaurants at least twice a week. The most popular drink on offer was lager beer, but Bilimoria found the lagers harsh, fizzy and bloating. 'They didn't accompany Indian food very well at all. People drank chilled lager because they felt like something cold and refreshing, but the quality wasn't right.'

A friend introduced him to real ale, which he loved, but the combination with Indian food did not work. On visits back to his family in India, the idea began to take hold that he would bring over his own lager beer from India, which would have all the refreshing qualities of a chilled lager but without all the gas.

Like most business ideas, it stemmed from a mix of passion and disappointment. 'It is pretty simple. You think, "I can do this product or service better." The difficulty is always making it happen. Ideally you want to change the marketplace into which you are going for ever.'

Bangalore

Bilimoria started the business on a fifty-fifty basis with a friend in late 1989. He had £20,000 in student debts and it was the start of a recession. 'We were lucky to have a mentor, my business partner's uncle. He was a retired businessman, who helped to guide us, motivate us, introduce us.

'I had never sold a bottle of beer in my life, let alone brewed one. We did a lot of research and really got to know the beer market well. In my mind, I knew exactly how I wanted our beer to taste.'

Bilimoria's mentor pointed them towards a brewery in Bangalore. 'We had a lot of luck in finding one of the best brewmasters in India, who had spent six years in the Czech Republic. To him, it was a challenge. "You want to produce the best ever Indian beer? Then let's do it." I worked with him at the brewery while my partner held the fort over here.'

Build credibility

Right from the start, Bilimoria's mission was to brew the finest-ever Indian beer and make it a global brand. 'Who was I to say this? I was a student in debt who knew nothing about brewing and was up against giants, some of whom had been around since the 14th century. Kingfisher had already been in the UK for eight years and 10 other Indian beers were trying to break into the market.

'The UK is the most competitive beer market in the world. Anyone can have a go, though nobody thought we had a chance. You face a real credibility gap. Nobody knows the product. Nobody knows the brand. So what makes anyone buy? You have to have complete confidence and faith in what you are selling. People have to be able to trust you to look after them.'

Indian restaurants

Cobra had two points in its favour. It found itself in a market with a thirst for lager: 50 years ago, lager accounted for 1 per cent of all the beer drunk; today, as tastes have become globalized, it stands at two-thirds.

The other plus for Cobra is the growth of Indian restaurants. 'They have become a way of life,' says Bilimoria, 44. 'People now go to Indian restaurants regardless of age or social standing. They are our base. Without their support, we would not be where we are today.

'If we can get people to discover our product in Indian restaurants, then eventually we can get our products sold in the supermarkets, which people will recognize as the lager that they drink with their curry. After that, we can think about getting it into the clubs and bars.'

Cobra is stocked by over 6,000 Indian restaurants, which continue to account for 50 per cent of sales, and is now carried by most major supermarkets and off-licences.

Take-off

For the first five years, business was tough. By 1995, Bilimoria's partner had had enough and left. Bilimoria bought him out and raised £0.5m through an enterprise investment scheme and a convertible preference share issue. It enabled him to start building a team and putting money into better point of sale.

'I always believed that we were a fuel-laden jet trundling along the runway which would eventually manage to take off,' he says. 'But it makes a difference working with the best advisers. In the early days it is tempting to cut costs, but you get what you pay for. You also get the credibility of working with a top firm.

'Once people see that your brand has potential, they start to want your shares. The challenge is to hold on to them, which means raising money through lots of different sources: overdrafts, small firms loan guarantees, bills of exchange, preference shares, factoring, invoice discounting, EIS, warrants, you name it.

'The result is that I still own 72 per cent of the shares and everyone in the company is in a share options scheme.'

Brewing partners

In 1996 Cobra doubled its sales, only to find that its problems importing from India had quadrupled. 'By then, we were bringing in hundreds of containers a year and I had to take the tough decision of whether or not to move our production to the UK.

'I was terrified that it might undermine the integrity of an Indian brand of beer. Would my customers stop drinking it? We ran a survey asking them to rank features of the beer in order of importance. The most important quality by a long shot was the extra-smooth taste and the least important was where it was brewed.'

Bilimoria chose Charles Wells in Bedford, Britain's largest independent brewer, as his manufacturing partner. 'All my problems disappeared in one go. We took the problem of availability and quality and turned it to our advantage.'

After a seven-year absence, Cobra is now once again producing beer in India, this time for the local market. Bilimoria's expectation is that annual consumption will take off in the same way as in China, which in 25 years has grown from 1 litre per person to 20 litres.

From cult to brand

Cobra's first piece of marketing was a green A5 flyer to put on tables in Indian restaurants. 'We couldn't afford full colour,' says Bilimoria. 'We started from the grass roots in Indian restaurants where people discovered the product. Word of mouth is the strongest foundation on which to build.'

In straddling the transition from a cult to a national brand, 1998 was a watershed year. 'We started our first ever mainstream advertising with Saatchi & Saatchi with the brief to establish Cobra as the best beer to drink with Indian food.

'When you are in a position to advertise, you have to be careful not to alienate your loyal following which has grown with you. If you commercialize the brand, you lose them. So any advertising has to appeal to existing customers.

'In 2003 we advertised on television for the first time. The original quotation was $1m for one commercial. Instead we produced two commercials for a fraction of $1m, because we persuaded Saatchi to use Indian resources. You do not have to be a multinational to engage with India.'

Cobra is now sponsoring all the movies on ITV 2, 3 and 4. 'We did not want the usual product shot and jingle. You have to entertain your public. The idea for the campaign, Global Vision, is that young filmmakers can submit their ideas and have a clip shown on national television to half a million viewers. As with everything we do, we are changing the marketplace.'

Ideas per hour

'A passion for our product underlies everything we do. Our values are not what you do, but how you do it. We have very few rules. There is no dress code. You do your own thing. Just trust and respect people, encourage them to come up with ideas and make it happen.

'One principle goes through everything we do: we make sure that we are different in some way. Ideally, we want to be better and change the marketplace.

'So, we have a Hoffman group [named after the man who first built a bridge over the Grand Canyon] every two months to generate ideas and measure its performance in IPH [ideas per hour].

'It is impossible to patent the beer, though you can trademark it. What you can't copy is the culture. Competitors are coming out with similar products all the time. The entrepreneurial spirit gives us the edge.

'We encourage people to try to change the market in everything that they do. Innovation is not just about new products, but design, channels to market and raising finance.'

In particular, Bilimoria likes to turn threats into opportunities. 'In 1999, at one of our management hideaways we identified that more and more wine was being consumed in Indian restaurants. Yes, it was a threat, because it meant that people were drinking less beer, but it was also an opportunity.

'We created a new category – premium house wine – branded after my father, General Bilimoria, who always said that we should do wine. We started in France, but extended to 10 other wine-growing countries, selecting balanced and easy-to-drink wines, which can be drunk on their own or with spicy foods. Again we were aiming to be different and to change the marketplace for ever.'

The power of innovation

Since 1997, Cobra has been growing at a rate of 40 per cent a year. To maintain momentum, Bilimoria is extending his range. 'Last year, we developed an alcohol-free lager. We hated all the ones round the world and eventually found a brewery in Holland with special technology. At long last, we have produced a drinkable non-alcoholic beer.'

He has also launched Cobra Lower Carb and is producing the world's first double-fermented lager, which is brewed in an old Belgian brewery at 8 per cent strength in old champagne bottles. 'Brewers might have been around for centuries, but a 16-year-old British company of Indian origin can still come up with firsts. That's the power of innovation.'

The bottling model

Instead of producing beer itself, Cobra prefers to work in partnership with other breweries. 'We don't own the premises, which has given us the ability to grow very rapidly,' says Bilimoria. 'We have our own people in there, so the beer is produced to our recipe and under our supervision.

'It is closer to the Coca-Cola model than to traditional brewers. Their main asset is their brand and a lot of the bottling is outsourced. For us, it was a conscious decision, even though we couldn't have afforded [to brew the beer ourselves] anyway.

'If we had bought a brewery, it would have had to be 10 times too big to grow into. For a rapid growth company like ours, the model we have followed is the best. Eventually we will own our breweries.'

Complexity of growth

Cobra is now brewing in five different countries and in the last 2½ years has expanded its product range from one variety, the original premium lager beer, to four. 'To manage the complexity of growth, we have to make sure you have a strong management team.

'The role of the chief executive should be an all-rounder supported by professionals who are much better than you could ever be,' says Bilimoria. 'You have to get them to work together, not in their sales, marketing or financial silos. The way I have found to do that is to make everyone feel part of every decision – so you get input on ideas and initiatives.'

Evolution of capital structure

In the next eight years, Bilimoria is aiming to grow sales sevenfold from $140m to $1bn. With new products and a new management team, he is aiming to push up the rate of growth to 50 per cent for each of the next three years.

By then, he is hoping to be in a position to float in London, although he will consider any serious offers to take over the company. 'The giants are interested in buying us out and we are getting quite a lot of offers. If someone makes us one we can't refuse, then we will consider it, but our plans are to float and build a global beer brand.'

For further details, go to www.cobrabeer.com.

Entrepreneurial leadership

For Philip Verity at Mazars, leadership determines the size to which a business will eventually grow

Leadership is the single biggest differentiator between a *good* business and a *great* business; a successful team and a winning, world-class team; a job that is enjoyable versus one that you regard as 'the best days of your life'.

Leadership is more than management; it's more potent, more powerful, more dynamic and yet more accessible and attainable. We lead people, but manage things. Sure, we need management, but a great business doesn't exist without a great leader. I'd even go as far as to say that the size of a business is constrained by the size of the leader.

If leadership is fundamental to a business's success, then it is also the key criterion in assessing the quality of management teams. Any funder or financial backer will be asking him- or herself, 'How good is the management team?'

We're not short of written material on leadership. But there is a dearth of true leadership skills in many businesses. Our job as business leaders is to be leadership enthusiasts: enthusiastic for our teams, for our businesses and for the stories we can create.

As a student of leadership, and certainly a learner, I've set out below what I believe to be the 10 key descriptors that sum up what we need to do to be entrepreneurial leaders.

1 Leaders imagine

Part of the role of the leader is to *imagine* and visualize the potential for the business. Vision and strategy can only be shared and communicated if the leader has first imagined the opportunity.

2 Leaders create opportunities

Entrepreneurial leaders will not be short of opportunities – in fact, the challenge will be to retain focus and purpose. Our role as leader is to create opportunities for our team and to encourage them to apply their talents and energies in the pursuit of opportunity.

3 Leaders are talent fanatics

At the heart of leadership is a genuine concern for others. No amount of 'active listening' can help a self-interested manager. If we can be as concerned about others as we are for ourselves, we can accomplish great things through our team and see others develop, flourish, grow and surpass us. In an age where businesses fight for their share of talent, we must understand that retention and development are as important as recruitment.

4 Leaders understand that it's all about people

One business leader described the art of strategy as 'getting the right people on the bus and in the right seats, whilst ensuring that the wrong people are taken off the bus'. A winning business is one in which there is a sound business model, some highly effective leaders and a skill-rich motivated team. Period. The formula hasn't changed... Have the right team, have good people who 'get it', and a plan to make it all happen.

5 Leaders are not the king of the castle

One of the privileges of leadership is that you don't always have to be right, don't have to be the best, the smartest or the loudest. The symphony conductor and the football coach almost certainly were not the best musician or footballer. Leaders understand the value of the team and get the best out of others.

6 Leaders are financial engineers

We can probably all be accused of being preoccupied with 'the numbers' at some point. But the numbers only tell us what has already happened, not how we got there. A leader's role is to understand the cause and effect of developing people and delivering world-class financial results.

7 Leaders make mistakes

Leaders don't always 'know' what to do. Knowledge in itself is not what sets a leader apart. Courageous leadership and leadership through uncertainty give leaders the opportunity to confront the issues and challenges with the team and to provide hope and direction at all times.

8 Leaders communicate

Leaders have the vision. There is an appropriate time for open and clear communication. The appropriate time is *all* the time!

Without an effective communications plan to deploy the strategic vision, there is no way for the team to understand and buy into it.

9 Leaders make things happen

Don't wait for everything to be perfect – go with 70 per cent to build commitment and momentum. The balance will sort itself out as you go. There is tension in many businesses between the people who are trying to do something, and the people who are trying to keep them from doing something! Leaders provide action.

10 Leaders develop other leaders

Ralph Nader said that 'the function of leadership is to produce more leaders, not more followers'. The key growth constraint in business today is one of leadership *capacity* and leadership *capability*. Attracting leadership talent into our businesses and retaining it is fundamental to growth, as those leaders will naturally develop other leaders and transform the business.

Philip Verity is a partner at Mazars, the international accounting and business advisory firm. Mazars acts for some of the fastest-growing entrepreneurial companies in the United Kingdom, offering a complete range of accountancy and business advisory services, including audit and assurance, tax advisory and compliance, corporate recovery and insolvency, consulting, forensic and investigations, corporate finance and financial services for private individuals.

Tel: 01908 664466
e-mail: Philip.verity@mazars.co.uk
www.mazars.co.uk

Creating effective strategies

To build real value, you have to think, plan and act differently says Mike Robson at SPS

Why some companies do not succeed

Many of us own the companies we are directors of. Sometimes we inherit the business but often we have launched and developed our companies from an early stage and have built our businesses around our individual skill sets, experience, preferences and personalities. That's fine in the early stages but it often means that vital parts of the business are run by people who are not specialists in that area, restricting the organization's ability to succeed. Many companies lack a full set of board- and management-level business skills. They are unable adequately to identify the risks and opportunities facing them and to create and implement plans to operate and develop their companies and create wealth for their owners.

The attributes of successful businesses

If we want to build real value in our businesses, we need to think, plan and act differently, taking time to step back from the day-to-day running of the business. Successful companies have longer time horizons, anticipate change and continually form, assess and implement plans for the growth and positioning of their businesses. They create effective systems and develop effective staff. They ensure they have access to a range of specialist skills, either internally or externally, from marketing through operations to finance. And they do so in a cost-effective way.

The most successful businesses in the United Kingdom have some, if not all, of these characteristics:

- They possess a clear strategy and vision.
- They know their market position or niche.
- They have an effective sales machine.
- They organize their business around systems, not people.
- They plan their finances.
- They 'manage' rather than 'do'.
- They have an effective board structure.
- They know when and how to exit their business.
- They seek advice.

The business owner's dilemma

Ten years ago I invested in a fledgling UK publishing company providing business-to-business products and services around the English-speaking world, mainly in the United States. At the end of the start-up period it was clear that the company lacked direction, was losing money and was likely to continue to do so.

I acquired the publishing company and invested both time and money building it up. Although I had been a director of a number of relatively large companies, I knew that I lacked a full range of relevant skills. My ability to plan and implement the development of the business was hampered in particular by my lack of both industry knowledge and marketing and sales skills. In common with many businesses of this size, I was unable to lure skilled personnel from large companies and I felt that although the consultancy firms might provide some interesting ideas, they would not be a viable source of assistance in the long term. Although the company developed well and I achieved a successful trade sale, I now realize that I could have done significantly better with external help.

Many readers will identify with the loneliness business owners feel and the difficulty they have in planning and implementing the development of their businesses and in sourcing valuable, practical and impartial assistance. The remainder of this chapter covers the contents of a strategic plan, the implementation process, the types of assistance you can access at each stage and what you should look for in an adviser.

The strategic plan

A strategic plan is a set of objectives and an action plan to achieve those objectives. Most business owners will tell you they have one, but often it is not formally drawn up or, more importantly, adhered to. To achieve an effective plan you need to have a clear understanding of the following:

- the goals and objectives of the owners and directors, including financial, retirement and work–life expectations;
- the market for your products or services: where do you fit into it, how will it change, what are the risks and opportunities?
- your customers: why and for how long will they need your products and services, what else do they need?
- your competitors: their strengths and weaknesses;
- the quality of your people, their ability to develop with the company, your ability to develop them and your ability to attract appropriate new staff;
- your suppliers: are they secure?
- the funding requirements of the business and how they can be best achieved;
- financial forecasts and the impact of all key variables on the results;
- how you will successfully implement the plan.

With this knowledge you can assess the risks and opportunities facing your business, set some informed objectives and create a plan to achieve them. You need to be certain that all relevant parties understand and accept both the objectives and the plan.

If the owners are planning to sell the business in the next few years, the planning process should also include an assessment of:

- the available exit route or routes; flotation, trade sale, MBO, etc;
- the profile of potential buyers;
- the likely range of valuations to be expected;
- an exit timetable;
- an action plan to achieve successful sale at an optimum value whilst continuing to operate the company effectively and whilst maintaining staff morale.

For many companies, strategic planning is a daunting, albeit rewarding, task. There are a number of organizations providing cost-effective and efficient assistance to business owners in creating their strategic plans or critically evaluating them once they have been drawn up. The advantage of using one of these organizations should be:

- a more structured planning process and resultant plan;
- a shorter delivery time;
- a critical assessment of your business model;
- input from a wider knowledge base;
- greater objectivity;
- the ability to benchmark your plan against businesses in similar markets;
- a reduction in 'groupthink'.

Implementation

There is no point in planning unless all the principal parties understand, accept and implement the plan. Often, business owners start off with good intentions but then become bogged down in the detail of the day-to-day working week, and the strategic plan becomes valueless. To maintain the direction of the company the principal parties need to meet regularly to:

■ critically review the business;
■ assess progress against predetermined benchmarks;
■ actively identify risks and opportunities;
■ constantly re-evaluate the strategic plan;
■ clearly define actions and responsibilities.

SMEs often fail to undertake this process successfully. There are a number of organizations that will, for a small proportion of the cost of a full-time director, assist business owners with the plan implementation process, providing them with:

■ the discipline of a regular, objective forward-looking review;
■ the active long-term support and encouragement of an experienced business professional;
■ a trusted and impartial adviser with a detailed understanding of the business;
■ increased contacts and knowledge.

Selecting advisers

Businesses seeking advice three or more times a year have twice the profit growth of people who do not seek advice. (Barclays/clearly business dot. com)

Innovation flourishes when knowledge, skills, energy and experience are allowed to interact. (The Alliance for Health and the Future)

Business owners can benefit tremendously from the services of business advisers if they pick the right adviser for their circumstances and develop a good relationship in which the skills and experience of the adviser are used effectively to achieve the objectives of the business. In general, business owners should look for the following attributes when selecting an adviser:

■ practical experience of growing businesses in a number of sectors;
■ practical experience of successfully advising other business owners;
■ supported when necessary by colleagues with a wide range of business skills;
■ independence and impartiality;
■ a willingness to support you in the long term;
■ flexibility: reasonable availability at short notice;
■ an enthusiasm for your business;
■ an understanding and sharing of your vision for your company;
■ good contacts;

- a willingness to challenge your thinking;
- the ability to take problems away from you and implement solutions independently;
- good decision-making ability;
- a good personal relationship with the business owners.

Mike Robson is an experienced and entrepreneurial businessman and a partner in SPS. In a varied business career Mike has steered one firm away from financial near-disaster and has launched, developed and successfully sold his own print and online publishing company. SPS is a nationwide partnership of 45 businessmen and women providing practical help to owners and managers of small and medium-sized businesses. Mike can be contacted on 08456 581185 or mike.robson@strategicplanningsolutions.co.uk.

How will people see your business?

A bright eye catching logo, strong descriptive text, memorable graphics: these all give a good first impression to new customers.

SNAP has an excellent **Design Team** who can talk through your initial ideas and come up with a selection of logos and layouts from which you can make your choice. From this they can then produce a range of business stationery and promotional literature to develop your brand.

If you already have a standard logo or association badge they can copy or develop it to allow you to produce new literature or a different customer incentive. They will also make sure your stationery fulfils any legal requirements with regard to registration numbers and director details.

From this concept, **SNAP** can **Print** anything you require to market your business or particular products. All this with a **guaranteed turnaround** so you can make that exhibition and meet that deadline!

They have excellent print capability in-house to be able to produce small runs of Stationery; large runs of flyers; Point of Sale Posters for outside as well as in!

The **Finishing** options are also second to none with varied Folder Options, Book Binding, Boxes and other Packaging; Credit Cards and Playing Cards; Mounted Posters and Banners to name just a few!

What about getting some new customers on board by sending out a **Mailshot**?

SNAP have the ability to personalise your letter or card with the correct data for name and address. In addition you can make your mailer stand out by presenting the customer contact name in a personalised and individual dynamic graphic.

STAND OUT from the CROWD!

What about a **Web** presence? The internet highway is visited daily by millions. Your graphics could be used to publicise your products in this open market place.

SNAP can also use e-mail to put your name in front of other new customers.

All businesses need Customers!

Use **SNAP** to help you **find and remind** those customers of your products and abilities.

Present them with an **Image** they won't forget and then provide a **Service** to them that is second to none and your business will grow!

Dealing with dilemmas

The boards of growing companies face a succession of dilemmas. Enormous value can be created, saved or lost depending on how these dilemmas are resolved, says Patrick Dunne of 3i

Introduction

Directors of growing businesses often make their most significant contribution when the board or individual directors face a dilemma. What's a dilemma? Well, let's assume here that it is simply a tricky situation with no immediately obvious conclusion and where all the alternative solutions involve some degree of pain.

The discovery that your Finance Director is incompetent may be a good example; dealing with boardroom conflict another. There are also the many straightforward commercial dilemmas facing growing businesses as well as all the personal ones for the leaders themselves.

Helping people through these magical moments of ownership and strategic, human or possibly moral challenge can be great fun. It can also be the key to subsequent success. However, watching a minor dilemma lead to a series of more damaging ones or seeing a successful enterprise destroyed by the wrong judgement at a pivotal moment can be a painful experience.

The nature of dilemmas

Dilemmas emerge for a whole range of reasons but you can usually put their root cause down to one or several of the following:

- The role of the board is unclear.
- There are humans involved.
- Situations change.
- There's money involved.

Lack of clarity or agreement over the role of the board produces a regular flow of dilemmas. So what is the role of the board? For me it is all about 'right strategy, right resources and keep out of jail'. By which I mean ensuring that the right strategy is in place and that it is being followed. That there are the right resources to meet that strategy, the most important of these being human and financial. Then, finally, that the company complies with all relevant regulations and agreements.

These three things are fundamental and won't change. However, as the company develops in terms of scale, breadth and ownership, the board needs to adapt. More often than not, it is *when* to change rather than *what* to change that presents the dilemma, particularly if it involves changing the people on the board.

Naturally, directors think and act as individuals as well as a group. Executive directors need to think as directors as well as managers or functional representatives, and shareholder representatives must be more than representatives. When the board's interests and those of the individuals on the board are perfectly aligned there is seldom a problem. However, there are times when they are not, and even the most committed team player will think personally once threatened. The threats that matter most to directors are those to their position, purse or pride.

Ironically, it was Richard Nixon who was quoted as saying, 'Don't let yourself become the issue.' It is easy to be critical of someone else, much harder to recognize or do something about our own limitations. One phenomenon that I have frequently observed is the 'entrepreneur's ear'. This amazingly effective selective hearing device, implanted at birth, gives entrepreneurs the ability to ignore the advice that would stop them doing the tremendously successful things they do. However, the entrepreneur's ear is only useful if combined with consistently good judgement and a number of other characteristics.

The feelings of invincibility that emerge following periods of success can often be the wax that turns a leader deaf. This is why leaders, no matter how successful, need at least one person who can act as a calibrator and challenger of their views.

Another thing that I have noticed is that just occasionally the boards of growing businesses start to exhibit teenage behaviour. If you are not sure what I mean, just think back to when you were about 14. Remember that heady mix of excitement and anxiety, confidence and insecurity, wanting to be grown up but not wanting to join in with rules of the game. Well, just as rational debate doesn't always get teenagers to do what you want to do, so it is with entrepreneurial boards. You need to understand what really motivates them at that particular moment.

Some principles for dealing with dilemmas

Assuming you're clear what the dilemma really is, the next thing is to decide how to tackle it. If you decide to become the principal 'resolver' yourself, you need to be clear why. Is it the survival instinct kicking in? Is it an opportunity to improve your own personal position? Perhaps people always look to you to sort things out. Whatever, it is always worth remembering that your motives may not be clear to others.

If you do decide you want to be the 'resolver' then there are a number of factors to consider before committing yourself. How good is your judgement? How strong are your influencing skills? What store of respect do you have with the rest of the board? It is very hard to influence people who don't respect you.

Deciding that you want to be the 'resolver' doesn't mean you have to do it all on your own. So who else needs to be involved in the process and when? If it is a boardroom conflict situation it is far easier to figure out what is going on if you are watching rather than fighting. Understanding how people feel about the different possibilities helps enormously. Many a rational decision has been ignored in favour of something worse.

Seizing the moment is also critical if the issue is a human one and especially if the likely outcome involves the removal of a director. Removing directors requires a great deal of skill and thought. Some people are talented at painting the pictures of what alternatives really mean and getting those who are going to suffer the most pain to recognize reality, accept it and then get on with it.

Is there a universally applicable way of dealing with dilemmas? I haven't found one. I have, however, always found it helpful to be clear what the dilemma is, how to resolve it, what to decide and then, apart from making the right judgement, most importantly how to bring the judgement to bear.

Summary

Enormous value can be created, saved or lost by resolving dilemmas. Getting a team in the boardroom that is well equipped to deal with them is therefore the key. Good judgement of people and of commercial situations is fundamental to successful outcomes. So, it is always worth asking, 'How good is the collective judgement of my board?' Finally, if you are going to be the 'resolver', make sure you know whether you are the cause of the problem or not before you start – and may I wish you the best of luck.

Patrick Dunne is Group Communications Director of 3i Group plc, a world leader in private equity and venture capital. He is also the author of three successful books about boards: *Running Board Meetings*, *Directors' Dilemmas* and *Tolley's Non-executive Director's Handbook*. He is a Visiting Professor at Cranfield and Chairman of the UK's leading charity in the field of conflict resolution for young adults, Leap – Confronting Conflict.

Tel: 020 7975 3283
e-mail: Patrick.Dunne@3i.comp

Prospects for growth

The performance of the UK economy has improved in 2006, but what more can companies and government do to raise the bar, asks David Fenton, Senior Economic Adviser, at The Royal Bank of Scotland Group

The end is nigh?

After three years of relatively plain sailing, global equity markets hit choppier waters in May. The turmoil brought an end to the longest bull market run for five decades and wiped out all the gains made in the first four months of the year.

It turned out to be a squall, but fears linger that it may signal the beginning of the end of the good times for the global economy. Are they right? In part, yes, but we would urge readers to bear in mind an astute observation made by former MPC member Stephen Nickel: 'There are always two views: one is that the world is going fine; the other is that everything is going to hell. And the stock market veers from one to the other without any particular logic to it.'

In other words, sentiment often matters as much to the short- to medium-term movements of equity markets as economic fundamentals. So if the FTSE is not an entirely reliable indicator of the prospects for UK growth, it falls to people like us to give our view, starting with a quick recap of what we said a year ago.

What a difference a year makes... not really

In the eighth edition of *The Growing Business Handbook* we outlined our forecast that the UK economy would grow by 2.0 per cent in 2005, followed by a mild acceleration to 2.4 per cent in 2006.

What has changed? Not much. The UK economy grew by 1.9 per cent in 2005, just shy of our forecast.[1] Scratching beneath the surface, 2005 will be remembered as the year that consumers took a breather. After an average growth rate of 3.5 per cent in the previous 10 years, 1.3 per cent must have felt like reverse for many consumer-facing industries in 2005. Indeed, exports made a bigger contribution to economic growth than consumer spending for the first time in 10 years.

If 2005 was slightly disappointing on the growth front, 2006 has been anything but. We now expect the UK economy to grow by 2.7 per cent in 2006 largely thanks to a revival in consumer spending. Those few extra percentage points should make 2006 that little bit better for growing business than 2005.

Companies are also getting in on the act. Contributions by employers with self-administered pensions rose to £12.2 billion in the first quarter of 2006, up from £7.7 billion a year ago, but companies still managed to spend a cool £30 billion on investment over the same three months.

High oil prices (Brent crude is in the low $60s a barrel as we write) and the changes to the rules governing company pensions are strong headwinds, but 2006 will be another decent year for investment if manufacturers keep spending. That's good news for anyone in the business-to-business sector.

2007 is a more difficult call. The August rate hike, with the prospect of more to come, may sap the consumer revival of some of its vitality, but we still expect GDP to grow broadly in line with its trend rate of 2.6–2.7 per cent. This is something the UK economy has gotten very good at. So good, in fact, that the Organisation for Economic Cooperation and Development (OECD) ranked the UK number one on 'macroeconomic performance' out of its 30 member countries. It noted that 'the stability and resilience of the economy have been impressive'. This is important: a less uncertain environment for business is usually a better one.

Stability versus ability

Now for the not-so-good news. The United Kingdom's labour and product markets may be among the most flexible in the OECD, but we score relatively poorly on most other counts of 'structural performance', which will determine the country's long-term economic performance and its ability to compete. These include productivity levels; skill levels; research and development (R&D) intensity; and infrastructure quality.

Take productivity per hour, for example. Despite a concerted effort by the government, this has not improved over the past 10 years. As a result, the United Kingdom ranked 15th (out of 27) on this count in 2003. This is hardly a recipe for success in an era of globalization.

Matters don't appear to have improved much since then. The United Kingdom climbed a few places in 2004, to 12th, but remains distinctly mid-table and well off the pace set by our main competitors (see Figure 1.5.1). To give some sense of what is at stake if we can raise our game, consider the United States. If the United Kingdom were as productive as the United States, we estimate that it would create around £200 billion more wealth per year. That translates to around £8,500 more income for the average household.

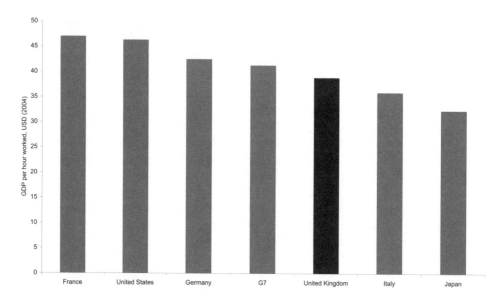

Source: OECD

Figure 1.5.1 Productivity of various OECD countries

So what needs to change? The OECD suggests that in order for the United Kingdom to improve, policy makers should address the following key challenges:

- raise the skill level of the workforce;
- address the apparently mediocre innovation performance;
- improve transport infrastructure;
- increase labour utilization by helping those claiming incapacity benefit into work;
- ensure that public money is spent efficiently to contain the tax burden.

So far, so sensible. But what about companies? A recent report by Proudfoot Consulting provides food for thought. Over the three years to 2005, more time was 'wasted' by UK companies (a whopping 36.6 per cent) than in any other nation/region studied, except Asia.[2]

More encouragingly, there was a dramatic improvement over the three years, from 39.9 per cent in 2003 to 31.5 per cent in 2005, though the fact that UK executives are, apparently, less ambitious in their target setting is disconcerting. Absolute gains in productivity count for nothing; relative gains are needed.

The good news is that the main causes of inefficiency as reported by executives – communication problems (between internal departments) and poor management (inefficient planning of work and organizational structure) – are eminently fixable. Skills shortages, legislation and regulation, and national transport infrastructure – the issues raised by the OECD – all matter, but come further down the list of complaints.

In this era of rapid globalization the old adage of 'doing what you do best, better' holds more firmly than ever. But don't forget about the basics, either!

Notes

1. All numbers from National Statistics, unless indicated otherwise.
2. Average percentage of unproductive time in companies reviewed by Proudfoot Consulting, which sets the optimum labour efficiency threshold at 85 per cent (no company can have 100 per cent labour utilization).

David Fenton is a Senior Economist with the RBS Group. He provides forecasts and strategic analysis on the UK economy for RBS and its customers.

Prior to joining RBS in 2002, David worked for Ernst & Young's Project Finance Team in Manchester. He has a Masters degree in Economics from the University of Glasgow.

Contact details:
Tel: 0131 626 3701
e-mail: david.fenton@rbs.co.uk

Want more regular updates on the economy? Please visit www.rbs.com/economics.

2

Exploiting ideas

Investing in Alpacas – for pleasure and profit
by Joy Whitehead, B.Sc., founder of Bozedown Alpacas

Investment potential

There is huge interest in alpacas – not only from people with land, but also from people simply wishing to invest in the future of these attractive, intelligent creatures, whose luxury fleece rivals cashmere. Alpacas are sought after by a variety of people, from those wishing to earn a sensible income from their land – even a small acreage can give good returns – to those wishing simply to have a few pets as pasture trimmers.

The number of alpaca owners in the UK has grown from a handful in 1989, when I first encountered alpacas, to around 800 in 2006. Alpacas now number around 16,000 in the UK – still a long way short of the estimated minimum of 100,000 needed to sustain a viable fibre industry; hence why the price of breeding stock remains high, ensuring good returns.

Females produce one offspring, or 'cria' per year. Embryo transfer costs are high and AI is virtually impossible in alpacas – hence with no way of increasing numbers quickly, prices of breeding females remain buoyant, and will continue to do so into the foreseeable future – especially those of the highest quality. We at Bozedown Alpacas specialise in importing and breeding these élite alpacas, and have achieved our unrivalled reputation by careful selection of the finest breeding stock in Peru and Australia, combined with a meticulous on-farm selective breeding programme. As well as supplying breeding stock to new and established breeders, we offer adjistment (livery) at very reasonable rates to enable non landowners to invest in the exciting future of alpacas.

Alpacas originate from the Andes of South America, where it freezes 300 nights of the year, but have adapted well to conditions in the UK and many other countries. The large eyes and fluffy coats of the more common huacaya subspecies make them very appealing, they communicate by humming – quite expressively! – and are easily trained to halter. They are sheared once a year, in May or June, and produce 3-5 kilos of luxury fibre per year. This compares with only 200 grams from a cashmere goat – a feral creature which is getting quite rare, giving alpaca a clear opening in the world luxury fibre market. Alpaca can be as fine as cashmere, but has the advantages of being smoother and more lustrous, making it highly desirable. The much rarer 'suri' subspecies has highly lustrous fibre which hangs in tight ringlets, and is used to produce fabulous worsted fabrics.

Alpaca fibre is an amazing commodity. Alpaca fibre fineness is measured in microns. 'Handle' is the softness and smoothness we feel on our skin. 28 micron alpaca fibre has the same handle as 18 micron sheep's wool. In other words it feels like finest merino wool. So even the alpacas which are producing relatively coarse (for alpacas!) 28 micron fleeces, are actually producing wonderful fibre which can be transformed into luxury garments. 18 micron alpaca fibre feels so soft it's like touching clouds! If we can reliably produce fibre less than 20 microns, then the world is our oyster. The demand for this quality natural fibre from the top producers of luxury garments will know no bounds! At Bozedown we already have many of these élite superfine alpacas in our breeding programme.

Marketing of British produced alpaca end product has thus far been quite restricted due to the relatively small amount of fibre available here, but there are now 2 major purchasers of raw fleece, who process the fleece into yarn and then either market and sell the yarn or continue to end product which is also marketed very successfully. In addition, several small mills now offer a service of spinning individual or multiple fleeces into yarn for returning to the grower for cottage industry use.

Why Alpacas?

Many people start out in alpacas as a hobby. And/or they are looking to change/improve their lifestyle. They are looking for animals to graze their paddock or pasture, and preferably something which won't end up on the dinner table! That's how I started back in 1989, when there were only about 150 alpacas in the country, mostly in zoos. So there was not much choice, and I bought the only alpacas I could find – 4 females and a male. My first male had excellent conformation, and good bone. I noticed that he passed this on to all his progeny, who showed great uniformity, and I realised that this was what breeding was about – this ability of a Sire to pass on his strong genetic traits. I was hooked!

Many people start out in alpacas as an investment. They want to enjoy the lifestyle associated with owning land, they want their land to work for them, and they want their investments to give reasonable returns. Alpacas can fulfil these aims.

Alpacas can change your life. For the complete alpaca experience Bozedown can be relied on to give a friendly advice and support service second to none. We offer Beginners Days, Breeders Seminars, Training Seminars, Fibre Workshops, Suri Workshops and Husbandry Days, as well as answering clients' queries on any aspect of keeping and breeding alpacas.

Sales and Support. We are a family business, and our highly experienced team offers genuine guidance on selection and purchase of alpacas, whether as pets or breeding stock. Lack of knowledge can lead to costly mistakes. However, we at Bozedown are keen to make sure clients get the best possible experience when starting out in alpacas. A fair and sensible pricing structure based on each alpaca's attributes ensures that clients are getting value for money, thus safeguarding their investment. We know we can't be beaten on quality. That is why we say "See us first and set your standard."

The Development of Alpaca Breeding in the UK

Breeding alpacas is both challenging and rewarding. The ancient indigenous peoples of Peru had developed their breeding programmes to a very high standard. We know this through the evidence of thousand-year-old mummified alpacas excavated in southern Peru. My challenge is to produce the same evenness, fineness and uniformity of fleece that I witnessed while working on those ancient mummies back in 1993. My reward is that with every succeeding generation of alpacas I have produced is nudging closer to that goal. As an industry we can still refine and improve our product, making it even more desirable.

Peru has a strong fibre industry, which encourages the Peruvian breeders to improve their own breeding to a high standard, and some of these have succeeded in producing very fine fibre with plenty of crimp, character and lustre, over the major part of the alpaca's body, called the 'blanket' area, then right up the neck and into the top knot, down under the belly, and down the legs. These are the Stud males and breeding females we look for when we select in Peru. Peru has the largest resource of alpaca genetics in the world, with 3 million alpacas, compared with 300,000 in Bolivia and only 30,000 in Chile. World famous breeder Don Julio Barredo, who died in March 2006, was line breeding his 'Accoyo' alpacas all his life, with the aim of producing 20 pounds weight of 20 micron fleece for 20 years of the alpaca's life. Some of the alpacas he bred are now found as far apart as North America, Australasia and Europe. Alpaca breeders around the world are also now taking forward the breeding of alpacas.

Bozedown's World Class breeding programme produces many Champion studs and outstanding females. Other alpaca breeders in the UK also taking up the challenge, and breeding their females to the very finest, densest Stud males they can find. Securing those outstanding stud males is taking UK breeding programmes forward in leaps and bounds. A few have been imported from Australia, where Peruvian alpacas have been bred for about 10 years longer than in the UK. Some have been selected directly from Peru, from breeders who take pride in their long association with the alpaca – the alpaca which legend says was given to them by the Earth goddess Pacha Mama, created out of the very earth of the Andes mountains.

Bozedown Alpacas has made 5 Peruvian selections, between 1998 and 2005. We have been able to secure some of the finest, densest alpacas in the world. Each time we have been able to sell a number of the selected alpacas to other breeders in the UK to enable them to go forward with their own breeding programmes, for the benefit of the entire UK industry. The interest our selections arouse is very evident, with breeders buzzing around like bees around a honey pot in the ensuing weeks after their arrival.

At Bozedown we have established our own bloodlines. Bozedown Alpacas has proved its ability to select and breed alpacas. The Show Ring is a tough place to parade your pride and joy. But over the years Bozedown Alpacas animals have been awarded many Supreme Champion and Champion prizes. However, this is no reason for complacency. There are plenty more good alpacas out there to challenge us and keep us on our breeding toes!

Each generation should be better than the last. However, each generation takes at least 3 years. Gestation lasts an average of 343 days, with the females being mated again 2-3 weeks after parturition A female can be bred at the earliest at about 14 months, providing she is well grown. So her cria can in theory be on the ground about 3 years after her own conception. A male matures between 2 and 3 years old. So, with a small amount of improvement in each generation it can take many years to upgrade quality significantly. Although there will still be many unimproved alpacas after this time, these animals are still of benefit to the National herd, as they are producing fibre which is useful to the industry as a whole.

Breeding strategy. The conformation of the animal plays a large part in any breeding decision. We need balanced animals, so that they work efficiently; with strong well-formed legs so that they can carry a cria without undue stress, or in the case of a male, mount the female and cause her to 'cush' for mating. The alpaca needs to have good dental formation, so that it can eat efficiently throughout its long lifetime – about 15 to 20 years. (Although minor dental problems such as slightly undershot teeth can be resolved easily by employing a horse dentist).

Good conformation is our first building block, and then we look at the fibre. We look for alpacas with good coverage, and producing a good weight of fine crimpy fibre, i.e. high density fleeces with good lock formation. Fleece samples are sent to a testing laboratory, and the test results give us further information on the fineness and evenness of the fleece.

Breeding for genetic improvement. While the use of top quality Stud males in our breeding programmes is paramount, it follows that, if we are to actually improve the fibre quality in the next generation, then we also have to use top quality females in our breeding progammes. The male and female each contribute 50% to the genetic make-up of the cria (offspring). If both the sire and dam are of similar quality, then there is a chance that an improvement over both parents can be achieved. Hence my continuing fascination in breeding. Hence also why the number of alpaca owners and breeders in the UK rises substantially year on year.

Bozedown Alpacas has been growing and developing since 1989. We are the leading British breeder, and have a very knowledgeable team working on breeding, sales and customer advice and support. See our web site **www.bozedown-alpacas.co.uk.** We have outstanding females for sale, in calf to Champion Studs, and offer Stud Services, Breeding Appraisals, Livery and Transport. We can offer good, sound, unrelated starting groups, depending on the individual client's aims, budget and special requirements. In addition, we cannot be beaten on value for money. Many of our clients, who are winning top Show prizes will testify on our behalf, as they return to us again and again for new purchases of breeding females, and for Stud Services. So remember, **"See us first and set your standard."**

Build it and they will come

As a fast-growing enterprise, how do you keep up the creative momentum, asks Andy Reid at ?What If!, an innovation company that trains companies in creative behaviours

One of my favourite films is *Field of Dreams*. In this 1989 film starring Kevin Costner, an Iowa farmer is inspired by a voice he can't ignore to build a full-size baseball pitch in his cornfield and, in turn, a place where dreams come true. For those who dare to dream, the film is a call to arms and a story to inspire our creative passions. For others, it's just a film about a farmer who annoys his neighbours. The point, however, is that those who dare to dream are often the ones who after all the struggles secure the last laugh; despite all the setbacks, ridicule and objection, finally overcome and inspire others to follow.

Sometimes you raise innovation up the commercial agenda by developing new products and services, sometimes you work on the retail experience and sometimes you work on the skills, behaviours and culture within organizations. In all instances, we see the same kinds of barriers to innovation regardless of the specific needs of enterprises. In recognizing early that these barriers exist, you can take steps to avoid them and turn them into enabling tools to ensure your success in the future. Here are some top tips in keeping creative momentum going.

Attitude: stay positive and 'can do'

When he wasn't choosing black paint for his cars, Henry Ford was also known for saying, 'Whether you think you can or you think you can't, either way, you're probably right.' It's true. A healthy attitude to problem solving is better than an unhealthy attitude. Consider all the times you've cracked something in the past and remember how you were at that time. My university lecturer insisted that the better theories were on the greater tide of common sense and that having a 'can do' approach to life works wonders – a philosophy I frequently adopted, given some of my grades!

My first top tip is to address your own attitude and challenge the beliefs that may not be serving you well. In being positive in any given situation you are more likely to happen across the answer, motivate others and develop confidence going forward than by constantly giving yourself reasons to feel useless every time you get stuck. If you have a positive attitude at the top of an organization, it's more likely to filter its way to the bottom too – positively. Watch your leaders as well as yourself!

Embrace risk and the irreverent

The larger an organization becomes, the more necessary systems and structures become in order to sustain the animal that has evolved. However, this doesn't create an environment conducive to having ideas.

At the start there is a great struggle whilst a company organizes itself (and, importantly, organizes who gets the tea) before business takes off. Then there is a period of growth that is rapid and prosperous (and everyone knows how everyone else likes their tea). Thereafter we see companies at a time of stagnation. Management is under pressure, things have got quite process driven; the company loses its 'mojo' (and no one feels like drinking tea).

My second top tip is embrace and reward risk taking and the irreverent. When companies grow, they tend to replicate what they did at the start; they systemize that success. Fast-growing enterprises, however, are organic and embrace free thinking alongside whatever structures are needed to survive. People are taking more ownership of their actions and are full of energy and excitement. It is ambition and positive attitude (and all that tea!) that keep you thinking creatively. Caution against systems that replace or attempt to replicate what essentially is a fabric of human behaviours interacting with each other.

A structure you can put in place here is agreeing on, identifying and rewarding frequently a set of values that best represent the company you have. At ?What *If*! our values of Love, Passion, Freshness, Bravery and Action are constantly exemplified in quarterly company meetings. Here we reward staff who have acted from the heart as well as the head, and as a result we're reminded of the values that have been core to the company for its lifetime. In summary, identify who you are, tune into your awareness of it and reward it publicly.

Laugh: take fun seriously

There is a misconception that playfulness is high-energy and needless distraction. I am not in the habit of 'crazytivity' or cat juggling in front of clients, nor am I an office clown because I like the attention. I take playfulness and the ability to 'let go' very seriously, as I recognize the value of having a relaxed mind. Here's the science, so pay attention!

When you're having fun, you relax. Fact. When you relax, your brain cools by one degree and the neurological pathways connecting the subconscious and cognitive parts of your brain open up more. You are more likely to make connections between disparate subjects and arrive at interesting and original ideas.

By embracing acts such as an impromptu office Olympics, singing, telling a joke and – wait for it – going outside for a walk with a colleague, you're allowing YOU to go to work. Curiosity (gossiping), intuition (listening to your gut) and playfulness (relaxing) are human characteristics and hard to suppress – so don't suppress them! In being human you will have more enjoyment at work and inspire others to want to share your company. Imagine that: a place where people go because they enjoy being there... can you imagine the productivity of a place like that?

Creativity is as much about the 'being' or 'how you are' as it is about following a method, or, as we say, 'the doing'. In summary, I think the best advice I can give for a small organization embarking on its innovation journey is to examine and challenge its attitudes, embrace risk and irreverence, and reward those who dare to dream and finally have some fun along the way: Build it and they will come.

At ?What If!, we dare to dream differently every day. We are 200 people worldwide with offices in London, Manchester, New York, Sydney and Shanghai. Last year we worked with 193 clients in raising innovation further up their commercial agenda.

Further details from:

?What If!
The Glassworks
3–4 Ashland Place
London W1U 4AH
Tel: 020 7535 7500
www.whatifinnovation.com

Innovation in smaller companies

Go deep before ever going broad, advises Gerard Burke of the Business Growth and Development Programme

Small business owners are regularly exhorted to 'innovate or die'. Given that this message often comes from government agencies and trade bodies, arguably some of the least innovative organizations of all, the words are often treated with some scepticism by those they are meant to enthuse! And if the purveyors of this message intend 'innovate' to mean diversification into new markets with new products/services, then this scepticism may well be justified.

Two separate studies that we have undertaken in recent years which correlate market focus with financial performance clearly show the same pattern. The best-performing smaller firms tend, overwhelmingly, to grow by selling more of their existing product and services to their existing customers and people just like them. In other words, they 'stick to the knitting'!

A compelling strategy for the growth-hungry firm is to find a profitable niche market and bring distinctive value to the customers within it. Some of the most successful businesses on our Business Growth and Development Programme (BGP) have done exactly that:

■ Pacific Direct supplies luxury branded toiletries to five-star hotels.
■ Cobra Beer offers a beer and wine portfolio to Indian restaurants.
■ Hotel Chocolat provides delivered handmade chocolate gifts.

The niche strategy comes with three great benefits for the owner-managed business. First, niches are frequently overlooked or not well served by big players. Second, a smaller business simply cannot fight on too many fronts. If it tries, there's a danger that it will fail to serve properly the needs of either the diversified market or the core customers. For instance, before participating in BGP, the founders of Hotel Chocolat had twice tried to grow through diversification – and failed both times. Following BGP, they renewed their focus on the core – and the resultant growth has been exponential.

Third, the business can focus on meeting the needs of a well-defined target group. This in turn builds a deep knowledge and understanding of their customers, which allows the business to be better than the competition at meeting those customers' needs.

Am I saying that these businesses don't innovate? Absolutely not! The best-performing smaller firms are highly innovative. Indeed, the three businesses I've mentioned above regularly win awards for their creativity and innovation.

However, their innovation is regular and usually *incremental*. Their deep knowledge of their niche allows them to respond quickly to, or even anticipate, their customers' needs. As a result, they can be seen to be constantly enhancing their products and services in ways that they already know will meet with their customers' approval.

This type of incremental innovation, based on deep sensitivity to customers' needs, is usually a perfectly natural and deeply ingrained behaviour within the business. In the successful growth business there is no need for a special 'innovation process', or for one person to be responsible for new ideas. Identifying new and better ways to service their customers is simply part of what everybody does and the business is sufficiently nimble and flexible to allow these improvements to be implemented quickly.

Of course, these high-performing businesses also occasionally diversify. But the sort of radical innovation and diversification that often seems to underlie the 'innovate or die' message is only undertaken once the foundations have been well laid within the core niche, and as part of a carefully thought through strategy.

For example, Pacific Direct built a strong position in hotels before moving to servicing airlines. Business and first-class airline passengers also tend to stay in five-star hotels and appreciate the same sort of luxury brands. Pacific Direct's credentials built in one niche bolstered its entry into the adjacent one and the company's infrastructure was robust enough to support the expansion.

Go deep *before* going broad, is the message. Unfortunately, too many ambitious businesses never make it past the first burst of growth because they start wandering too far, too fast from what they really know how to do.

Gerard Burke is the programme director and lead designer of the Business Growth and Development Programme (BGP). BGP is the United Kingdom's biggest and most successful development programme for ambitious owner-managers. The programme is now in its 19th consecutive year of operation and during that time has helped nearly 1,000 owner-managers to achieve their business and personal ambitions. Businesses that participate in BGP grow sales and profit more quickly than their peers and grow more quickly after the programme than they did before. For example, here's what Karan Bilimoria of Cobra Beer said about it:

> *BGP has been a real turning point in my business and my career. This unique programme has given me the personal and hands-on development I required. It exceeded my expectations and was excellent value for money. I really wish I'd done it earlier.*

BGP has recently been recognized as one of the 'Seven Pillars of Wisdom' for entrepreneurs by *Real Business* magazine.

You can find out more about BGP at www.som.cranfield.ac.uk/som/enterprise/credo.

The innovation process

There is nothing random about innovation, says Peter Ives at Business Dynamix. It is a creative problem-solving process that is central to the development and survival of any business

'Innovate or Die!' the Department for Trade and Industry used to cry, to try to convince businesses that they needed to change to become competitive. But in many cases the call fell on deaf ears, as innovation has become a very hackneyed word giving mixed messages. In fact, we no longer include innovation in the titles of our conferences or workshops, as it has become a 'turn-off' for many businesspeople.

The famous quotation from *Star Wars*, 'May the Force be with you', sums up the impression that many people have, and one often-used definition of innovation, 'the profitable exploitation of new ideas', adds to the belief that it is almost a mystical power linked to 'Eureka' moments. There is confusion as to whether invention and innovation are the same thing. In fact, they are two different skills.

Many small businesses think that innovation is a random event, intrinsic and incapable of being taught; it is difficult to manage and therefore something to be left to specialists. Businesses survive and grow by developing and improving strategic processes, and innovation is felt not to fall into this category. However, if we consider the definition of innovation as shown in *Innovation Management and the Knowledge-driven Economy*, a report from the EU Directorate-General for Enterprise, we see that it is a process – and, more importantly, a creative problem-solving process. Managing and seeking to solve problems is something that most businesspeople will find easy to understand.

Innovation enables the businessperson to challenge and improve his or her business model. It is the framework that underpins the successful growth of businesses.

Innovation is:

■ A process, more specifically a problem-solving process.
■ A process occurring primarily within commercial firms, where the role of government agencies or public laboratories is to a certain extent secondary.
■ An interactive process involving relationships between firms with different actors. These relationships are both formal and informal, and position firms within commercial networks.
■ A diversified learning process. Learning may arise from different issues: learning by using, learning by doing or learning by sharing, internal or external sources of knowledge and the absorption capacity of firms.
■ A process involving the exchange of codified or tacit knowledge.
■ An interactive process of learning and exchange where interdependence between actors generates an innovative system or an innovation cluster.

Source: *Innovation Management and the Knowledge-driven Economy*, a report from the EU Directorate-General for Enterprise.

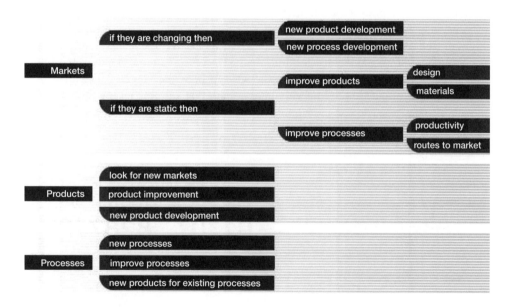

Figure 2.3.1 Strategies for innovation

But just being innovative is not enough. As with every other process, we need to be able to measure it to manage it and we need to ensure that our strategies and actions are all linked so as to achieve effective outcomes. The Balanced Business Scorecard is an ideal method to ensure that we are accurately assessing the performance of our business in the four key areas.

So what makes innovation happen? Like most things, it will only happen if senior management champion it and devote time to considering the future and understanding the needs of the marketplace.

A working environment that encourages creativity and a willingness to experiment is needed. Recognize that there will be failures, but these should be learning points. I think the old saying 'the person who never made a mistake never made anything' sums it up.

There needs to be a willingness to engage in joint ventures and collaborative efforts designed to develop and commercialize innovative solutions. No company holds all the skills, nor should it. Businesses need to understand where they fit within the innovation curve; are they developers of 'bleeding-edge' solutions or products? Or market developers who create or drive growth in a marketplace?

Good project management is designed to identify, develop and commercialize innovative solutions.

So how do businesses achieve these revolutionary insights? They use tried and tested tools and techniques to assess the potential of their business or product.

I'm sure that there are few of you who have not use the legendary SWOT (Strengths, Weaknesses, Opportunities, Threats) analysis to look at the effectiveness of your businesses. It's a simple tool, but one that produces results, especially when strengthened by using PEST or the enhanced PESTEC (Political, Economic, Social, Technological, Environmental, Cultural) analysis to look in more depth at the future trends that could impact upon your business. It ensures that you consider all market environment dynamics, both internal and external, that can impact on your business model. Too many businesses are internally focused and neglect to consider outside

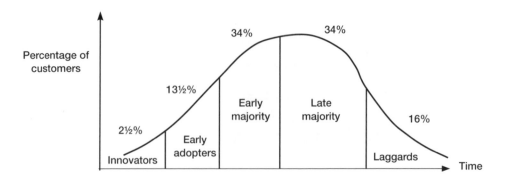

Source: Adapted from E. M. Rogers, *The Diffusion of Innovations*, Macmillan, 1962

Figure 2.3.2 The adoption process

Internal

External

Figure 2.3.3   SWOT analysis

forces, such as new technologies, that have the potential to change market processes and relationships. Of course, some of those forces may not be as high-profile as new technological advances; they may merely be local. In London, how many shops failed to think about the negative impact that the introduction of the Congestion Charge would have upon their passing trade!

Innovation is an inclusive process and only works when all parts of the business contribute to the process. Brainstorming is without doubt one of the most effective analysis tools for a business and a way to ensure 'buy-in' from all key personnel. However, the process must stay true to its 'blank sheet of paper' concept, with freedom to contribute by all, with no initial assessment as to the value of suggestions. It is often difficult for those involved in the business to remain impartial, and an external facilitator is required to ensure things remain on track.

Remember, you don't have to do it alone. There are a number of external influencers that can help you to identify and evaluate opportunities. The knowledge available from universities and other higher education institutes (HEIs) is often 'leading edge' and the resources that they have available are far superior to those that the average business can contemplate. Most, if not all, of the Regional Development Agencies actively support or fund initiatives that match businesses with HEIs, so strengthening the transfer of knowledge and innovation within their regions.

Having identified opportunities to be innovative, the next step is to evaluate them, consider the risks and develop a strong business case for implementation. As regards risks, consider what will be the 'blockers' or 'drivers' to implementation. There are a range of tools that help you to evaluate these and they include, among others:

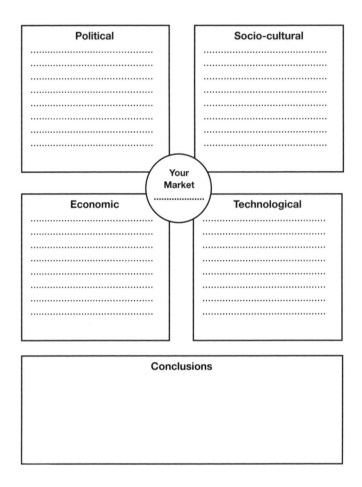

Figure 2.3.4 PEST analysis

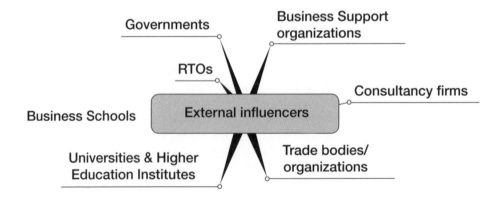

Figure 2.3.5 External influencers

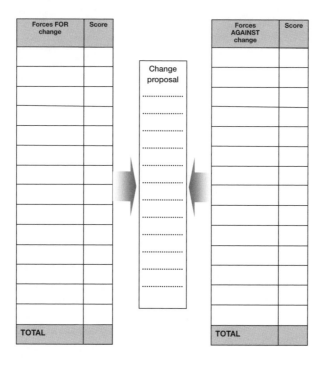

Forces FOR change	Score			Forces AGAINST change	Score

Change proposal

Figure 2.3.6   Force field analysis

Thinking Hat	Focus	Insights
	• Available data • Past trends • Gaps in the data	
	• Intuition • Gut reaction • Emotion	
	• The pessimistic • viewpoint • Why might it NOT work?	
	• The optimistic viewpoint	
	• Creativity • Other ways of doing things	
	• Process control	

Figure 2.3.7   The six hats technique

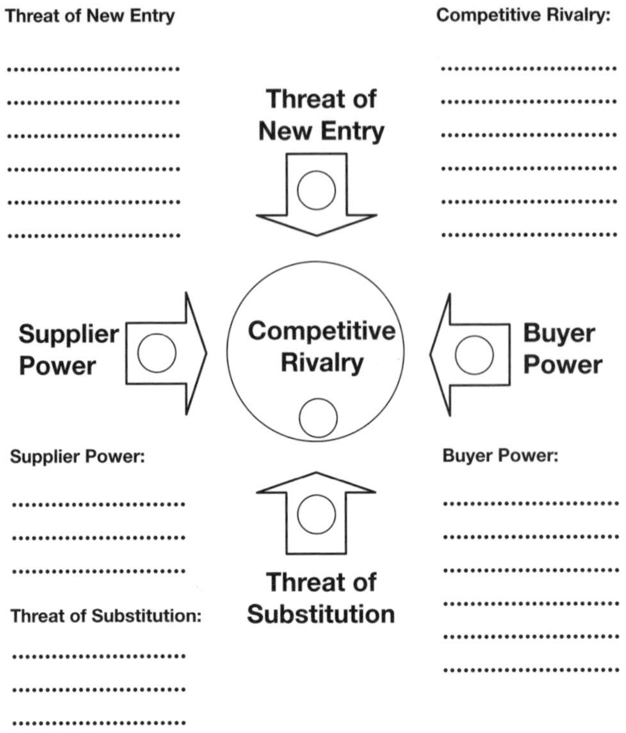

Threat of New Entry

....
....
....
....
....
....

Competitive Rivalry:

....
....
....
....
....
....

Threat of New Entry

Supplier Power

Competitive Rivalry

Buyer Power

Supplier Power:

....
....
....

Buyer Power:

....
....
....
....
....
....

Threat of Substitution:

....
....
....

Threat of Substitution

Figure 2.3.8 Michael Porter's five forces

- force field analysis;
- the six hats technique;
- Michael Porter's five forces.

Whilst it is natural to favour one or two of these tools and techniques, I would recommend that several of them are used in each case to ensure that a well-rounded evaluation is made.

Innovation is often linked with product development. Many businesses will only consider the short-term financial reward, but a careful evaluation of the value of products to the business needs to consider the life cycle of the product as well as its position within the business's portfolio of products. One of the classic tools used to evaluate product value is the Boston Matrix, developed by the Boston Consulting Group, which takes into account the future potential of products together with their financial contribution. In a similar way, businesses who have teams of account managers should conduct a similar evaluation of individual portfolios against a matrix of values, including financial ones, to ensure that maximum value is obtained from their client base.

This chapter has concentrated primarily upon the impact on business processes of what is best regarded as incremental innovation but can lead to major innovation.

Stars
Question Marks
Cash Cows
Dogs
C
D
B
A
E
F
H
G
I
% Market Growth Rate
20
10
10
5
0
x5
x2
1
x.5
x.2
Relative Market Share

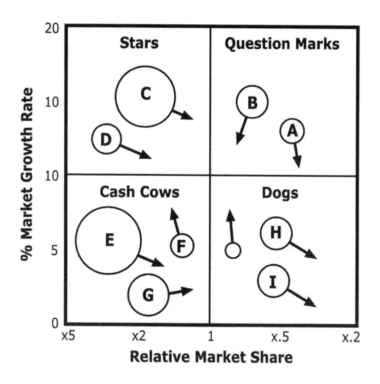

Figure 2.3.9 The Boston Matrix

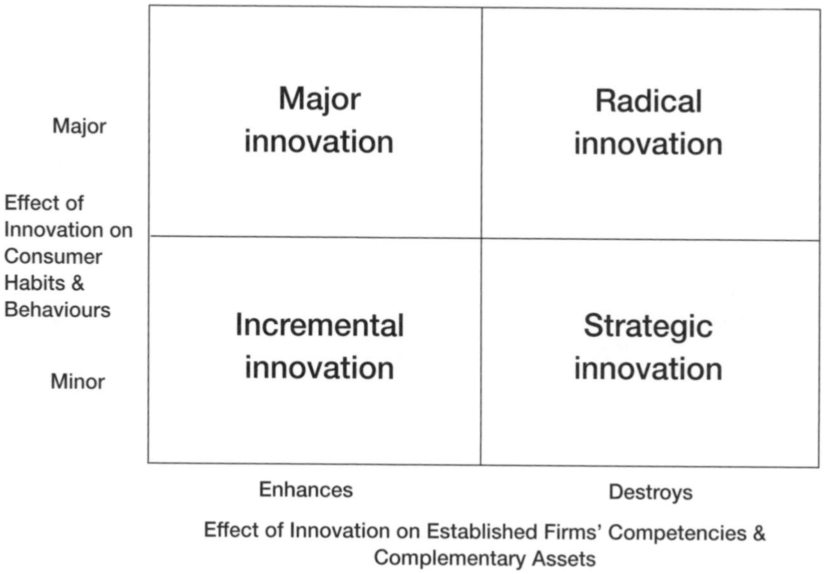

Major
Effect of Innovation on Consumer Habits & Behaviours
Minor
Major innovation
Radical innovation
Incremental innovation
Strategic innovation
Enhances
Destroys
Effect of Innovation on Established Firms' Competencies & Complementary Assets

Figure 2.3.10 Different types of innovation

To really benefit, businesses need to make innovation a strategic priority. They need to consider how they can best use their skills and resources to maximize their profit potential. They could be Pioneers, introducing radical new products with a view to obtaining an early profit, or Innovators that develop the market after a design or standard has become dominant, using their marketing and process skills to grow the initial market to achieve substantial profits. These two strategic positions require very different, and potentially conflicting, skill sets. Pioneers require small, highly flexible business structures with a focus upon technological skills, whilst Innovators inhabit large businesses with all the associated resources and teams required to implement large-scale marketing plans.

As you can see, innovation is fundamental to the development and survival of any business. To ignore the potential of innovation is to condemn a business to 'death by stagnation'. We need to continue to challenge businesses to continually re-examine every aspect of their business to achieve their potential.

Business Dynamix was established just over six years ago with the aim of enabling businesses to achieve their potential. Working with sectors ranging from nanotechnology to vehicle immobilization has enabled us to develop a unique range of tools and techniques to assist businesses to maximize their human and intellectual capital as well as their strategic planning and processes.

Peter Ives is the Managing Director of Business Dynamix and founded the business on the premise of accessing the best skills and technological advantages to develop sustainable high-growth businesses in the United Kingdom and continental Europe.

Peter Ives
Business Dynamix Ltd
Maple House
High Street
Potters Bar
Hertfordshire EN6 5BS
Tel: 01707 828712
Mobile: 07771 642266
www.businessdynamix.co.uk

Knowledge transfer

The United Kingdom has a world-class knowledge base. Jo Wheeler of Knowledge Transfer Partnerships reports on a programme that helps you draw on this expertise and boost your profits

With businesses today facing global competition like never before, the concept of 'knowledge transfer' has risen high on the national agenda. Amid trade liberalization and falling production costs in the emerging economies, innovation is the key for many small and medium-sized enterprises (SMEs). But how do directors ensure that new ventures survive in a global marketplace? According to the Government, knowledge transfer is the answer.

In today's progressive, information-driven economy, knowledge transfer is all about transferring good ideas, research results and skills between universities, other research organizations, business and the wider community, to enable innovative new products and services to be developed.

The Government has firmly placed knowledge transfer as a priority for the future, with one of the Department for Trade and Industry's objectives being '[to] promote effective transfer of knowledge to improve UK innovation performance and accelerate business exploitation of science and new and existing technologies'.

Key concerns central to SMEs looking to innovate often include:

- How do you begin to innovate?
- Where do you get your ideas from?
- How can you fund it?
- Can you minimize the risks?

Knowledge
Transfer
Partnerships

I need...

to find an innovative
solution to help my
business grow

to increase my
competitive
advantage

recently qualified
people to spearhead
a new project

access to experts who
can help me take my
business forward

And that's what you'll get!

Knowledge Transfer Partnerships provide resources and expertise to thriving organisations who wish to innovate, expand or improve their performance.

To find out how your business could benefit from a tailor-made Knowledge Transfer Partnership visit **www.ktponline.org.uk/companies** or call **0870 190 2829**

Investment in research provides much of the foundation for innovation, and the new products and services that result, but with growing financial pressures, companies are struggling to fund research and, furthermore, to exploit the findings commercially.

One of the Government's flagship schemes, which aims to address these issues and help companies improve their competitiveness and productivity, and promote innovation, is the DTI-led Knowledge Transfer Partnerships (KTP) programme. The Lincolnshire-based company Infranor, manufacturer of precision motion control systems, undertook a recent KTP in response to the September 11 terrorist attacks, which destroyed its business overnight as its customers immediately migrated to low-cost manufacturing centres in China. Dr Lee Fenney, Managing Director of Infranor, says of the KTP, 'The project before was intended to be a means of getting more profits out of the business. Now the project has given us a route to survival and also to tremendous growth.'

KTP utilizes the knowledge, technology and skills that reside within UK knowledge bases (academic or research institutions). A partnership is created between a company and the knowledge base in response to a specific and strategic project within the company. Each partnership employs one or more high-calibre Associates (recently qualified people) to work in the company on the project, which can last from one to three years. The Associates are supported by a knowledge base that has experience relevant to the project.

In the case of Infranor, the KTP project, supported by IT expertise from the University of Portsmouth, identified a market opportunity ideal for the company. Infranor developed an intelligent database that could remotely monitor and report on product performance. The technology was quickly delivered to market, with stunning sales results.

'Fortunately, in the UK we have a world-beating science and technology base. With Knowledge Transfer Partnerships we want to engage with this area of expertise to really improve the innovation performance of the UK economy,' says Kevin Knappett, head of the UK Knowledge Transfer Unit at the DTI.

KTP has proved to be an important platform from which SMEs can drive their business forward. Currently representing about 87 per cent of the KTP portfolio, the growing number of SMEs involved with KTP reflects the enormous benefits companies enjoy. Perhaps most important is the dedicated resource of experts the company is allocated, which in management consultancy terms would often be financially out of reach.

'We didn't just get the Associate, we got the university, and we didn't just get the one professor half a day a week, we actually got his friends, his colleagues. As they hit problems they were talking around the world... It was that shared benefit that you can't put a price on,' says Bob Andrews, Managing Director of High Wycombe-based Fulcrum Systems.

Business performance outputs vary considerably from case to case, given the rich variety of projects. Latest information shows that, on average, the business benefits that can be expected from a single KTP project are:

■ an increase of over £220,000 in annual profits before tax;
■ the creation of three genuine new jobs;
■ an increase in the skills of existing staff.

Innovation is the essential response to the vital challenge of globalization. According to the DTI, innovation must be embedded throughout British business, not just in products but in processes too. 'Innovation is not just a one-off event, it's a state of mind, a hunger for what's new: new ways of marketing, new organizational structures and better ways of using people's skills,' says Alan Johnson, MP.

An MIT study estimated that 80 per cent of all productivity growth in the past century has been due to innovation, and knowledge transfer, it claims, is vital in achieving this. KTP delivers economic benefits in three areas central to innovation, namely collaboration, the lowering of risks, and the diffusion of technology and best practice.

Collaboration

The collaboration between businesses and knowledge bases helps to solve barriers to innovation. A much wider range of research can be undertaken and captured, increasing the chances of a successful technological and commercial outcome. 'The KTP Associate provided the company with a focus for research, development and innovation... we got clarity, and projects started to happen. Getting involved with KTP... had the effect of broadening our horizons and I have no doubt it will help us enter new markets,' says Hugh Stewart, Chairman of Caledonian Alloys Ltd.

Lowering risks

High-technology SMEs that wish, or need, to grow quickly often have to undertake R&D projects that are relatively large in relation to the financial value of the company. KTP projects are part-funded by the Government, with the balance of the costs coming from the company partner. An SME can expect to contribute a third of the project costs while a large company would contribute half. Currently, the average annual project costs are around £60,000. Bearing in mind the dedicated resource of experts the company receives throughout the course of the project, the investment the company makes in a KTP project is significantly lower than the cost of raising external finance.

'There was a tremendous advantage to a Knowledge Transfer Partnership with the university. You would probably have to raise a couple of million pounds minimum to carry this out on a purely commercial scale,' says Adrian Godwin, Chairman of Lerch Bates & Associates.

Diffusion of technology and best practice

Increasingly, firms are having to incorporate a number of technologies into their products and processes whilst keeping up with an escalating number of changes in business practice. Combined with the quickening pace of technological change, this imposes a burden that is felt particularly heavily by SMEs. As a result, many SMEs are not adopting new technologies and business practices as soon as they should. KTP provides businesses with information and solutions to these important issues, encouraging companies to improve their service offerings, based on the application of business best practice. Through KTP, companies can exploit economies of scale that would otherwise be unavailable to them.

A company that has benefited greatly from the innovation that KTP facilitates is P&L Systems. The company recognized that it had got about as far as it could selling one product, fly-killers. A KTP project with Northumbria University gave it the expertise and support it needed to embed design-led product innovation into the company's culture. 'It's really changed the company. The turnover's significantly increased, the profit of the business has significantly increased, and… there's a lot of future development,' says P&L Systems' Managing Director, Chris Lee. Tom Holmes, the Associate involved in the project, comments, 'We've now got the mechanism to develop innovative products; we've now got a number of quality products that we know are right for the market. It's a case of "let's go out there and grab hold of that".'

Key facts:

■ During the course of 2004/05, over £32 million of grant support was committed to new Knowledge Transfer Partnerships (KTPs), augmented by over £53m from participating companies.
■ During 2004/05, grants were offered on behalf of sponsors to 425 new partnerships and at the close of the year there were 858 active partnerships, with places for 958 Associates.
■ The main areas of technology/knowledge for KTP during 2004/05 are:
  – social science and marketing: 13%;
  – management science: 10%;
  – science: 16%;
  – engineering (including design): 40%;
  – IT: 21%.
■ The distribution of company size of the 858 partnerships as at March 2005 was as follows:
  – micro-businesses (fewer than 10 employees): 14%;
  – small enterprises (10–49 employees): 45%;
  – medium-sized enterprises (50–249 employees): 28%;
  – large enterprises (250 or more employees): 13%.

If you would like further information on the benefits that Knowledge Transfer Partnerships can offer, visit the website www.ktponline.org.uk or call 0870 190 2829 or e-mail companies@ktponline.org.uk. You can also obtain information about Knowledge Transfer Partnerships from the business support network Business Link (tel: 0845 600 9006; website: www.businesslink.gov.uk). Knowledge Transfer Partnerships is one of the DTI's business support products.

Research and development tax relief for SMEs

If you spend £20,000 on research and development, then you could set £30,000 against your profits. Jon Sutton, a partner at Dixon Wilson, explains how to qualify

The aim of this chapter is to set out the operation of the research and development (R&D) tax relief that may be claimed by small and medium-sized companies, the qualifying conditions that must be satisfied and the items for which relief may be obtained.

Qualifying companies

This chapter only addresses the relief available to small or medium-sized companies. A company is regarded as small or medium-sized if it, 1) has fewer than 250 employees and either or both of an annual turnover not exceeding 40m euros and a balance sheet total not exceeding 27m euros; and 2) has less than 25 per cent of its capital or voting rights owned by one or more companies that are not small or medium-sized (with certain limited exceptions).

Qualifying expenditure

The expenditure qualifying for relief must satisfy certain criteria, as follows:

■ The expenditure must be at least £10,000 per accounting period.
■ If the accounting period is more or less than 12 months in duration then the £10,000 is adjusted pro rata.
■ the expenditure must be revenue expenditure attributable to R&D that is related to the trade of the company and is carried out by the company or on its behalf.
■ The expenditure must relate to:
  – the cost of employing qualifying staff;
  – consumable stores;
  – subcontractor costs (with restrictions).

The company claiming the relief should own the intellectual property that is developed as a result of the work.

Specific detail concerning the qualifying costs

Qualifying staff

Qualifying staff are staff who are directly involved in the R&D. They could be researchers or managers. The staff costs must be apportioned between R&D and other activity where the staff are not involved full time with the research and development. The staff need not be directly employed by the company but certain conditions must be met. Costs that qualify include salaries, bonuses and national insurance contributions as well as pension contributions.

Consumable stores

Consumable stores are items directly utilized in the R&D. They include materials and equipment where the latter has a short useful life. Computer software and transformable materials also qualify. Transformable materials include water, fuel and power. Equipment that will be retained for the longer term and provide benefits over a number of periods is capital expenditure and does not qualify for this relief, although other allowances may be available.

Subcontractor costs

Typically, a subcontractor who is providing services in relation to R&D to a company cannot claim relief on its costs because it does not own the intellectual property that is created. The subcontractor does not have to be small or medium-sized and it need not be a UK company. There are special reliefs available where the subcontractor and the company claiming the relief are connected, so as to ensure that proper relief is given for the costs incurred.

Ownership of the intellectual property

The company claiming the relief must own the intellectual property. Even if the R&D fails, the cost still qualifies for relief provided it would have qualified had it been a success. There is one exception to this, which is for small and medium-sized companies where work is subcontracted to them.

Nature of the relief

The relief is a deduction from profits for tax purposes. However, if the business is loss making, the additional loss can be surrendered in exchange for an immediate repayment of tax rather than be carried forward to be set against future profits.

Claim against profits

If the R&D relief is to be claimed as a cost against profits, then the relief is calculated by adding a further 50 per cent to the qualifying expenditure for tax purposes. This is then claimed in addition to the 100 per cent of the costs already available. For a tax-paying company this reduces the liability. For a loss-making company it increases the loss available to carry forward (or backward) or to use against other income or to surrender to other companies. So, for instance, if a company spent £20,000 on qualifying expenditure, then it would get relief against its profits totalling £30,000; this is the £20,000 of cost and the extra £10,000 of relief.

Claim as a tax credit

If the company is loss making, then it may be that a relief as a deduction from profits is not attractive. In this situation the company can obtain a repayment of tax from HMRC but only up to the lower of:

■ 16% of the surrenderable loss (ie 24% of the qualifying expenditure);
■ the total PAYE and Class 1 national insurance paid by the company in that accounting period.

The loss surrendered to a tax credit is equal to the lower of:
■ 150% of the qualifying expenditure;
■ the total loss of the trade after any claims made or that could be made against other profits or gains of the same period, and other reliefs claimed in respect of the losses.

Making a claim for relief

A claim for relief made by claiming the enhanced cost against the income of the company must be done via the company's corporation tax return in the relevant period. This must be made within two years for periods ending after 31 March 2006. If instead a repayment is to be claimed, then the claim must be made within one year of filing the tax return for the company.

Other relevant issues

Pre-trading expenditure

Where a company has not yet commenced its trade, it can still claim the R&D tax relief provided the R&D is related to the trade it is anticipated will be commenced in due course.

Joint ventures

It is quite common for a company to carry on R&D through a joint venture so as to bring together the skills and abilities of two complementary companies. Where a corporate joint venture is used, it is the joint venture company that needs to claim the relief. Where instead there is a non-corporate joint venture, each company will normally own the R&D that it itself creates. Each of the two companies will be able to claim the relief on the relevant part of its expenditure.

Grants and subsidies

Where some form of qualifying government grant or subsidy is received by the company, none of the cost for the project qualifies for the R&D tax relief. This is the position irrespective of whether the entire cost of the project is covered by that grant or subsidy. However, companies receiving such a grant or subsidy may be able to claim large company relief, as that is not classed as a state aid. There are certain exceptions where the grant or subsidy provided by the company is not paid state aid.

Jon Sutton is a partner at Dixon Wilson Chartered Accountants, working closely with and advising the owners and managers of unquoted, often family-owned, companies. To contact him, please e-mail him at jonsutton@dixonwilson.co.uk or call 020 7680 8100.

New ideas need expert protection if you want them to soar

Intellectual property

Exclusivity improves your returns, so make an early start in developing your intellectual property, says Stephen Carter at Mewburn Ellis LLP

Intellectual property (eg technical innovations, brands and designs) is an important asset for any business. Intellectual property rights, if exercised correctly, provide businesses with the opportunity to gain exclusivity in their intellectual property, allowing them to maximize the return on the investment needed to create the intellectual property in the first instance.

Some intellectual property (IP) rights come into existence automatically. One example is copyright. Stronger rights, however, need to be actively sought. Without at least a basic understanding of what these rights are and how they are obtained, businesses run the risk of missing the opportunity for protection altogether.

For small companies in particular, securing appropriate protection for their IP can be absolutely critical to success. This is especially the case for rapidly growing businesses that must look to outside sources for funds to support their growth, as adequate IP protection is more often than not a prerequisite for such investments. At the same time, it must be appreciated that there can be significant costs associated with obtaining intellectual property protection, so any IP strategy must strike a balance between these costs and the commercial value of owning the IP. Every small business should therefore develop an IP strategy at the earliest opportunity as part of its overall business strategy, and update the strategy regularly as it grows.

This chapter provides an introduction to the three principal forms of registered intellectual property protection: patents, registered trade marks and designs. It is of course impossible to explain in a limited number of pages all the nuances of the law, and it is always advisable to seek specific advice from a specialist in any given situation. However, armed with the practical guidance given here, businesses should be in a better position to start developing an IP strategy to protect their intellectual assets, which today are very often the foundations on which a business is built.

Patents

A patent is a legal right granted for a new invention. It allows the owner of the patent to take legal action against others who use the invention without the patent owner's permission. The right has a maximum lifetime of 20 years in most countries, from the date of the patent application. What a patent does *not* do is give the owner an automatic right to use the invention. He or she still needs to take care to avoid infringing other people's rights.

Increasingly it is advisable to obtain protection not only in the United Kingdom but also in other countries, which can be achieved by filing applications directly in the countries of interest, with a European patent or, especially if cover is required in many countries outside Europe, via the Patent Cooperation Treaty (PCT). A European patent can cover your invention in some of or all of the member countries of the European Patent Organisation (there are currently 31 members, including all of the EU countries except Malta), while a PCT also covers many other countries. The appropriate route to take will depend on the specific circumstances of the case, although the PCT route is often an attractive one for businesses that want to keep their options open in the short term whilst minimizing costs.

It is not strictly necessary to obtain a patent, as you are free to exploit your invention without one, although only if no one else already has patent rights to it. However, if you do not have a patent, it can be very hard to stop other people copying your invention. Note that even if you do have a patent, you do not automatically have the right to use your invention.

A patent belongs to the inventor, unless he or she has given the rights to someone else. Normally, if the inventor is an employee and makes the invention in the course of his or her work, the rights belong to the employer. It is important to know which person(s) actually made an inventive contribution to the technology covered by a patent application, in order to know who will own the rights in any resulting patent. It is generally easier to sort out the chain of ownership and any possible ownership disputes at an early stage of the application procedure rather than leaving things until later, when matters may have become much more contentious and relevant evidence may have been lost or forgotten. In some countries (eg the United States) the inventorship issue is so important that deliberately falsifying it in a patent application can invalidate any patent resulting from the application.

The owner of the patent may license it, allowing others to use the invention, and can sell it to someone else.

To be patentable, your invention must be new; that is, the invention must never have been made public *in any way* before you apply to the relevant Patent Office(s). This means that your invention must not have been published by someone else before you. It also means that if you want a patent, you *must not* tell anyone about your invention, except in confidence, until your application is filed with the Patent Office. Also, it must involve an inventive step. This means that the invention must not simply be an obvious development of something that is already known. Also, it must be capable of being made or used in any kind of industry, including agriculture. Most inventions satisfy this final requirement.

An invention is typically an apparatus, a product, a manufacturing process, etc. Your invention must not fall into an excluded category (eg works of art, scientific theories, mathematical methods and the presentation of information).

The fact that you own a patent will often deter competitors from using your invention. It helps to refer to it in your product literature once your patent has been granted. However, if your invention is being used by someone without your consent – the patent is being infringed – you can obtain an injunction to stop them and claim damages (compensation).

You cannot sue for infringement until your patent is granted (in the United Kingdom this usually takes about four years from the first application date). However, once your patent is granted, you may be able to claim damages in retrospect from the date your patent application was published.

Trade marks

For hundreds of years, traders have put symbols or marks on their goods to indicate their origin. For centuries there have been cases in the United Kingdom involving trade marks, which can be traced as far back as the reign of James I, almost 400 years ago. Nowadays it is possible (and often advisable), as it is with patents, to register a trade mark not only in the United Kingdom but in other countries using the Community Trade Mark system or the Madrid Protocol (like the PCT, the Madrid Protocol has members throughout the world and is the nearest thing existing to an international trade mark system).

A trade mark is something (eg a word or sign) that enables customers to identify goods or services as coming from a particular source, even though they may not know the source's identity. A reputable trader will want his or her products or services to have desirable and reliable qualities, so that the customer will come to regard the trader's trade mark as a guarantee of quality.

Marks can be very valuable and important if properly developed by advertising, promotion and correct use on quality products or services. Thus, it is vitally important for the mark's repute and the producer's repute to protect the mark in the United Kingdom and abroad.

The strongest means of protecting a mark is to register it. An unregistered mark can be used, but without registration your rights are far harder (and potentially more expensive) to enforce. You should always consider registering a new mark when the cost of changing the mark is likely to exceed the cost of registration. If advertising costs are taken into consideration, this will almost certainly be the case when you are introducing a significant new mark or brand name. It is particularly beneficial to register any mark you believe has a future beyond a few months.

To be registrable, a mark must be distinctive. It can be anything that can be depicted graphically: a single word, logo, picture or a mixture of any of these. A mark can be a three-dimensional shape as long as this is not the result of the function of the object or container. A mark must not be descriptive or deceptive; it cannot be a common surname or geographical name, a national flag, or someone else's heraldic device (though sometimes parts of such items can be acceptable); it must not be confusable with any earlier registered mark.

In principle, a trade mark registration gives the proprietor the right to stop others from using confusingly similar marks in relation to similar goods or services. In some circumstances the owner of a registered mark can even stop others from using a mark for goods or services that are not similar to those for which it is registered. A UK or Madrid registration also gives the proprietor a potential defence to an infringement action brought by a third party.

Designs

In the context of intellectual property the 'design' of a product is generally its shape, or ornamentation applied to it, although the exact definition varies between different types of protection. Essentially, the design of a product relates to its appearance, rather than to technical principles of its construction or operation. Designs may be registered in the United Kingdom (UK registered designs) and/or in the European Union (registered Community designs). There are also certain automatic rights conferred in the United Kingdom and the European Union on unregistered designs. Registered protection is also available abroad, but there is less harmonization of design laws around the world than there is with patents and trade marks, so the requirements and procedures vary significantly from one country to another. The following focuses on UK and EU rights.

A UK-registered design or a registered Community design gives a 'monopoly' right; that is, a right to stop anybody else using the registered design irrespective of whether they copied it.

A design may be the appearance of the whole or a part of a product (including its inside) and may arise from the lines, contours, colours, shape, texture, material or ornamentation of the product. The product may even be a graphic symbol such as a computer icon or a typographical typeface.

A design registration cannot protect features of a design that are solely dictated by the product's technical function, or features that are required to permit the product to be connected to or placed in, around or against another product so that either product may perform its function. However, a design that serves the purpose of allowing the assembly of modular products may be registered.

A UK registered design (in the United Kingdom) or a registered Community design (in the European Union) gives its proprietor the exclusive right to make, use, sell, import and export any product embodying the design, if it is a shape, or bearing the design if it is ornamentation. These rights extend to similar designs that do not produce a substantially different impression on the informed user.

The proprietor can take action against any third party who carries out any of the rights exclusive to the proprietor within the designated area without the proprietor's permission, even if they are using a design that they created independently and without copying.

A registration can last 25 years if renewed (through payment of a fee) at five-yearly intervals.

Unregistered design right (UDR) in the United Kingdom and unregistered Community design (UCD) in the European Union come into existence automatically. UK UDR gives its owner the right to prevent unauthorized copying of the design in the United Kingdom; UCD gives its owner the right to prevent unauthorized copying of the design throughout the European Union. In contrast to registered design rights, these are not monopoly rights, in the sense that only if a third party produces an article by copying is design right infringed. The owner may also prevent unauthorized dealing, eg by importation, possession, sale, hire, offer to sell or hire, in infringing articles provided the party who does so has knowledge or reason to believe he or she is dealing in an infringing article.

A UK UDR comes into being upon the making of an article to a particular design or by the creation of a 'design document' (a record of the design, which may take any form such as a drawing, photograph, written description – even a knitting pattern) by a 'qualified person' (or as a result of employment by or a commission from such a person). A qualified person is a national or resident of the European Union or of certain non-EU countries that offer reciprocal rights to UK nationals. A company may count as a 'qualified person'.

Protection is for 15 years for UK UDR (during the last five years, protection is reduced) and for 3 years for UCD.

Stephen Carter has a degree and a Master's in Mechanical Engineering from the University of Bath. He joined Mewburn Ellis in 1994 and is a Chartered Patent Attorney and European Patent Attorney. He worked for a law firm from 2000 to 2004, gaining experience in IP litigation and due diligence work for corporate transactions and IPOs. He rejoined Mewburn Ellis as a partner in 2004. Stephen does patent work in general, engineering and software fields and also some designs work. Further details:

Mewburn Ellis LLP
York House
23 Kingsway
London WC2B 6HP
Tel: 020 7240 4405
e-mail: mail@mewburn.com
www.mewburn.com

MEWBURN ELLIS LLP is one of the UK's largest firms of Chartered Patent Attorneys, European Patent Attorneys, European Trade Mark Attorneys and European Design Attorneys. We have over 50 patent and trade mark attorneys and technical specialists, covering the full range of intellectual property issues: Patents, Trade Marks, Designs, Industrial Copyright and related matters.

Our clients are numerous and varied, from innovative start-up companies to some of the world's leading businesses, as well as private individuals, academic institutions and charitable organisations. They are involved in a wide range of business activities, reflecting our expertise across the technical and Intellectual Property disciplines.

A significant amount of our work comes from UK based clients. We work closely with these clients to prepare and file patent, trade mark and design applications in the UK, Europe and elsewhere. We also have extensive experience in contentious IP matters, including oppositions at the European Patent Office, OHIM (Community Trade Marks Office) and the UK Patent Office.

Day to day handling of European and UK intellectual property rights inevitably brings us special expertise in European/UK intellectual property practice. We also have a good understanding of practices in other important jurisdictions, gained in part through a programme of secondments that over the past few years has seen many of our qualified attorneys spend a period of 2 or 3 months with law firms in the US, China and Japan.

We believe strongly that our role is to provide a positive service giving the benefit of that expertise to every client, whether British or from overseas. Our first aim is therefore always to be responsive and alert to the instructions and information which our client provides. We do not carry out instructions passively, but seek positively to make additional contributions using our special expertise, whilst being sensitive to a client's budget. This distinctive approach often leads to beneficial changes in a proposed course of action, and has value for all of our clients.

We aim also to treat our clients' intellectual property rights not in isolation, but as part of their legal, commercial and industrial environment.

"Peers regard **Mewburn Ellis** as a top firm"

LLP

Legal 500, 2004

Want to know why?

Mewburn Ellis is one of the UK's largest firms of Chartered Patent Attorneys, European Patent Attorneys, European Trade Mark Attorneys and European Design Attorneys.

Day to day handling of European and UK intellectual property rights brings us special expertise in European/UK intellectual property practice. We believe strongly that our role is to provide a positive service giving the benefit of that expertise to every client, whether British or from overseas.

Our first aim is always to be responsive and alert to the instructions and information which our client provides.

We do not carry out instructions passively, but seek positively to make additional contributions using our special expertise. This distinctive approach often leads to beneficial changes in a proposed course of action, and has particular value for overseas clients.

We aim to treat our clients' intellectual property rights not in isolation, but as part of their legal, commercial and industrial environment.

LONDON	**BRISTOL**	**MANCHESTER**	**CAMBRIDGE**
York House	No. 1	Bridgewater House	Newnham House
23 Kingsway	Redcliff Street	Whitworth Street	Cambridge Business Park
London WC2B 6HP	Bristol BS1 6NP	Manchester M1 6LT	Cambridge CB4 0WZ
Tel: 020 7240 4405	**Tel: 0117 926 6411**	**Tel: 0161 247 7722**	**Tel: 01223 420383**
Fax: 020 7240 9339	Fax: 0117 926 5692	Fax: 0161 247 7766	Fax: 01223 423792

patents • trademarks • designs • copyright

www.mewburn.com

Making standards work

Standards are at the heart of successful innovation, says Marcus Long, Head of External Affairs, British Standards Institution

At heart, a standard is simply an agreed means of achieving a shared goal. Standards make life safer, healthier and easier for people, organizations and enterprises. They enable communication and trade, and promote efficiency and growth.

Business benefits of standards

All businesses can benefit from standards, from local firms to multinationals. The key advantages of standards include:

- improved products or services;
- greater competitive advantage;
- increased size and satisfaction of customer base;
- simplified regulatory compliance;
- reduction of business costs and the likelihood of mistakes.

Maintaining and demonstrating high quality is amongst the most effective ways of retaining existing customers and attracting new ones. Standards offer a key way to convince potential customers that you meet the highest and most widely respected levels of quality, safety and reliability.

By applying technical standards you can ensure that your products or services are compatible with those manufactured or provided by others. This interoperability can be particularly beneficial when exporting, and can provide a reliable and consistent reference point to reduce the risk of errors and misunderstandings.

Compliance with standards can help you to meet mandatory legal obligations regarding such things as product safety and environmental protection as well as assist in opening up new markets.

Standards are at the heart of successful innovation. Defining and measuring product performance while protecting intellectual property, they provide a framework for enhanced research and development, shared knowledge and increased efficiency. Using established standards reduces the time, effort and costs involved in the development of new products, increasing their likelihood of success in the marketplace.

Types of standards

There are three basic types of standards:

∎ formal consensus standards;
∎ informal commissioned standards;
∎ regulatory standards.

Formal consensus standards

Formal consensus standards fall into two main categories. Technical standards detail specifications that businesses can use to shape their products or services so that they fit market or regulatory needs. Quality management system (QMS) standards establish recognized best practice for the way processes should be managed.

Formal consensus standards are established by a broad consensus of industry experts and representatives of government, business and society. New standards are created when a genuine societal or commercial need has been identified, often when a business develops a new product, process or service to which no existing standard can be applied. These standards are revised as necessary to keep pace with societal and/or commercial needs.

Informal commissioned standards

Informal commissioned standards vary from simple guidelines on telephone answering procedures to joint ventures between organizations to establish a dominant technological format. Informal standards offer many benefits in terms of quality and efficiency.

Regulatory standards

Standards are designed primarily for voluntary use. However, some laws and regulations refer specifically to certain standards, or use them as the simplest way of showing compliance. Developed collaboratively, these standards form a passport for business, offering a simple and effective means of meeting regulatory requirements and securing a voice for business in the standards development process.

British Standards

The British Standards Institution (BSI) is the world's leading standards and quality services organization. Formed in 1901 and incorporated under Royal Charter in 1929 it is also the oldest standards making body in the world. BSI is independent of government, industry and trade associations and is a non-profit distributing organization. It is a globally recognised impartial body that serves both public and private sectors.

Standards cover every area of life and are codes of best practice that improve safety, efficiency, interoperability and facilitate trade. British Standards is the National Standards Body of the UK responsible for facilitating, drafting, publishing and marketing standards and related information products. BSI provides organizations with leading-edge best practice solutions that support and represent the needs of UK business and society at home and abroad.

British Standards facilitates the production of British, European and international standards by working with manufacturing and service industries, businesses and governments. Over the last decade BSI has evolved from being largely a standards setting organization to develop a commercial portfolio of global products and services in the quality sector. In 2002 a Memorandum of Understanding was signed with HM Government, whereby the Government agreed to consult with BSI on standard issues.

In the UK, BSI's 27,000 standards cover every area of life from technical guidelines for production processes in a diverse range of industries to specifications for 'making things happen', such as in the service sector and in systems for the management of CCTV systems, customer loyalty and sustainable development. BSI represents UK interests both at home and abroad, and the standards have been proven through independent research commissioned by the DTI to contribute £2.5bn to annual GDP.

In 2006, BSI acquired major German certification business NIS ZERT and Entropy International Ltd, one of the world's leading providers of performance and sustainability software solutions. As a result of these strategic moves, and through more than a century of growth, the BSI Group now delivers a comprehensive business services portfolio to our clients, helping them raise their performance and enhance their competitiveness world-wide.

"Standards helped our business grow."

"Through standards we doubled food service production and improved our quality too."

Mark Smith, Production Controller, Wilkin & Sons Ltd

COMMITTED TO STANDARDS.

For Wilkin & Sons, the British Retail Consortium (BRC) Global Standard for Food has led to improvements that have dramatically increased production in just one year. Production Controller Mark Smith explains: "As part of our commitment to standards we established continuous improvement meetings, the outcome of these has led to changes on our production lines which has improved productivity in some areas by more than 100%."

Greater efficiencies on the production line mean the business has been able to cut costs and therefore compete more aggressively on price for new contracts. As a result Wilkin & Sons recorded the biggest sales increase to airlines in over 30 years and they are still providing the benchmark for quality. The business is now looking at adopting new standards to boost performance further.

From streamlining your efficiency to honing your competitive advantage, standards can boost your business too. To find out more visit www.StandardsWork.co.uk

Selecting and applying standards

Choosing the right standards to adopt and implementing them can be a quick and easy process. Advice and additional information are available through such organizations as the British Standards Institution's Business Information Consultancy, or from www. StandardsWork.co.uk. The following factors are important to consider when selecting standards:

■ evaluating the market;
■ considering your customers;
■ consulting the professionals.

Market research will provide valuable information on the standards used by competitors, and the market access opportunities that standards have provided for them. Trade associations may also be able to recommend suitable standards, while BSI's online standards directory, www.bsonline.bsi-global.com, may prove an invaluable source of up-to-date information.

Buying and introducing a standard

Once the most appropriate standard for your business has been identified and purchased, implementation can be a surprisingly straightforward process. On receiving your standard, it is advisable to devise a plan for its implementation, to ensure that the standard is applied efficiently and effectively. Once the standards' requirements are understood, all employees and company representatives should be made aware of the changes called for and, most importantly, the benefits to be gained.

Certification and product marking

A product certification mark provides assurances to customers that a recognized standard has been met. In some cases this is mandatory. For example, certain types of product are required to bear the CE mark to indicate compliance with European Directives. Even where certification is not mandatory, many organizations opt for independent verification that they have introduced a standard correctly. Voluntary certification makes a powerful statement to customers and competitors, and should be carried out by a body approved by the United Kingdom Accreditation Service (UKAS).

The certification process

When an application for certification is made, representatives from the certification body visit the business to examine how the standard is being used. The time taken and the cost involved depend upon such factors as the number of employees the business has and which standard has been implemented. Following this inspection, the certifying body either issues a compliance certificate or provides guidance about where things need to be improved so that compliance can be achieved. Another visit is arranged to check whether the necessary improvements have been made. Once issued, compliance certificates need to be renewed periodically.

Case study: Anglo Felt

Anglo Felt Industries, based in Rochdale, manufactures a range of products made from recycled and waste fibres. The company was founded in 1939 and has 30 full-time employees. The Managing Director, Simon Macaulay, explains how the implementation of ISO 9000 has helped the business achieve the following benefits:

- all-round improvements to business;
- increased customer satisfaction through monitoring of product quality;
- implementation of a complaints management system;
- a continual assessment process leading to enhanced performance.

How much time does it take?

Anglo Felt Industries spends about one day per month on administration relating to the use of the standard. Simon Macaulay says, 'As far as we are concerned it's time very well spent. Once you've introduced a standard into your business, it's important to publicize the fact. We put information on our letterheads, because we feel it makes a statement about our commitment to quality.'

Why comply with standards?

Compliance with ISO 9000 ensures that an organization achieves consistently high standards, and gives added assurance to customers about the quality of products and services. Simon Macaulay says, 'I also think it is quite hard to do business in certain areas without standards – sometimes customers won't buy from you unless you are compliant. In my opinion, many small firms can be quite disorganized, so introducing standards helps to improve the structure of a business.'

With which standards does Anglo Felt Industries comply?

Anglo Felt decided to sign up to ISO 9000:1994 over 10 years ago. Since then, the quality management standard has been updated in response to the changing needs of business, and is now called ISO 9001:2000. Simon Macaulay says, 'Our products also conform to BS 5808 for carpet underlay, and water holding standard DIN 53923.'

Is Anglo Felt Industries working toward compliance with further standards?

Anglo Felt Industries competes in a highly specialized marketplace. Standards provide a powerful message in terms of product differentiation, and can open doors to new markets. Simon Macaulay says, 'We're trying to get our products to meet more standards all the time. At the moment we're aiming to meet the standard for flame-retardant material that is suitable for use in the shipping industry.'

Marcus Long joined the British Standards Institution in April 2005 as Head of External Affairs. With responsibility for key relationships, Marcus interfaces with government, business and consumer groups to develop standards and spread the messages about the advantages of standards and standardization to a wider audience.

British Standards is the National Standards Body of the United Kingdom responsible for facilitating, drafting, publishing and marketing standards and related information products. British Standards provides organizations with leading-edge best practice solutions that represent and support the needs of UK business and society at home and abroad.

For more information about standards and the benefits they can bring to your business, visit www.StandardsWork.co.uk.

Accreditation

Proper evaluation of your goods and services helps build confidence through the supply chain, says Jon Murthy at UKAS

If you are busy running a business, sourcing the right people and organizations to carry out your certification, inspection, testing or calibration work can be time-consuming and fraught with unknowns.

There is an answer. Decide to use UKAS-accredited evaluation services and you will find that finding the right supplier is made easier, saving your business time and money in a whole host of ways. Doors to new markets will also open up, whether they are public service organizations, or customers in overseas markets.

Businesses need to have confidence in the goods and services that they procure. There is a means of building trust in the marketplace in the supply of goods and services. Accreditation by the United Kingdom Accreditation Service (UKAS) is the key to ensuring that suppliers, purchasers and specifiers can have confidence in the quality of goods and in the provision of services throughout the supply chain.

Companies big and small buy independent evaluations either through choice (to reduce the risk of product failure, for example) or as a consequence of legal requirements (such as health and safety regulations). Most commonly these evaluations are calibration of equipment, product testing, inspection of equipment, and certification systems. It is the ability to distinguish between a proven, competent evaluator that ensures that the selection is an informed choice and not a gamble. UKAS accreditation means the evaluator can show to its customer that it has been successful in meeting the requirements of international accreditation standards.

Too many of Britain's companies run the risk of undermining their long-term success by purchasing independent evaluations that are not UKAS accredited.

Examples of such risks are product failure caused by invalid test results, increased costs caused by inaccurate measurement, legal action arising from inadequately inspected equipment resulting in accidents, and rejected tenders and orders citing lack of a UKAS-accredited certificate or test report.

Rob Blackburn of Redhill Analysts confirms this point: 'Using a UKAS-accredited laboratory militates against risk – commercial, safety, and legal. It's a way of saying "relax".'

What is accreditation?

Accreditation is the procedure by which an authoritative body gives formal recognition that a body or person is *competent* to carry out specific tasks. Accreditation is an ongoing business process rather than a one-off achievement. If an organization wishes to be accredited and is operating in an area in which UKAS has existing expertise, an assessment will be carried out to establish that:

- the evaluator is impartial;
- the evaluator is technically competent to do the work in question;
- the resources and facilities are appropriate and sufficient for the work;
- the evaluator's actual performance is to the required standard;
- the evaluator is capable of sustaining the required level of performance.

Once an organization is accredited, an assessment is carried out annually at the customer's premises by a team of experienced UKAS assessment managers, supported, where required, by independent assessors with specialist technical expertise. They work closely with the customer's management team and use structured, rigorous and proven assessment methodology. They test the customer's management systems and technical competence in the field for which the customer is seeking accreditation.

UKAS assessors act on behalf of the customer's industry sector but they are also conscious of the customer's business objectives. The assessors check that the customer is achieving what it claims to be achieving and they provide constructive criticism and will advise on best practice. A UKAS assessment is a comprehensive and transparent health check on a business by a respected and independent third party. Once accredited, businesses are monitored annually, as already mentioned, and are reassessed every four years. This continuous assessment cycle ensures that UKAS customers adopt and develop practices that are consistent with the demands of the sectors in which they operate.

What are the benefits?

An evaluation service accredited by UKAS has proved that it complies with best practice and is competent to deliver a consistently reliable, impartial and accurate service to an appropriate and internationally recognized standard. By choosing a UKAS-accredited supplier, not only can you be assured that you are receiving the best and most appropriate service for your needs but you will also discover that the UKAS 'mark' on your documentation brings with it national and international recognition and credibility for your business.

Together, these attributes can:

■ reduce paperwork and increase efficiency by reducing the necessity to re-audit your business or retest your products for new markets;
■ de-risk your procurement by taking the guesswork out of choosing an evaluation body and by giving you confidence that you will get the service that best fulfils your requirements;
■ win new business, particularly since the use of accredited services is increasingly a stipulation of specifiers, most notably in the public sector;
■ facilitate access to international markets, since UKAS-accredited certificates have global recognition;
■ help you in the adoption of best practice, since your evaluating body is required to have appropriate knowledge of your business sector;
■ control costs, because accurate testing, calibration and other evaluation services along with the adoption of best practice can limit product failure and downtime;
■ help with knowledge transfer and product development, since accredited evaluation bodies can be a good source of impartial advice;
■ offer market differentiation and leadership by showing to others credible evidence of good practice, for instance in your environmental management systems;
■ demonstrate due diligence in the event of legal action.

These benefits are summarized by Andy Scott, CBI's Director of International Competitiveness:

> It is important that those in the business community have a good awareness and understanding of the benefits that accreditation can offer and the service available from UKAS. As we enter an era of increasingly rapid change, it is important for businesses to be able to demonstrate their products are fit for purpose. The CBI fully endorses the view that, for markets to function properly, purchasers must have confidence the standards are being met.

Whatever your business priorities and whatever sector your business is in, using accredited services offers value for money and will have a positive effect on your bottom line.

Are accredited services relevant to your business?

Certification

You may spend considerable time, effort and resource in the certification process because you have been persuaded of its importance as a business tool and because of the business benefits it can bring. But unless you have used a UKAS-accredited certification body, the benefits of certification could fall short of your expectations. Prospective customers may be unsure of the credibility of your certification and you may find yourself suffering from internal inefficiencies because your management systems have not been identified as inappropriate to your needs.

In the United Kingdom, UKAS accredits around 130 certification bodies, ranging from small specialists to large, multinational organizations employing many hundreds of people. You can be sure that one of these UKAS-accredited certification bodies will have the right people, technical expertise, management systems and track record to assess and certify your business competently.

What types of certification are accredited?

While Quality Management System certification (the ISO 9000 series) accounts for the bulk of work undertaken by certification bodies, there are other equally important areas of work, namely:

- product certification;
- personnel certification;
- certification of information security management systems;
- certification of environmental management systems;
- certification of IT service management systems;
- certification of food safety management systems;
- certification of occupational health and safety management systems.

Many of the UKAS-accredited certification bodies specialize in just one of these areas. Others may have specialist teams working in several or all the areas listed.

Inspection

Typically, inspections will cover product design, products, materials and equipment, installations, plant, processes and services. Some of these areas will be covered by legislation that demands that regular inspection is undertaken.

The competence of any inspection body you appoint may be crucial in maintaining your reputation as a responsible organization. You will want to make sure that the organization you pay to undertake inspections on your behalf has the people, facilities, technical expertise, management systems and track record to undertake the inspection professionally and competently.

Rather than leave your reputation to chance, ensure that your inspection body is up to the task by using one that has been accredited by UKAS. By doing so, you can be sure that you have invested your money wisely and have taken the necessary steps to manage and minimize your risks.

Save your business money by using UKAS-accredited services

Make an informed choice and have confidence in your suppliers—*look for the UKAS Mark*

If your business uses testing, calibration, certification or inspection services, choosing a supplier that is UKAS- accredited will deliver the following benefits to your business.

Raise your bottom line

- Increase your efficiency by removing duplication of audits
- Win new business and tenders where UKAS-accredited services are specified or demanded by regulators
- Differentiate your business with a best-in-class supply chain

Reduce your risk

- Reduce failure by ensuring goods meet specification
- Avoid a damaged reputation
- Be protected against potential legal action through enhanced due diligence

Please contact

If you wish to find out how accreditation could help your business please contact: Jon Murthy, Marketing & Communications Manager Telephone **020 8917 8493** email **jon.murthy@ukas.com** Or visit our website at **www.ukas.com**

The United Kingdom Accreditation Service is the sole accreditation body recognised by Government for assessment and verification against international standards. Our aim is to promote quality assurance to ensure that buyers have confidence and trust in the service you receive. We are a strong supporter of 'self-regulation' as opposed to Government legislation, in order to cut the cost burden of additional red tape or unnecessary bureaucracy.

"The number of customer audits of the Overseal site has vastly reduced since obtaining UKAS-accredited certification, from 20 in 2000 to only 7 in 2004."
Andrew Wainwright, Overseal

"Using a UKAS-accredited laboratory mitigates against risk—commercial, safety, and legal. It's a way of saying 'relax'."
Rob Blackburn, Redhill Analysts

UKAS
UNITED
KINGDOM
ACCREDITATION
SERVICE

The UKAS mark is recognised and supported by business both large and small, as well as public service procurement departments, who value independent quality assessment.

DELIVERING CONFIDENCE
UNITED KINGDOM ACCREDITATION SERVICE (UKAS)

"It is important that those in the business community have a good awareness and understanding of the benefits that accreditation can offer and the service available from UKAS."

Andy Scott, Director International Competitiveness, CBI

As we enter an era of increasingly rapid change, it is important for businesses to be able to demonstrate their products are fit for purpose. The CBI fully endorses the view that, for markets to function properly, purchasers must have confidence the standards are being met.

We all want to have confidence in the goods and services that we use. Trust is essential whether in the high street, the supermarket, or buying as a business. We also want to have reliable public services.

There is a means of building trust in the market place and in public services. Accreditation by the United Kingdom Accreditation Service (UKAS) is the key to ensuring that consumers, suppliers, purchasers and specifiers can have confidence in the quality of goods and in the provision of services throughout the supply chain.

Companies big and small buy independent evaluations either through choice (to reduce the risk of product failure for example) or as a consequence of legal requirements (such as health and safety regulations). Most commonly these evaluations are calibration of equipment, product testing, inspection of equipment and certification systems. It is the ability to distinguish between a proven, competent evaluator that ensures that the selection is an informed choice and not a gamble. UKAS accreditation means the evaluator can show to its customer that it has been successful at meeting the requirements of international accreditation standards.

UKAS believes that too many of Britain's companies run the risk of undermining their long-term success by purchasing independent evaluations that are not UKAS-accredited. Examples of such risks are product failure caused by invalid test results, increased costs caused by inaccurate measurement, legal action arising from inadequately inspected equipment resulting in accidents, and rejected tenders and orders citing lack of UKAS-accredited certificate or test report.

Businesses who choose to use accredited service providers also share in a number of benefits, including enhanced international market access (such as the European Union), demonstrable due diligence in the event of legal action, and a superb source of impartial advice and knowledge transfer in product development opportunities.

There is no legal requirement for the providers of certification services to be accredited, yet the UK Government recommends the use of UKAS-accredited certification services wherever this is an option.

Businesses are being encouraged to choose wisely by looking for the UKAS Mark featuring the Royal Crown when purchasing certification services. There is one symbol that is common to all activities accredited by UKAS – the Royal Crown. This signifies government recognition. The Department of Trade and Industry has licensed UKAS to use accreditation Marks featuring the Royal Crown and to sub-license these Marks to UKAS accredited organisations.

"If a small business chooses to take the certification route we are strongly in favour that they select a certification body carrying UKAS accreditation."

Ian Handford, Chairman, Federation of Small Businesses

Founded in 1995, UKAS is recognised by the government as the sole national body for the accreditation of laboratories and certification and inspection bodies and is allowed to use the powerfully symbolic Royal Crown in its national accreditation marks, denoting government approval and international recognition. It is the ability to distinguish between a proven, competent evaluator that ensures the selection of a laboratory, certification or inspection body is an informed choice and not a gamble. This informed choice reduces the risk of selecting an incompetent evaluator and paying for, or more seriously, acting upon invalid results.

Details of all UKAS-accredited calibration and testing laboratories (whether by name, location, parameter or a range of parameters) are available at our website: **www.ukas.org**

For general enquiries about UKAS, please call **+44 (0)20 8917 8400** or email **info@ukas.com**

Testing and calibration

Product testing is used to show that a product meets a specification. This may be a customer requirement or legal obligation, or part of your own product development regime.

You need to be absolutely sure that the laboratory carrying out your testing for you has the people, facilities and track record to produce valid and accurate data and results each and every time. The same must be true of any laboratory carrying out calibrations on your behalf.

The United Kingdom Accreditation Service (UKAS) is the sole body recognized by government to carry out accreditation of businesses offering conformity assessment services such as certification, inspection, testing and calibration. It assesses these bodies against internationally agreed standards. To locate a UKAS-accredited evaluation body in your area or one that provides a particular specialist service, help is at hand. Visit www.ukas.com for full details of all UKAS-accredited organizations. Alternatively, for further information about UKAS and its accreditation role, telephone +44 (0)20 8917 8400 or e-mail info@ukas.com.

3

Gaining market share

Smarter marketing

Want to boost your marketing? Paul Hewerdine at Loewy, the leading brand communications agency, has some tried and tested tips

You want results from your marketing. And chances are you want them fast. You need every campaign to sparkle – to deliver maximum bang for your bucks. But are you finding it easier said than done?

So why can success be so hard to achieve every time? Why is it the exception, not the norm?

What your brand means to customers

Want to know what your brand means to customers? Just ask them. Do customers think you're dynamic, market leading, innovative – all those great words? Or are they thinking something not quite as complimentary?

Tip 1: Focus groups to focus your mind

Conducting focus groups does not have to be prohibitively costly or time-consuming. Think about who those in your target audience are and what you'd like to learn from them, then bring in a professional facilitator who can tease this from them.

Tip 2: Be prepared to act

If the focus groups and research suggest change, then don't shy away from it. You're getting the opportunity to fix things before they become a major headache later.

Tip 3: It's just the tip of the iceberg

Your brand cannot mean everything to everyone. Don't try to say everything. Communicate a single brand message and stick with it. Only evolve your brand when it's needed – and not just because people are getting bored internally.

Tip 4: Get internal buy-in

Evolving your brand can cause an internal backlash unless you involve people on the 'journey'. Share the research findings with them, promote what you're doing, and get their understanding and buy-in before you show them the end result.

Tip 5: Be honest

Your customers know more than you think – and they're often pretty cynical. Don't try to position yourself as something you're not. Your audience won't be fooled. If you need to evolve, then involve your audience; don't leave them behind and hope they'll catch up.

Tip 6: Don't change for the sake of it

If your brand isn't broke, don't try to fix it. Don't change messages or value propositions too often. Even in today's fast-paced world it still takes time for messages to sink in. The best brand campaigns are the ones that run and run...

Put the wow factor into your campaigns

Five seconds. A cursory glance. Yes? No. Bin/delete/turn the page. A campaign – six, maybe eight, weeks in development – ignored.

So how can you put the real impact and pizzazz into your campaigns – make them truly resonate with your audience? Whether you've got the big-cheese CFO in your sights or the techiest of techies, never forget, almost above all, that these people are living, breathing humans too.

Tip 1: Think like them

They're busy. They're cynical. They've got worries. What are they? Tap into them. Analyse how your proposition can empathize and help them out.

Tip 2: Make them smile

Don't make them groan. Make them smile in the mind. They get the subtle gag but know others won't. They'll drop their guard – and best still, read on.

Tip 3: Make sure there's a big idea

Always make sure your campaign is built on the strongest premise – a single big idea that's simple, got legs and will give you cut-through. It beats pictures of men in suits any day.

Tip 4: Add an extra dimension

Quite literally. Why not trial 3D direct mailers for increased impact and recall? With careful targeting, they needn't cost you the earth. Chances are you'll get a better return too. Or go digital and really engage with your audience.

Tip 5: Be relevant

Target. Tailor. Better still, personalize (more on that later). Just make sure your proposition never gets lost.

Tip 6: If you're not bowled over, your audience won't be either

Don't just tick the boxes – or settle for second best. Average campaigns at best get average results. Don't play it safe; the campaigns we all remember had a brave marketer driving them!

Think multiple channels for multiple impact

Do you ever get the feeling your campaign plans are lacking a certain degree of cohesion? Are you concerned that response rates from previously tried and tested channels aren't reaching the dizzy heights they once did?

You could say there are just too many channels to market now. Too many ways to spend and dilute your marketing budget. So how can you plan and deliver truly integrated campaigns for truly exceptional results?

Tip 1: Clearly define your target audience

Define. Segment. Understand. Get to grips with the media they use and how they consume it. You'll be halfway home.

Tip 2: Understand how to use different media to best effect

Don't fall into the trap of thinking the same execution will work across everything. Learn what works for each media – one size certainly doesn't fit all.

Tip 3: View your customer interaction as a journey

Plan your interactions over time. Don't try to say everything in one go – to keep you front of mind and to streamline the sales process, 'drip-feed' your message.

Tip 4: Be flexible but in the main stick to the plan

Keep a strategic head – don't undertake tactical knee-jerk activity. Is that £3k last-minute discounted ad really worth its salt?

Tip 5: How much can you save by moving more activity online?

Online activity shouldn't be an afterthought. How about running a web seminar that's available on demand on your website after the event rather than a poorly attended seminar in Norwich?

Tip 6: Measure and benchmark your performance across all channels

Whatever the route to market, ensure there's some way of measuring the performance of your activity. That way, you can learn what works best.

Remember your salespeople are your best channel to market

How can you ensure that all the members of your sales force are fully behind all your campaigns? How can you make sure they're truly a force to be reckoned with?

Tip 1: Engage early to ensure sales buy-in

Involving one or two influential sales folk at the campaign planning stage provides valuable customer insight and market intelligence. And it makes them feel part of the campaign, helping get that all-important buy-in.

Tip 2: Less tends to be more

They've got targets to meet – and don't want anything to get in their way. Punchy and relevant communications about your campaigns that talk their language will get noticed.

Tip 3: Make sure they know what's in it for them

Tell them how you're going to help them sell more and they're more likely to listen. Nice sales incentives that tie in with the campaign also pay dividends.

Tip 4: Use the wonders of new technology

Why not use a simple text message on the day your campaign is hitting, to remind them to call their customers? Or even consider a podcast.

Tip 5: Give them the tools to help them sell

Not necessarily brochures. Think smart sales presentations. Think return on investment (ROI) calculators. Think online product or service demos. Best of all, think case studies.

Tip 6: Make them aware of the results

If you make them aware of the results, then with time they'll start to realize that marketing can and does deliver results.

When they search, make sure you get noticed

Your prospects are looking for information on a company or product. They're looking for a solution to their problem. So where do they start?

First off, they'll probably ask a friend or colleague for advice – but clearly, with your fine brand reputation, you've got that base covered. As a second option (and increasingly as a first), they'll hop on to the internet – and a friendly neighbourhood search engine. So the big question: if they search for information around any of your key propositions, will they find you?

Tip 1: Take ownership of search engine optimization

Don't just leave it to your webmaster. Understand how it works and make sure your website tops the search engine in results for relevant search terms.

Tip 2: Recognize that search engine ranking isn't just about good design

Yes, it's about page layout, HTML meta-tags, the content management system (CMS) you use and the submission process. However, it's also about the site content: the right messages and the right copy.

Tip 3: Support your campaigns with pay-per-click

Ensure you top the listings with a sponsored link. With smart bidding, you can maximize your web presence and, best of all, only pay for results. Organic search should be the mainstay of your search strategy, but while you're developing this, get to market quickly with a targeted pay-per-click campaign.

Tip 4: Select as many variations on your search terms as possible

Out-think your competitors; ensure you've got all the different permutations of your keywords and phrases covered.

Tip 5: Consider the local aspect of the world wide web

If your site or campaign has a target audience beyond the United Kingdom, make sure you cover the local language versions of search terms. You'll also need to understand how searches work differently across regions.

Tip 6: Refine, refine, refine for best results

With regular reporting, you can keep a check on your campaign and constantly refine your keywords, content and ad copy to boost results.

Next time, make it personal

Mention the word 'personalization' and, in the past, it brought four words to mind for many marketing execs: 'My mail merge hell'. With it come thoughts of address labels and Word documents incorrectly addressed, named and titled – enough to put anyone off personalization for life.

However, casting aside doubts about your data integrity, personalization has moved on. Used effectively, it can now significantly boost your campaign effectiveness.

Tip 1: Always make sure your data are up to scratch first

Rather than using a scattergun approach, carefully define the audience for your campaign, then undertake a quick data cleaning and profiling exercise. If the data aren't clean, don't risk personalizing. Why not market to a small number of highly qualified names, rather than doing a mass mailing?

Tip 2: Make the most of Variable Digital Print

Professional print personalization can now be achieved easily and cost-effectively. More than just text personalization – it's now even possible to personalize imagery. Now that's powerful.

Tip 3: Personalize the content – not just the name

It's easy to personalize with an individual's name or company name but why not tailor the core content of your communication? How about including a company-specific business case with real numbers?

Tip 4: Personalize online content too

Don't just think in terms of personalizing print. Online content – whether e-mail bulletins, web content or online ads – can be personalized just as readily.

Tip 5: Develop account-based marketing campaigns

Personalization can also be used effectively to engage multiple decision makers and influencers within the same organization – as part of a marketing programme to build your relationships with a target customer group of one.

Tip 6: Constantly seek to capture data and keep them clean

Use your activities to capture more and more intelligence on your customers and prospects, enabling you to target and tailor campaigns further still. Your customer knowledge is your competitive advantage.

A little packaging of services goes a long way

How easy is it to market a service with a £500k price tag? Worse still, what happens if your salespeople are more used to selling £5k products?

It's a challenge we see again and again: how to move from product-based selling to a services-led business model. The key here is to develop services propositions that are clear, compelling and, above all, easy for the sales force to sell to their existing customers.

It's about being realistic. You won't change things overnight, so take a step in the right direction with a number of 'value propositions' that will get the buy-in of your internal people and won't confuse your customers.

Tip 1: Keep it simple

Business-to-business communications are awash with complicated propositions that customers simply fail to grasp. Simplicity is a virtue. If customers have to work too hard to 'get it', they just won't bother.

Tip 2: Use real language

Here's where you leave the acronyms at the door. Customers will appreciate clear, jargon-free English that explains clearly what your proposition is, and the value it brings.

Tip 3: Focus on value

Ask yourself, does this service really add value for customers? What pains does the service solve, and how is it genuinely different from your competitors' offerings?

Tip 4: Ask your customers

The best way to develop a strong service proposition is to involve your customers. They will be forthright and helpful in saying whether the service would be of interest to them – and if not, why not.

Tip 5: Put half your effort into internal communications

There's no point packaging a service if the salespeople don't know how to sell it, or even don't know it exists! Spend half your time internally; develop a 'how to sell guide', FAQs and any other tools the sales force could want. Speak to them individually if possible; don't let 'I didn't get the e-mail' be an excuse!

Tip 6: One step at a time

A healthy dose of realism is critical. You need to involve your sales force, rather than purely imposing new services to sell. You also can't change a business overnight, so try to influence a number of salespeople and get them on board; they will act as champions for the new packaged services.

Loewy is one of the United Kingdom's fastest-growing integrated brand communications agencies. Our dedicated B2B team work with B2B marketers to help them plan, deliver and manage their marketing activities for maximum impact – and results.

We're big on integration – and always have been. We'll help you choose the right channels to market – and exploit them to best effect using a combination of smart thinking and creativity. All the time, we make sure everything is joined up. It makes your life easier and ensures we exceed your expectations – every time.

For further information, contact Paul Hewerdine (tel: 020 7798 2006; e-mail: paul.hewerdine@loewygroup.com).

Building a reputation

Your company's reputation is one of its most valuable assets. Why then do most firms leave reputation to chance? Louise Third, a partner at Integra Communications, makes the case for boardroom-level buy-in for sustained reputation management

When is your next board meeting or senior management get-together? Does reputation management or measurement signify on the agenda? I guess not. Attention will no doubt focus on such items as monthly sales results, staff recruitment, the factory expansion and the usual financial reports. Marketing might creep on to the agenda if there is some slack in the budget for advertising. If your board-level agenda looks like this, I suggest you are omitting a vital management function, that of reputation creation and protection. The corporate climate changes rapidly without warning, so you should prepare for all weathers.

Gathering storm clouds

A good reputation is an asset in times of need. It is the best defence when anything goes wrong, the licence to operate when things get controversial. During the US stock market crash of 1987, shares in the 10 most admired companies recovered faster and suffered less, while shares in the 10 least admired companies fell three times as far. Measuring reputation is difficult, but a *Management Today* report from 1998 suggested that a positive reputation is worth around a year's turnover. Your firm may be able to recover from a factory fire but rebuilding reputation after media criticism of the company's financial management can take much longer. Dwindling sales and loyalty switched to your competition hit the bottom line: the cost of acquiring a new customer is 5 to 20 times greater than the cost of retaining existing ones, according to the American Consumer Association.

the enterprise PR specialists

public relations and communications specialists to the national small firms sector

Our Services

Strategic Consultancy:

Integra can help you plan to ensure that your communications are focused, co-ordinated and flexible.

Publications:

Our expert writers and editors will enable you to produce effective and well written publications, from newsletters to web sites and professional magazines.

PR Coaching:

Smaller companies sometimes want to do the media relations leg work themselves but be guided by a professional. For this reason we offer a PR coaching service which provides advice and contacts at a price smaller businesses can afford.

Media Relations:

Our experience will enable you to present what you need to say in a way that interests the media, resulting in a steady stream of positive messages. We can advise on avoiding problems and managing a crisis.

Sponsorship, Exhibitions and Conferences:

We know where our clients need to be seen and can ensure that you make the most of the opportunities to be in the right place at the right time.

Presentation Skills Coaching:

Our in-house expertise ensures that when a client is in front of an audience their performance is first class, delivering the right messages with the desired results.

Contact Louise Third for further information.

Storm protection

Your company has a reputation whether you like it or not. It relates to past activity as well as current perception. If you don't like it, active steps must be taken to secure change. If you do like it, the debate must move on to how it can be maintained. But a good reputation is one that works for commercial benefit, not simply the one you or your board likes. Let's draft an agenda for your next board meeting that will begin the process for you and your business.

Agenda item 1: A reputation that works for us

First up on that agenda should be a discussion around what type of reputation will best enhance the prospects of the business – which means being clear about what the business is *for* and what it wants to be *known for*. Let's assume you own a business travel company and you specialize in trade visits to China. You want to be known not only as a company that gets people there and back safely but as one that understands *guanxi* (pronounced 'GWAN-shee'), the exchange of favours and art of doing business in China through contacts. As a result, your clients meet the right people, benefit from your 'localized' Chinese interpreters and come home with contracts. Build your reputation on simple but solid foundations.

Agenda item 2: Our communications plan

You operate within a complex set of relationships, and those who have a view about you and the business are many and varied. This is best illustrated in Figure 3.2.1, taken from John Clare's *Guide to Media Handling* (Gower, 2001).

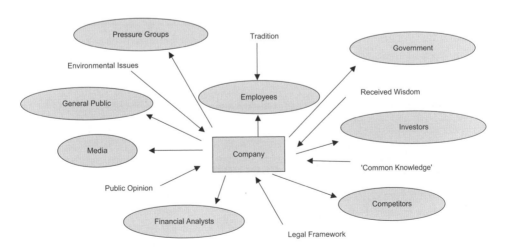

Figure 3.2.1   A typical communications environment

Public relations (PR) is the business tool most often wheeled out to either change people's behaviour or to change attitudes. Used well, PR is an important contributor to commercial success and can consolidate your reputation. Never underestimate the power of a persuasive story, so take a few to the board meeting to illustrate how PR works.

Restaurant recipe for a good reputation

Kevin and Dawn Hartley, the owners of Mozart's Restaurant in Nottingham, understand the power of reputation, having strategically developed their business using PR tactics and customer communications. The couple opened the 40-seat restaurant in November 2002 and were keen to establish it as a quality evening venue where diners from across the East Midlands could enjoy fresh cuisine in a friendly setting.

The couple encourage customer feedback in the form of a simple card completed as credit cards are swiped. Collecting e-mail addresses has enabled them to launch a regular e-bulletin to customers, carrying both restaurant and, occasionally, family news.

Kevin positioned himself as spokesman for the restaurant, utilizing his articulate and friendly manner to offer expert comment to the local press and radio. The opening of their restaurant in November 2002 was marked on Trent FM with champagne and canapés and followed a month later by a two-hour Christmas show, broadcast live from the restaurant. BBC Radio Nottingham carried a Valentine's recipe on the website and 50,000 listeners enjoyed a live cooking session in association with the Nottingham Restaurant Awards.

'As well as increasing awareness of Mozart's, we were keen to develop our brand by establishing it as Nottingham's first entirely non-smoking restaurant. Announcing this policy on National No-Smoking Day in 2004 brought us a high level of media coverage and gave a new dimension to our reputation. Indeed, when the government White Paper on smoking was published last November, we were bombarded with requests for interviews and featured on several local radio stations and regional television news,' says Kevin.

Mozart's Restaurant has enjoyed a 15 per cent rise in trade as a direct result of both their no-smoking policy and the coverage it has generated.

Agenda item 3: Getting everyone on board

You might get your external communications plans well honed, but a failure to involve staff, no matter how few, in reputation building could leave you exposed. Good PR – initiated through listening and reporting back – can act as the conscience of the organization and inform top management decision making. However, many managers worry that they do not have a good enough radar for emerging issues. So, consult staff from the start, as they are probably more aware of the firm's reputation – with suppliers, customers, the general public – than you are. Make sure your reputation management is engaging, ongoing and active, ensuring that the company's brand and behaviour match.

If at all practical, appoint a board member to take responsibility for communications strategy, planning, delivery and measurement. It might well have to be you. As the owner or manager of a growing firm, you probably personify all that the business stands for and offers. What better opportunity than this to actively manage your firm's 'personality' and performance?

Agenda item 4: Getting external advice

If you decide to appoint a professional consultant, in either public relations, public affairs or, specifically, reputation management, choose someone with relevant experience and contacts. If they are a Member of the Chartered Institute of Public Relations or other recognized body, so much the better. Provide them with a clear briefing and explain what you expect of them. If budgets are tight and you want to do much of the work yourselves, using a PR coach or mentor is another way forward.

Sunnier times

So, the board meeting went well; you began a period of staff consultation, carried out some perception research and appointed the PR consultant to oversee your communications strategy. Now, 10 years on, you have sold a growing, profitable business. Little did you realize as you made those decisions that the company's reputation would so positively determine the value and price paid over and above your other asset valuation. The investment in time, effort and resources was worth every penny.

Louise Third is a public relations practitioner and founder of Integra Communications, the enterprise PR specialists. A former small business adviser, Louise combines her knowledge, TV, radio and writing experience in working with both public and private-sector clients. She is editor of the *Business Adviser* journal. For further details, telephone 0115 906 1377 or e-mail louise@integra. gb.com. Integra's website is www.integra.gb.com.

Franchising

The success of UK franchising is based around the nature of the relationship between the franchisee and franchisor, explains Dan Archer of the British Franchise Association (bfa)

The 2006 NatWest/BFA Franchise Survey highlights the fact that franchised businesses contribute £10.3bn a year to UK GDP. The sector continues to grow, with some 759 franchisors taking responsibility for 33,500 franchisees. Notably, franchising is responsible for 369,000 UK jobs. Part of the appeal of franchising is the breadth of operational businesses that have chosen the franchising route to growth. Industries as diverse as fast food retail, cost reduction consultancy, home maintenance and even pet food supply have all been touched by franchising.

Another attractive facet of the draw of UK franchising is its success compared to that of stand-alone businesses. New business start-ups, depending on the level of support that the owner receives, experience between 60 per cent at best and 90 per cent at worst failure rates. By virtue of the fact that franchising provides for the repetition of proven business success, the figures present an almost mirror image for franchisee business starts of a less than 10 per cent failure rate.

Franchising is more popular than ever and presents an attractive option to either those wanting to go into business under the umbrella of an established brand with a proven concept (*franchisees*) or those choosing franchising to grow their business (*franchisors*) So what does each party bring to the relationship and what are the benefits to them?

Franchisees

Entering franchising as a franchisee allows a new business owner a licence to trade under the brand that has been established by the franchisor. The franchisee benefits from a proven business concept, systems and procedures for successfully running that business, an initial and ongoing support network, and a legal agreement between the two parties. Moreover, the franchisee receives help and guidance, together with training, from the franchisor. Because the system is an established one, there is less risk and a statistically higher success rate.

What the franchisee brings to franchising is a capital injection to start the business and a local knowledge and focus. Franchisees provide an enterprising perspective and the often talked-about enthusiasm of the owner-operator. In real terms, the commitment of a franchisee can lead to the same outlet in the same town with the same product and customer base performing better under a franchised structure. The franchisee cares that the business succeeds because it is theirs.

Franchisors

For established businesses using franchising to grow their network, expand into new territories or gain a productivity advantage there are several benefits. As each new franchisee invests in the business, the franchisor can grow without the relatively heavy capital investment needed by the entrepreneur in a corporate organization. The franchisor also mitigates some of the risk of expanding into new territories. Most notably, the enthusiasm of the owner-operator can lead to profitability, turnover and customer satisfaction being greater in franchised outlets compared to similar managed operations.

The franchisor contributes the business concept and undertakes to prove its success. They will also establish a means for transferring the intellectual property regarding how to run that business to the franchisee through training and operational manuals. They will support the franchisee to help ensure their success and actively protect the established brand from both internal and external damage.

'The bfa draws a distinction between a good way of franchising and other ways,' Archer comments. 'The association's accreditation process measures franchisors against the bfa code of ethics and the European code of ethics in franchising. There is a duty of care on the franchisor, and our membership have been inspected to measure them against recognized standards.'

While franchising is a successful sector, bfa director-general Brian Smart warns people thinking of entering franchising as either a franchisor or a franchisee to do the proper research and their own due diligence. There is a distinction between the right way of franchising, accredited by bodies such as the bfa, and other, more ad hoc ways. New franchisors and franchisees should realize that the relationship in franchising is a long-term one, so neither party should enter it lightly. The secret is to err on the side of caution and do your homework.

Researching a business investment deserves dedicated time. Just because a franchise business is up and running, this does not mean that the franchisee does not need to do the same amount of research. Equally, a successful stand-alone business may not be suitable for franchising, so prospective franchisors should also undertake proper research.

The British Franchise Association is a voluntary self-regulating body, set up in 1977 from within the franchising industry itself. Accredited bfa members have proved that they are an established business and that they offer a fair and ethical franchising opportunity. More than 330 accredited franchise brands proudly display their bfa membership, and as part of this membership are reaccredited on a regular basis against the bfa's Code of Ethics.

The bfa works to increase awareness about good business practice within franchising. All members must adhere to its code of practice, and this helps assure individuals buying into a bfa-accredited franchise business that they are dealing with an established company offering a fair and ethical franchise opportunity.

In addition, bfa membership is a benchmark of quality providing public recognition for franchisors. This quality standard adds not only to the franchisor's brand but to the value of each and every franchisee within the bfa-accredited franchise network.

The bfa runs educational seminars ranging from two-hour introductions to franchising up to full one-day workshops and discovery days for both those considering becoming a franchisee and businesses looking at growth through franchising. In addition, its online bookshop contains a diverse range of titles covering key concepts in reference book, workbook and DVD format.

For further details, contact:

The British Franchise Association
Thames View
Newtown Road
Henley-on-Thames
Oxon RG9 1HG
Tel: 01491 578050
www.thebfa.org.

Licensing: a good way to grow

Robert Sales of Swindell & Pearson suggests that growing companies should include licensing in their strategic thinking, as a potential way of increasing revenue, obtaining revenue from new areas, and hence achieving growth without some of the pain this usually involves

Licensing

Licensing usually entails a company allowing a third party to use one or more of its rights, and the third party pays for the privilege of using those rights.

Free beer?

It may sound too good to be true, but effective licensing can come close to approaching the 'free beer' ideal. By licensing, a company can seek rewards by allowing somebody else to work its rights, in places or ways that the company presently cannot or does not work these rights itself.

A good licence arrangement may provide a steady income stream for a company, for little effort on its part. This income can significantly assist a company in its growth.

Why license?

Aside from obtaining 'free beer', there may be one or more markets out there that a company is unable to supply. This may be because the company is too small, too busy, does not have appropriate expertise, or does not have sufficient capacity to supply a particular market. Alternatively, it may be a market that the company cannot supply satisfactorily without significant investment in arranging distribution, local partners and the like. A licensee may already be established in this market, and may readily be able to add the company's products, services or other rights to its existing business in this market.

Another scenario is that the rights are in a field in which the company does not have sufficient knowledge and/or reputation. It may be that the company's rights are applicable in a field in which the company has no track record or experience. Or it may be that a company cannot, or is not ready to, enter a particular geographical market. Accordingly, rights in that market could be licensed, perhaps to a company established in that area, which may be a local partner.

Licensing can be carried out by all sizes of companies, and throughout their existence. Microsoft has recently launched a programme to spin off its unused intellectual property with the hope of generating licensing revenue from its unused innovations. IBM is famous for its extensive licensing activities. Licensing also takes place in many smaller companies.

What do you need to be able to license?

The usual rights to be licensed are intellectual property rights (IPRs) such as patents, designs, copyright, trade marks or know-how. In view of this, care must be taken when seeking to obtain these rights. Strategic thinking is necessary in deciding which types of protection to seek, how broad the protection sought should be, and geographically where to seek protection.

For instance, if a company knows it can only service the UK market, it may seek for a licensee for the US market, and therefore protection should be sought in both the United Kingdom and the United States.

Particular rights that may be licensed

Let's share the big idea

Concepts are generally protected by patents, which can be granted for a wide range of inventions as long as the invention is novel and inventive relative to previous arrangements. Ron Hickman became a multi-millionaire by licensing the Workmate® to Black & Decker®. Mr Hickman struggled for many years in achieving his success, and also when necessary bringing legal proceedings against various infringers of his patent rights.

Most licensing of ideas is not so dramatic. A possible licensing scenario might be a start-up UK firm making electronic testing equipment. Its new testing product has proved very successful and it is hard pressed even to meet the demands in the United Kingdom and the rest of the European Union for this product. In view of this, it has licensed an established US company to make and sell the product in the United States. This provides profits from a market that the company cannot service itself.

A West Country manufacturer of traffic cones has developed a new moulding process that helps to provide a stable base for its cones. This moulding process has a wide range of potential applications. It has already signed a licensing deal with a Northern Ireland firm that makes garden furniture, and negotiations are about to start with a Scottish manufacturer of children's toys with a view to using the moulding process on its products. Again, this provides profits from a market the company cannot itself operate in.

A grand design?

There are many instances of the licensing of designs. For instance, men's suits and also pottery dinner sets bearing designs by Jeff Banks are available in our high streets.

A wallpaper manufacturer may turn to licensing its very successful designs for use on other products such as bed linen or general furnishings, for use as coordinated items, or as stand-alone ranges. In both cases, profits are being obtained from markets for which the licensor does not have manufacturing experience.

Copyright: how far can it be spread?

Again there are many instances of copyright being licensed. For example, the copyright in a character in a film, television series or cartoon may be widely licensed on diverse products such as yogurts, T-shirts, board games, footballs, bed linen, etc. The income from such licensing deals can significantly supplement the income from the original film or other work, without the film company needing to establish itself in these other markets.

Exploit the brand

A company's brand can be its most valued asset. The brand may be what attracts customers, and may provide a guarantee of quality, durability, value, exclusiveness or reliability.

The goodwill in a brand can be taken into new areas by licensing. For example, the well-known and respected brand JCB®, originally known for agricultural and earth-moving equipment, has been taken by licensing into the field of power tools, lawnmowers and elsewhere, to provide the same message of quality to purchasers of these products.

An example of potential licensing would be a company purchasing the assets, including the main trade mark, of a well-known brand in the baby care field. This mark has been used for over 100 years by a UK family firm that has now fallen on hard times, in no small part because of competition from the Far East.

The purchaser of the assets now intends to make only a small number of high-quality premium products under the brand, which is where its expertise lies. This company also, though, intends licensing the trade mark on other products, still in the baby care field and bearing the well-known UK brand, but which will be made and sold by a foreign company. Strict provisions have been put in place to ensure that the quality of the foreign-made products will be appropriate to this esteemed UK brand. Thus, the licensor gains profits from markets outside its own expertise by careful choice and control of a licensee.

Know-how: tell others how to

Know-how covers trade secrets such as recipes, process steps and conditions, and the like. As the only protection for know-how is confidentiality, care must always be exercised to retain this confidentiality. Once a secret has been lost, it can never be regained.

An example of licensing here is the recipe of a particular biscuit. The recipe is licensed for manufacture abroad, and particularly for sale into the expatriate market in the United States for Britons there who wish to purchase this special, typically British biscuit. Strict provisions are provided in the licence to maintain the secrecy of the recipe, and also to ensure the quality of the product. The British manufacturer is able to gain profits from the expatriate market without setting up overseas.

What you should be looking for in a licence

Where it should cover

Normally it will cover markets you are not active in, or those that can be penetrated much further by the licensee.

What it should cover

It might cover products or services similar to your own, or could be restricted to products, services or activities away from your main activities.

What's in it for you

Most commonly you will receive a royalty, which may be a percentage or a fixed figure. The royalty can vary, dependent for instance on the volume of sales.

When negotiating a royalty figure, it is always worth bearing in mind that 2 per cent of a lot of sales is usually more than 20 per cent of a very small amount of sales. Therefore, any royalties should aim to be realistic for both parties so as to enable significant sales to take place whilst providing an appropriate income for the rights owner. Taking advice is important.

Summary: don't miss out on a potential bonus

Licensing can provide growth in bringing in extra revenue, and especially from markets that a company may not be able to serve itself. To be able to license successfully, it is necessary to have in place appropriate IP rights covering what you wish to license and where.

Therefore, strategic thinking is required at the outset to decide how and where there is a potential for any new innovation, and whether one or more third parties may be required to fully develop and realize the potential of the innovation.

Robert Sales is a partner with Chartered UK and European Patent and Trade Mark Attorneys, Swindell & Pearson based at the firm's Head Office in Derby, but also carrying out work in the firm's Stoke-on-Trent office. Robert has been with Swindell & Pearson for over 20 years but would like to point out he was very young when he started!

Robert acts for a diverse range of clients from the aerospace industry to yogurt manufacturers, in relation to their varied IP interests. He obtains patent, trade mark and design protection for his clients around the world, as well as advising on potential infringement of such rights. He also advises his clients on the rights held by their competitors and others, helps to evaluate those rights, and advises on how to avoid infringing such rights and if appropriate how to attack those rights.

Away from work Robert enjoys (?) watching Nottingham Forest. He also enjoys skiing, including skiing up mountains as well as down them. When there is no snow he still likes climbing mountains, and tries to drag his family along with him.

4

Customer service

Service on the move

Pay-as-you-go mobile technology can transform the delivery of service to customers, argues Martin Taylor, Managing Director of Impact Applications

Financial burden

Business and commercial markets have become more crowded than ever, with organizations turning to new technologies to help elevate them above the bustling competition. Mobile is one such technology and is proving to be a particular favourite thanks to its ability to improve the quality and relevance of service delivery to the customer whilst reducing overall costs.

However, many smaller companies cannot afford to compete with larger organizations with what are perceived to be expensive mobile technologies and IT infrastructures. In addition to this, in many cases mobile solutions have been complex and expensive to deploy, relying on dated client–server technology that requires significant contractor training. Given the cost and risk associated with such deployments, it is little wonder that the majority of growing organizations are unwilling or unable to invest in technology that could potentially transform the efficiency of their businesses.

But it's not all bad news. There *is* a way for mobile technology to achieve widespread business adoption. By combining the use of standard web browsers – used by over 50 per cent of the UK population – with familiar personal digital assistant (PDA) technology, organizations can very easily and cost-effectively provide their operatives with access to key information, such as job details and information on authorized suppliers, in real time.

Meeting objectives

By providing operatives with access to information from a familiar, easy-to-use PDA, organizations are transforming working practices, from updating jobs to placing orders with suppliers. Real-time information not only ensures that job details are up to date, but also accurately indicates the availability of products such as spare parts – in either van or depot. Productivity is increased by reducing the time spent trawling suppliers to purchase parts, while stock control is transformed.

Response Maintenance and Building Services is a Wolverhampton-based provider of emergency response and general building services to local authorities, housing associations and insurance groups. Founded by Andrew Cornaby in 1994, the company has seen significant market change over the past few years, with low margins and demands for increased accountability within the social housing sector sending many competitors out of business or towards a different client base. With over £60,000 worth of stock held in a warehouse, it had no cost-effective way of allocating materials to contractors, resulting in significant additional purchasing of materials – with attendant lost time whilst contractors undertook the purchase process.

It adopted a mobile solution that provided end-to-end management of Response Maintenance's key business processes, delivering client management, stock control, estimating and scheduling, health and safety, job management, and invoicing through a web-based application accessible from the office, at home and on the road.

Rugged, handheld PDAs provide Response Maintenance's 25 service engineers with real-time remote access to the system, providing both job information and materials allocation. If the materials are not already within the standard product set in the van, contractors can either collect materials from the warehouse or use the PDA to purchase goods from specific suppliers determined by the organization. Once completed, the customer signs off the job on-screen – and an invoice is generated automatically.

'Simply reducing paperwork and duplication has enabled Response Maintenance to reduce its office personnel to seven,' commented Andrew Cornaby, founder of Response Maintenance. 'Invoicing is now being completed up to four weeks earlier than previously, which has significantly improved credit control. In fact, we now have so much more time that the company is embarking upon its first major marketing campaign.'

Another organization that has leveraged the benefits of a mobile solution is Brunelcare, a Bristol-based charity providing residential homes, sheltered housing and very sheltered housing to the elderly. Established during the Second World War to provide the first 'Meals on Wheels' for elderly people, Brunelcare now provides care and housing for thousands of people living within 1,000 sheltered housing units, six care homes and their own homes. It adopted a web-based operations management system (OMS), which, through mobile technology, is providing the charity's workforce with up-to-date information about jobs – including location and a detailed overview of what is required. Using a 'zero-client' model, the PDA is constantly connected to Brunelcare's back office via the internet.

The quality of service now delivered by Brunelcare is excellent, with emergency repairs being dealt with within two hours, urgent ones within three to four days and routine ones within days – well within the key performance indicators (KPIs) set by the Housing Corporation. Critically, the charity now has complete visibility over operations, which has driven significant productivity improvements and cost reduction. Improved central visibility has enabled the repair coordinators to improve scheduling, reducing the amount of time that operatives waste in the notorious Bristol traffic.

Keeping ahead

Essentially, mobile technology can transform and is transforming the delivery of service. However, many local contractors and organizations are deterred by the idea of investing in this technology because of the perceived cost. Yet evidence shows that businesses that can deliver a good customer experience – based on good communication and information – can actually transform the cost of delivery.

Whatever solution a growing business is looking to adopt, a managed service provides organizations with a platform for embracing mobile technology without requiring a potentially business-breaking technology investment. Critically, the service can now be provided in a pay-as-you-go model, removing the need for major up-front investment. Using the managed service, jobs are paid for on a per incident basis, enabling contractors of all sizes to attain maximum benefit with minimum investment or risk.

With such cost-effective and easy-to-deploy solutions readily available, now is the time for growing businesses to adopt these mobile technologies and benefit from the tools that the solutions provide, helping companies keep abreast of the competition and stand shoulder to shoulder with – and even outpace – the larger organizations in their crowded markets.

Impact Applications, with its e-business and mobile data solutions experts, specializes in web-based business solutions that improve the effectiveness, productivity and value of today's mobile workforce. Martin Taylor is its co-founder and Managing Director.

Further information:

Tel: +44 (0)870 046 3356
e-mail: martintaylor@impactapplications.com
www.impactapplications.com

Just one number

0800? 0845? 0870? 0871? Georgette Jones discusses the options for replacing all your customer contact numbers with one number

Many small and medium-sized businesses are recognizing the benefits of using a single telephone number solution to represent their business throughout the United Kingdom. One Number services have long been used by large businesses, but now, with the flexibility of hosted service providers, these solutions are being successfully deployed into businesses of all sizes in all market sectors.

What a One Number-hosted telephone solution can do for your business

A hosted telephony solution can replace all your customer contact numbers across the United Kingdom with a single number without affecting your existing telephone system. This enables you to improve the customer service experience by directing the caller to the first available employee regardless of his or her location. What's more, it can provide an opportunity for your company to generate revenue from calls that were previously a cost to your business.

Available types of marketing telephone numbers

- *0800 free phone:* Free-phone numbers are one of the most dynamic response mechanisms available. Research by AT & T in 1998 has shown that advertising responses increase by up to 300% when a free-phone number is used. The caller does not pay for any part of the call, so these numbers are usually associated with selling a product or service.

■ *0845 local rate:* Local-rate numbers mean that callers are charged at their local rate when calling your business irrespective of where in the United Kingdom they are calling from. These numbers give your company the perception of being a national business and encourage callers from all over the United Kingdom to contact your business instead of their local firm.

■ *0870 national rate:* National-rate numbers are used to give your business a 'national presence' and promote it as a large firm. This number can also be used to generate revenue in periods when a large volume of calls are being received; these numbers are often used for customer support lines.

■ *0871 special rate:* Special-rate numbers are used in many cases for generating income from inbound calls, as the caller is charged for all of the call at the same rate, 24 hours per day. These numbers are very popular with businesses that have a lot of weekend and evening calls.

■ *090 premium rate:* Premium-rate numbers are used by companies that provide a value added service or content through their telephone service – for example, helpdesk or information lines. There are a range of tariffs available from 5p to 150p per minute and they are excellent ways of generating revenue from callers who do not have a support contract, for example.

Business benefits of using a One Number telephone solution

Simplification

By replacing all your business contact numbers with one telephone number you are making your business more accessible to existing and new trade. Callers can then be answered by a professionally scripted welcome greeting; in addition, promotional messages can be played during the on-hold function to encourage repeat business and new products and services.

Customer satisfaction

With a One Number solution, all calls are answered quickly and efficiently by the correct person, so calling into your company becomes a pleasant and rewarding experience. The level of customer service can also be graded according to the type of customer. For example, VIP customers can be prioritized in the call queue.

Maximizing of marketing efforts

Advertising one easy-to-remember number on marketing and promotional materials instead of several regional numbers maximizes your marketing efforts. If you make this a free phone number, response rates are significantly increased. Marketing response to adverts can now be measured by campaign.

Call routeing

One Number telephone solutions unifies businesses with disparate locations, enabling them to act as one large company. As a hosted service, all calls are automatically routed through a single network. When a call is made, whether from a land line or a mobile phone, the call is instantly routed to the caller's nearest location/office. If the nearest location is busy, the call can be automatically diverted to the next nearest available location, so callers never receive an engaged tone. Time-and-day routeing ensures that all calls are answered no matter when they arrive: callers can either listen to a message informing them about your opening hours or be connected to an out-of-hours service.

Revenue protection

Managing some types of calls can be a costly business, particularly if the nature of the call is to provide advice or a service. Using a revenue-generating number such as 0870 or 0871 numbers transforms these calls from a cost to immediate revenue.

If you can't measure it, you can't manage it

Most businesses are unaware of the number of calls they are handling and, more importantly, the number of calls they are losing. These lost calls represent lost revenue and it is crucial for businesses of any size to capture real-time information on their incoming calls so that problems with service delivery can be quickly identified.

Managed telephony service

In reality, few companies are capable of predicting their future telecommunication needs. Technological innovations, new ideas and the sudden appearance of new business opportunities can render hardware systems obsolete overnight. It is a particular challenge for small and medium-sized enterprises (SMEs) to balance the initial cost of investment with the long-term benefits. Hosted services should deliver a fully integrated platform of inbound solutions at a fraction of the investment cost of traditional hardware solutions. More importantly, solutions can be changed on a 'pay per use, per month' basis to ensure you only pay for what you use.

Add new features quickly and painlessly.

Customer expectations and market trends change rapidly. With a hosted solution you can quickly upgrade your services with minimal disruption to your operation – it's as simple as flicking a switch. In addition, you can tailor the service according to the type of call, for example using VIP routeing to connect your best customers directly to their account contact.

Eliminate over- and undercapacity

With a pay-as-you-go on-demand hosted solution you can scale your service up or down at any time to adjust to customer demand. You pay a little more when you are busy and less during quiet periods. A hosted One Number solution will help you stay in step with a continually changing market.

Eliminate maintenance and upgrade costs

In reality, few SMEs have the technical expertise in-house to keep up with current technical trends. Hosted solutions are monitored 24/7 by a team of highly skilled technical support staff, ensuring guaranteed performance and reliability of service. In addition, the technical infrastructure is constantly upgraded to ensure best-in-class functionality and service sophistication. Traditional hardware telephony solutions require servicing and on-site support by technical engineers, and can be a financial burden to developing businesses.

Think you're too small for a telephony solution?

Many small businesses are unaware of the flexibility and scalability a One Number, hosted telephony solution can deliver, and, more importantly, the dramatic business benefits that can be gained. Traditional hardware telephony suppliers have given One Number telephony solutions an expensive reputation. However, telephony solutions from a hosted service provider grow alongside the needs of your business. In addition, you should have the luxury of advanced functionality 'on tap', as and when your business demands. No business should be too small or too large for a hosted solution.

For further information on Consorte solutions, please e-mail info@consorte.com or call a member of the sales team on 08450 803 070.

Complaints

Complaints are valuable to all organizations. Treasure them, says Paul Cooper of the Institute of Customer Service

Britons are shedding their reserved natures and turning into hot-blooded consumers willing to argue at the drop of a hat and stand up for their rights, and we are becoming more 'passionate'.

More than half of people now complain all or most of the time if they are unhappy with a product. Complaining has become so prevalent that two-thirds of people now believe that we are better at it than before. But it is age over youth and inexperience which increases the chances of making a complaint, according to the National Complaints Culture Survey (NCCS). Two-thirds of those over 50 complain all or most of the time if they are dissatisfied, while the under-21s are the least likely to complain – a lesson for the future. (BBC News coverage of the ICS/TMI National Complaints Culture Survey (now in its sixth year)

Also, Professor Bob Johnson of Warwick Business School, in his ICS Breakthrough Research reports *Service Excellence = Reputation = Profit* and *Delivering Service Excellence: The View from the Front Line*, has clearly demonstrated that 'what makes excellent service "excellent" and poor service "poor" is very much about how organisations deal with problems and complaints'.

Therefore, the professional and efficient handling of complaints is a critical factor for all organizations, in both the private and the public sector, and regardless of the size of the organization; in fact, for small and medium-sized enterprises (SMEs) it is critical.

Real benefits in prioritizing and improving complaints handling

The following are some more issues from NCCS, 2000–06:

- Nearly all customers would recommend a company to their friends if a complaint had been resolved efficiently.
- Four out of five customers would spread the word if a complaint had been handled badly, and it is the most common reason for customers to switch suppliers.
- Many companies still seem not to be listening to this key customer service point, so there are advantages to starting now.
- Despite the rise in the number of complaints, only one in four employees feel qualified to deal with them.
- Only one in three customer-facing staff are actually trained to deal with angry customers.

Definition of a complaint

A complaint is 'an expression of dissatisfaction whether justified or not' (BS 8600).

Golden rules of complaints handling for organizations

Strategic plan

- *Have a clear, flexible, welcoming and open policy on complaints.* A complaint is a gift and you should consider yourself lucky that a customer is prepared to give up valuable time to help you improve your organization.
- *Train your staff and management in complaints handling.* Give them confidence to tackle the difficult customers and support their actions. Excellent complaint handling isn't easy and can sometimes be stressful and feel unrewarding. Confirm its importance in providing great customer service.
- *Give complaining enough priority and authority.* Staff should be aware that complaints are a top priority item for your operation, and *anyone* who deals with them must have sufficient authority to resolve them completely.
- *Ensure that you can process complaints from all sources.* Nowadays there are four main ways to complain: in person, by telephone, by mail or by e-mail/internet. Your organization must be able to handle all of these efficiently and, more importantly, effectively.
- *Set up a process to log and analyse all complaints and share them with everyone.* One can learn so much about problems concerning internal processes, training, specific employees or managers, and products – free.

Process and actions

- *Thank the customer for complaining.* Remember, you are lucky that the customer is prepared to give up time and money to let you know he or she has a problem, instead of just walking away. A complaint is a gift.
- *Say that you are sorry that the problem has happened.* This is *not* an admission of guilt on your part; it's just good manners.
- *Put yourself in the place of the customer.* This will instantly give you an advantage, as not only will you have more empathy with the customer, but also you know your business better than the customer does and so, hopefully, will be able to see the solution more quickly.
- *Start with the view that the customer has a valid point, not that he or she is trying to rip you off.* It is true that there are some professional complainers out there, but they are in the minority, and, if you are a local store, you probably know them anyway. Accepting that the customer may well have a point, even internally, may well trigger off ideas for an acceptable resolution.
- *Get all the facts first.* Letting the customer give you all of the information helps you fully understand the situation *and*, if the customer is emotional, will give him or her time to calm down.
- *Don't leap straight to the 'free gift' route.* It's very tempting to give the customer a gift or vouchers, and in many cases, done properly, it is good service. However, too often it is done *instead* of solving the problem, which can lead to more complaints about the same thing because it hasn't been fixed, and also to the 'training' of more professional complainers.
- *Correct the mistake.* None of the other points is really valid if you don't fix the problem! Make sure that your definition of the right fix is the same as the customer's.
- *Learn from every complaint.* Do something! Fix the process; train staff in the issue; eliminate the fault. Wherever possible, let the complaining customer know that he or she has helped you resolve a problem. The customer will feel great and come back again and again (and will probably tell friends!).
- *Minimize reasons for complaints.* Do you have a continuous improvement culture? Do you check customer (and employee) satisfaction regularly? Do you check the quality of the goods sold in your organization?
- *Remember, it costs at least five times as much to gain a new customer as to keep an existing one.* Keeping this complaining customer should be the top priority, and at these cost ratios you can afford to be generous with your time and effort.
- *ALWAYS respond.* In-person complainers hopefully always get dealt with, but make sure that *everyone* who complains on the telephone, by letter or by e-mail gets a rapid and appropriate response.
- *Listen to your staff.* They nearly always care about your company and doing a good job, and are much closer to the customers than you are. Ask their views regularly and make changes when they are sensible. Make sure *their* complaints are handled too.

■ *Lead by example.* It's not that your staff *don't* listen to what you say, it's that they *do* listen, so make sure that you are always setting the right example and giving complaints your personal priority. Reward good complaints handling.

Overall, the most important thing to understand is that it is usually OK to make some mistakes (unless they are *really* stupid!); customers don't expect you to be perfect. However, they do then expect you to handle the complaint brilliantly. Interestingly enough, this is also true of your staff, who have respect for their organization if it is good at handling complaints and has an open and honest approach to them within a no-blame culture.

The real no-no is to keep receiving the same complaint and not doing anything about it! Complaints are free research, a free audit and a free process check all in one and must be used to learn from with regard to product, process and training.

Paul Cooper is communications director of the Institute of Customer Service (tel: 01787 278180; e-mail: paul.cooper@icsmail.co.uk; website: www.institute ofcustomerservice.com).

The latest ICS/TMI National Complaints Culture Survey 2006 was launched in May 2006, and copies can be obtained direct from the ICS website www.instituteofcustomerservice.com or on 01206 571716. Copies of Bob Johnston's research can also be obtained through the website or Colchester office.

Rewarding customer service

Paul Cooper, Communications Director of the Institute of Customer Service, reports on how reward and recognition can help to deliver your customer service strategy.

Everyone instinctively realizes that salaries and associated benefits have an effect on performance, but what is that effect? To find out, the Institute of Customer Service and the Chartered Institute of Personnel and Development commissioned Aston Business School to carry out comprehensive breakthrough research into this area, with particular reference to customer service performance. The research was done by Professors Michael West and Gary Fisher, and Dr Judy Scully.

Previous Aston research has already shown that people management is a powerful predictor of organizational performance, and that the more organizations actively *involve*, *develop* and *engage* the *willing* contribution of their employees, the better those organizations perform. This new research builds on this to look at the importance of people management and customer service for business performance and how organizations can use reward more effectively.

The aims of the research were to:

- identify the impact of good reward and recognition practices on customer service and satisfaction;
- highlight which practices are most effective;
- determine the extent of employee satisfaction with reward and recognition;

■ identify the approaches to reward and recognition most associated with employee commitment and motivation;
■ understand how factors such as culture and employee characteristics affect satisfaction;
■ study the effects of autonomy, participation and involvement on satisfaction.

The research was conducted on 22 sites in 15 organizations, involving 11 call centres, 7 face-to-face customer services or 4 combinations of both. It was on a national basis in the public, private and not-for-profit sectors, with responses from over 800 customer service staff.

Major conclusions

Organizations with the best customer service:

■ make extensive use of performance-related pay and team-based reward and recognition;
■ emphasize career development of staff, and work–life balance issues;
■ have few differences between reward and benefits policies for managers and staff respectively;
■ have contingent pay based on customer satisfaction and service quality rather than just on productivity;
■ have high levels of employee satisfaction.

For example, on the issue of non-variation of benefits the following are direct quotations from participants:

Our managers would feel quite strange about having different things. (Kent County Council)

For managers the same performance management system is used. (Scottish Water)

At one point we had different holiday allowances, but we realized it's important, as everybody's working just as hard, to ensure that everyone has the same type of benefit. (Unite)

As mentioned above, a further key issue was that customer service organizations need to ensure that staff are rewarded and recognized for delivering high-quality customer service, but many organizations have adopted models that were developed for organizations with different cultures and processes, such as manufacturing. This is particularly true of contingent pay, and there was a significant difference on the spread of constituent parts of the make-up of this between the better organizations and the rest, as follows:

Assessment criteria used by companies for contingent pay:

	Top 5	Others
Customer satisfaction	100%	18%
Service quality	100%	29%
Productivity	70%	70%

Overall, this gave 'a quality, not just a quantity, emphasis'.

Another key differentiator was employee satisfaction. Employees in the top organizations saw their employers as:

■ fair;
■ looking after them;
■ consultative and open to suggestions;
■ involving them in decision making;
■ fair payers;
■ providing high levels of feedback;
■ warm and supportive.

And so, in essence, of course salary is important, but satisfaction with pay is highest when employees:

■ have high levels of commitment;
■ feel proud;
■ have a sense of belonging;
■ are intent on staying;
■ have a strong sense of attachment.

Therefore, 'pay practices should be internally equitable and externally competitive'.

But salary is not enough. Employees want:

■ greater freedom and autonomy;
■ responsibility – to be more involved;
■ recognition;
■ praise;
■ achievement;
■ trust;
■ personal growth – ongoing learning and development, qualifications, career.

Again there is a distinctive difference between organizations in relation to their approach to reward strategies. The percentages of companies using different reward strategies are as follows:

	Top	Others
Performance-related pay	60%	29%
Individual recognition	80%	47%
Team-based reward	60%	12%
Team-based recognition	100%	12%
Work–life balance policies	100%	59%
Career development	100%	71%
Company pension	100%	71%
Restaurant facilities	100%	53%

And there was a much stronger prevalence of the usage of other benefits, including (by frequency):

- company sick pay;
- nationally/professionally recognized training;
- in-house training courses;
- external/off-site training courses;
- career development programmes/policies;
- contributory pension;
- work–life balance policies;
- relocation packages;
- transferable pension;
- medical insurance;
- career counselling;
- workplace nurseries and crèches;
- social facilities;
- non-contributory pension;
- sports facilities;
- retail vouchers.

Differences were also noticeable in the area of work–life balance provision – an area that is surprisingly important for staff. For example:

- flexible start/finish times;
- individual control over hours of work;
- career-break schemes;
- term-time working contracts;
- childcare assistance – crèche/nursery;
- supported study;
- sabbaticals;
- home working.

Overall, a good reward policy has:

■ market competitiveness;
■ internal equity and fairness;
■ variation through contingent pay – motivational/message/equity;
■ individual/team rewards;
■ employee benefits;
■ reward priorities;
■ a good mix for the 'total reward'.

If it's good, then it will:

■ establish a clear relationship between pay and performance, competence and skill;
■ recognize achievement;
■ reinforce performance-related culture;
■ demonstrate that the organization values skill development and competencies;
■ reinforce team and individual effort;
■ concentrate on the priority areas;
■ attract and retain the best people;
■ improve pay competitiveness;
■ increase employee commitment.

'Everyone has targets that are linked to our company strategy, which is focused on customers, people and shareholders... in that order'(Shane Speirs, Unite Group).

The research has shown, yet again, that the service–value–profit chain holds good. In this case, it is clear that organizations that fairly treat, value, respect and support their staff tend to get:

■ staff who are satisfied with pay, recognition, involvement...
■ who are also staff with high commitment to the organization...
■ which provides the organization with high-quality customer service...
■ which enhances the reputation of the organization...
■ which directly leads to increased profitability.

An important issue does come up in the treatment of staff, and especially feedback: 'Managers must give employees accurate and supportive feedback on performance, but negative feedback should constitute, if any, only a tiny proportion (probably less than 5 per cent).'

And so, the conclusions of the research are as follows:

■ Reward and recognition can only be understood in a cultural context.
■ Employees must feel valued, respected and supported.
■ Employees must be fairly treated and looked after.
■ It is important to monitor their treatment by means of regular employee surveys.

- Constantly seek ways to improve the well-being of employees, especially in terms of work–life balance.
- Utilize employee knowledge of how service can be improved.
- Reward innovation.
- Staff enjoy working in organizations that emphasize the importance of good customer service.
- These actions should lead to much lower staff turnover – therefore career development plans take on even greater importance.

Paul Cooper is Communications Director of the Institute of Customer Service (tel: 01787 278180; e-mail: paul.cooper@icsmail.co.uk; website: www.institute ofcustomerservice.com).

The ICS/CIM research *Rewarding Customer Service? Using reward and recognition to deliver your customer service strategy* is available for just £50 directly from the online shop at the ICS website www.instituteofcustomerservic e.com, or call Vicky Woollard at ICS Colchester on 01206 571716.

Perfect PA: The ready-to-use Personal Assistant

Remember the good old-fashioned secretary who took care of the typing, data entry, filing and all the other 101 essential but time-intensive administrative tasks around the office?

If like most businesses you no longer have a dedicated, central resource organizing all these activities, you must sometimes wonder why so much senior and junior management time is wasted fulfilling such a function, when they should be focused on sales and marketing, business development, formulating strategy and other recognised management activities.

What does it do? Product summary

Help is at hand with Green Button's Perfect PA v2.2, which not only provides a secretarial function but also contains all the communications management, operations features and target marketing requirements a small business or organisation needs. What's more, it's easy to use, requires no additional programming and is genuinely cross-platform for sharing between Mac and PC users.

Once you've used Perfect PA, you'll wonder how you got by without it –
Whether you're an SME, sole trader or partnership organization, Perfect PA will save you time because it performs routine tasks and has been designed specifically with your needs in mind, covering:

- Outgoing and incoming eMails are automatically filed against the contact alongside all paper communications, including mailshots;
- Amongst the operations features is easy conversion of a quotation to invoice;
- Your target marketing requirements are met by a user-definable categories feature with a simple entry routine for defining and allocating categories to contacts;
- Select all those with the required categories and create your mailshot or eMailshot – Perfect PA's address formatting facilitates worldwide variations.

With Perfect P.A.

Without Perfect P.A.

Who is Perfect PA for?

We have identified corporate user groups, smaller businesses, individuals and people who run a number of activities as users who would most benefit from using Perfect PA.

Small businesses and corporate user groups

Perfect PA was specifically developed and designed to help corporate user group managers, small business owners and sole traders run their businesses more efficiently. By saving time on routine administrative tasks, more time can be devoted to developing the business itself.

How much do you value 18 days a year of your time? That's how much you could save just by eliminating *five minutes* per working day of your time currently spent doing routine tasks… tasks that Perfect PA could be doing for you.

Start-ups

Contacts and networking are the life-blood of any new business. By using Perfect PA from day one, a new business start-up can stay on top of its communications – saving time and working smarter. When combined with an accounts package, Perfect PA will provide the new business owner with a software solution that provides everything needed to run the business.

Membership organisations

Perfect PA's combination of contact information and marketing tools is ideal for any type of membership organisation needing to contact its members frequently, for example Chambers of Commerce, sports clubs, charities.

Perfect PA features overview

Providing an essential CRM tool for all small and medium sized businesses, Perfect PA offers ease of use and value for money in a powerful application for contact and communications management which also facilitates target marketing. By tracking incoming and outgoing communication, Perfect PA provides instant access to all the information needed when contacting customers, suppliers, members and other categories as defined by the user.

Perfect PA's simple 'point and click' style design means there is no need for expensive customization, enabling you to:
- Be productive straightaway
- Organize all your communication information in one place
- Share information with other programs and people in your workgroup
- Protect your most valuable assets - your customers

You can also:
- Manage your customer contacts quickly and easily
- Instantly access previous communications with contacts or businesses
- Keep up to date and track individual projects
- Produce targeted mailings by post eMail and fax
- Automatically record outgoing letters, eMails and faxes

Perfect PA also has:
- Categories for easier contact management and target marketing
- Powerful post code map for targeted mailing activities
- Powerful search capabilities
- Single user or small network functionality

Cross-platform capability

Perfect PA's award winning technology allows you to share data with users on other platforms. No problem if you work on an Apple Mac and your accounts department works on PC (Windows) – Perfect PA's file structure is fully compatible with all platforms.

*If you would like to speak to somebody to find out more about the features and functions of Perfect PA, please call our sales team on **0870 446 0580**.*

CAN'T FIND THE TIME TO GROW YOUR BUSINESS?

INSTALL PERFECT PA – THE CONTACT & COMMUNICATIONS MANAGEMENT SYSTEM FOR SMALL BUSINESSES

- Automatically log and file e-mail, letters and invoices
- Instantly view communication history of each contact
- Easily categorise them for more effective contact management
- Quickly produce segmented lists and targeted mailings
- Update and track individual projects for each contact

Perfect PA has been designed specifically to help the small business owner and will save you time by performing routine tasks

'Ready-to-use... no additional programming... cross-platform'

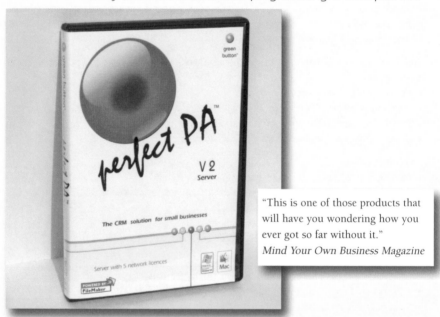

"This is one of those products that will have you wondering how you ever got so far without it."
Mind Your Own Business Magazine

You may download Perfect PA from our website www.greenbutton.uk.com

Customer relationship management for small businesses

Growth allows senior executives less time to spend with individual customers. Mark Staniszewski, Managing Director of Green Button Software, discusses how to maintain a friendly, personal and attentive service

Let's start with a definition of customer relationship management (CRM), for which I am indebted to Wikipedia, the free encyclopedia. 'CRM, in its broadest sense, means managing all interactions and business with customers. A good CRM program will allow a business to acquire customers, service the customer, increase the value of the customer to the company and retain good customers.' The concept therefore is not exactly rocket science, although if you read the marketing press you might think it was, because the whole subject seems to have become obscured by the use of pseudo-scientific jargon. It is not rocket science, because CRM is what any business will be instinctively doing whatever its size and whatever its business sector. It pre-dates computers. If you think back to the days of the small greengrocer on your local high street, you would have received personal, friendly, attentive service from the owner, who might even have arranged for your purchases to be delivered to your home. It has taken supermarkets 40 years to reinvent this particular level of service. What has changed is the amount of information that can be collected on each individual customer. So in the computer age, what does CRM mean for small businesses?

Definition of a small business

So that we are clear about the size of businesses we are talking about, let us make a brief foray into the world of government statistics. According to the Department of Trade and Industry (DTI), Britain had a total of 4.3 million business enterprises at the start of 2004, of which 99.3 per cent were small businesses employing between 0 and 49 employees. However, the vast majority of these businesses – 3.1 million – had no employees. So the small businesses we are talking about comprise two different segments: 1) sole traders or partnerships comprising only the self-employed owner-managers, and companies comprising only an employee-director; and 2) companies employing fewer than 50 employees. It is worth pointing out that these businesses account for 46.8 per cent of employment and 37.0 per cent of business turnover in the United Kingdom.

CRM for the sole trader

So what does CRM mean for the sole trader? Although it does depend on the type of business, most sole traders will know each of their customers personally, they will have a clear idea of their needs, likes and dislikes, and will have managed the relationship with a paper-based system (or a good memory). With the advent of off-the-shelf CRM software solutions, paper-based systems are a criminal waste of the proprietor's time. By automatically recording and filing electronic correspondence and outgoing letters, delivery notes and invoices in one computer file, a huge amount of routine administrative work can be streamlined. This will allow the sole trader more time to develop his or her business.

CRM for the small business with employees

It is once a business starts taking on employees that CRM software becomes essential. The proprietor/managing director will no longer have personal knowledge of each customer. Some aspects of the interaction or relationship will now be handled by other members of the team. There may be a separate and distinct sales team. Customer complaints may be handled by a different department. It is vital therefore that all the interactions with customers can be gathered and filed on the computer for easy access so that all members of the team can track the relationship with each customer. However, this is only one aspect of the capability of these CRM packages.

CRM and marketing

Marketing is potentially where CRM should be of most positive benefit to the bottom line. Because the software is capturing all the information it can from the company's relationship with each customer, this information can be analysed and utilized to maximize the value from each relationship. However, CRM software does not and cannot tell you what to do. It is up to you to decide how and when to contact your customers and what to offer. So does your customer prefer a personal sales visit, a letter, electronic mail, postcard, newsletter, etc? Your CRM program can tell you when your customer last bought something from you, what it was, how much they paid. So, is it time to try to cross-sell, make them a special offer or give them some free information? The relationship still depends on you and your marketing strategy – but CRM software facilitates the process and makes targeted mailings of whatever kind easier to implement and manage.

Acquisition of new customers

Everyone knows that their best potential customer is an existing customer, but inevitably some customers will desert you over time. So, part of your marketing strategy will be dedicated to the acquisition of new customers. CRM packages will help by giving you the information to profile your existing customers, so you can narrow down your target audience to potential customers with the same or similar characteristics.

Choosing a CRM package for your business

You may have been put off buying a CRM package because of the envisaged cost; this is no longer a concern, as there are a number of off-the-shelf packages that are targeted at the small business market and priced accordingly. Products that would be worth looking at include Act!!, Goldmine and Perfect PA. These do not cost the earth and have similar features. I have not included Microsoft's offering, as this requires training and implementation by an outside consultancy, which may put it beyond the budget limits of most small businesses.

When comparing the software packages mentioned, it is worth considering whether they have the in-built flexibility to cope with your business requirements, because customization will probably cost more than the original software itself. Some companies, particularly those in the creative sector, may well have a mixed platform network and therefore require a system that can transfer data across Macs and PCs – something to bear in mind when comparing systems. In addition, the basic software package may not include all the essential features that you need and you may then find it necessary to buy add-ons that make the original purchase price misleading. Read the small print and download a trial!

CRM and your company

However, we are probably getting ahead of ourselves. Because CRM has been a buzzword for so long, you may feel that you need a system without really thinking it through properly. You must be certain that your company will actually benefit from the customer information that such a system can provide and that you have the necessary expertise to utilize it to get a return on your investment. The decision should not be taken in isolation as it requires all potential users to buy in to the concept, because it is how well the system is used that will determine how much benefit the company derives from it. And it is not just about buying in, because levels of computer literacy will vary between individuals and it is no use buying a system that some of your team cannot get to grips with. Ease of use is an overused term in this marketplace, but if it is a reality, then you might actually have a system that 100 per cent of the team can use.

It is possible for CRM software to help you run an entire business, but you must have the vision and desire to make it happen.

Green Button Software was established in 2001. It specializes in the design of off-the-shelf solutions for small businesses and is a member of the FileMaker Solutions Alliance. Its product targeted at this sector is Perfect PA communications management and target marketing for sole traders and small businesses employing up to 100 people.

For more information, ring 0870 446 0580 or visit www.greenbutton. uk.com.

5

People and performance

Stress and ill health can drain a fortune from your business

For £1 a week help plug the leak with HealthSure One's better benefits

£601* per employee per year disappears down the tubes because of sickness absence.

For as little as £1 per head per week **HealthSure One** is a company-funded healthcare scheme for your workforce.

Policyholders can claim back **100%** of the cost of treatment in all the categories covered (up to policy limits).

Better still, stress counselling is included in the confidential 24-hour helpline, with the option of adding 6 face-to-face sessions for an extra 25p per week per employee. By offering your employees this you could reduce the risk of legal action and help meet your duty of care requirements.

Call now for full details of how **HealthSure One** can enhance the health of your business.

0845 075 0063
www.healthsure.co.uk

*The average figure according to the CIPD Absence Management 2005

Weekly premium one adult†		Entry level £1.00	
			Payback Amount
Dental Full cost of treatment within any 12-month period up to:	ADULT	£50	100%
Optical Full cost of spectacles, contact lenses or eye tests within any 24-month period up to:	ADULT	£50	100%
Health Screening Full cost of diagnostic health screen within any 12-month period up to:	ADULT	£100	100%
Specialist Consultations Full cost of diagnostic consultations within any 12-month period up to:	ADULT	£200	100%
Acupuncture, Chiropractic, Osteopathy, Chiropody, Physiotherapy Full cost of treatment within any 12-month period up to:	ADULT	£150	100%
Personal Accident Cover Benefits are underwritten by Chubb Insurance Company of Europe, through Marsh UK Limited.	ADULT	£5,000	
Confidential 24-hour Helpline Stress counselling, bereavement, legal, debt, household emergency and medical advice		✓	
Additional premium per week to include up to 6 face-to-face counselling sessions		£0.25	

†This table shows one of the nine different policy levels, full information on levels of cover can be found in the product leaflet. Premiums correct at time of going to press.

HealthSure One
IT PAYS TO LOOK AFTER YOUR EMPLOYEES

Employee well-being – work it out

Many businesses happily invest money in the development of their products and services but few invest in the health of one of their most vital assets – their employees.

Russ Piper, director of channel acquisition at HealthSure looks at why it is important for employers to look after the health of their employees.

"Many businesses recognise that employee well-being is a priority, but feel that staff training and development is perhaps more important," commented Russ.

"This really shouldn't be the case. Health-related sickness absence is a real issue for national productivity. Costing in excess of £3.8 billion per annum[1], it is responsible for more than 40 million working days lost each year in the UK[2].

"This has a significant, detrimental effect on businesses bottom lines – particularly if the organisation is middle market or an SME."

Absenteeism is not merely caused by employees pulling one day 'sickies'. The increased pace of today's working environment has affected the daily workloads of the majority of employees forcing them to cope with longer working hours, increased demands and greater pressure to achieve.

Providing further food for thought, Health & Safety Executive (HSE) guidelines have made healthcare a legal priority for employers.

It is now an employer's duty by law to make sure their employees are not made ill by their work and firms have been forced to look in detail at their healthcare strategies.

Employers who don't take stress or health issues in the workplace seriously leave themselves wide open to the threat of litigation and compensation claims from employees who feel that they have suffered as a result of their work.

It's important that employers put healthcare strategies in place to address this issue. While some sickness cannot be prevented, it is important to realise that fast and easy access to professional health advice and care can be a decisive factor in reducing time away from the workplace.

---

[1] CBI Statistics 2004, http://www.hse.gov.uk/sicknessabsence/index.htm 2005.
[2] IHC, online recruitment 2005

"There are many products on the market to help. Private medical insurance is the most well known, however costly premiums often mean that companies have little option but to only offer them to senior employees," Russ continued.

Healthcare cash plans such as HealthSure's can complement PMI or even be a more affordable alternative. By investing from as little as £1 per employee per week, managers can ensure that they are providing an easy to use solution to employee healthcare requirements.

"Healthcare cash plans allow all businesses, regardless of their size, industry or budget to offer healthcare to their employees. They are becoming increasingly popular with SMEs looking after the health of their workforce on a budget" he said.

Policies allow employees to claim money up to agreed limits towards the cost of treatments such as a dental check-up or filling, an eye test, a new pair of glasses or contact lenses and more specialised treatments such as a health screen and consultations. In addition, policies also include a 24 hour, confidential employee helpline and the option to add face to face counselling sessions.

With HSE guidelines highlighting companies' responsibility towards employee well-being, the counselling and helpline can help to address the issue of stress. Furthermore, with the 'dental crisis' continuing to hit national headlines, the cover towards dental treatments ensures that managers are offering a benefit that is relevant to all.

Russ Piper concludes, "Essentially, by providing a cost effective solution to combating absenteeism, businesses not only address the impact that health-related absenteeism has on performance and business success, they also play a role in ensuring that their workforce stays healthy and happy."

Company paid health policies are one of the fastest growing employee benefit with employer and employee enjoying the perks of a healthier, happier and more productive workforce that is motivated and takes less time off sick.

For further information on how they can help your business contact HealthSure on 0845 075 0063 or visit **www.healthsure.co.uk**

For further information please contact Jessica Davenport at Mere PR
Tel: 0161 929 8700   Fax: 0161 929 8300   E:mail: jessica@mere.co.uk

Twenty-first-century HR services for SMEs

In a global economy, we have to learn to work smarter and improve our people practices, says Laura Firth, Managing Director of Reed Consulting

In today's global marketplace, manual work is increasingly being 'off-shored'. Many UK businesses have recognized that it is difficult to compete globally on the basis of brawn (ie unskilled labour), so many companies are seeking to compete on brain. This can be done by working smarter, demonstrating outstanding people practice that improves both efficiency and quality, and innovating to ensure that the organization stays ahead of its global competitors. Since an organization, at its most basic level, is a group of people working together to a common aim, it is perhaps not surprising that so much innovation has taken place over the past decade in the HR services market. Gone are the days when HR (or Personnel, as it was formerly referred to) was purely about tea, sympathy and admin. The in-house HR professional has been given a lively wake-up call – a 'call to action' – to prove that he or she can make a difference to the organization's performance or risk being 'outsourced' or replaced by an 'on demand' service provider. In this chapter I cite just four of the many advances in HR services available to SMEs to transform their business performance in demonstrable ways.

Most business professionals will look at the chart of the life cycle of an organization shown in Figure 5.1.1 and will relate to having operated at one or more of the stages illustrated. As you reflect on the different businesses you have been in, and the different stages they were at, it is common for you to relate to the good and bad of those situations, much as you do when you think about the different stages of your own

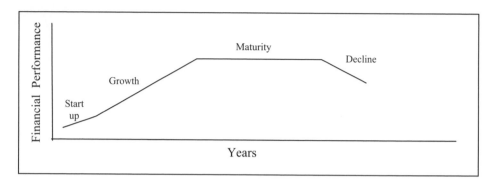

Figure 5.1.1

life. Some you look back on with nostalgia, some – perhaps the teenage (growth) years – you may look back on and remember the growing pains. The important parallel, which most experienced business professionals will recognize in this analogy, is that the different stages of an organization's growth place different demands on its people and require a different approach to people practice in order to be effective.

Executive development to lead and engage employees in the change

Many seasoned successful business leaders will tell you that doggedly sticking to the same style and approach to people practice as their organization made the transition through the stages illustrated in the figure actually inhibited the speed of growth and success that their businesses achieved. Clearly, all SME owners are striving to achieve success. However, recognizing that the first step in that change process might mean changing your approach personally can be an uncomfortable realization for any business owner. In the light of this fact, funding is increasingly being provided through business links to firms of psychologists, such as our own, to work with the senior managers of SMEs to enable them to receive independent support in this. Through a diagnostic consultation, which is then followed by an intensive executive coaching programme, senior managers and directors are helped to change their behaviours, growing their skills and repertoire to be more effective.

When a business makes the transition from being a small start-up with hands-on involvement by the owners into a larger organization with less personally committed employees, it takes a strong, adept leader to engage with all the new employees to ensure they are fully committed to the standards, principles and values of the organization. Executive development helps to equip the leaders of these organizations to harness these skills and to secure the engagement of employees to achieve the organizations' goals. This used to be a service that only senior managers in large FTSE organizations received, but opening this out to support MDs of SMEs seems to be making a real difference – according to the clients we have worked with, at least.

Outsourcing HR services: focused, value-driven HR interventions

As an organization makes a transition from start-up into the growth phase of its life cycle, it increasingly becomes apparent to the owners that there comes a need for rules and processes to be put in place. One can draw a parallel between this and football; you need to know that all of your players are working in the same direction, towards the same goal. They need to know where they should be and how they should support the other players, and, importantly, what is and is not 'fair play'.

Traditionally, at this point most SMEs would either: 1) grow the role of the company PA to encompass 'HR matters'; or 2) hire a junior HR person. The problem with this traditional approach has been, in case 1), that this relatively unskilled person could not advise on more complicated matters (eg legislation – and hence solicitors would still need to be consulted), and, in case 2), that these persons are not equipped to be able to support the senior management team in getting the best out of their people, so the organization would lose what could otherwise have been a strong competitive edge. These challenges gave rise to an increasing number of organizations, such as our own, that provide 'on demand' or 'outsourced' modular HR services. Table 5.1.1 illustrates the range of services available from these 'one-stop shops'.

Table 5.1.1 Services available from 'one-stop shops' offering modular HR services

Employment law	Not qualified solicitors (hence not at the same hourly rate) but experienced HR specialists providing employment-law-abiding advice.
Web-based HR information/ documents	Web portals, on a pay-for-access basis, providing HR policies, procedures, contracts and other useful documentation.
Web-based HR database for SMEs	Cost-effective online HR database, particularly helpful for SMEs in different sites that want full visibility of absence records, performance ratings, development records, etc across their sites.
Outsourced HR	Providers who provide the above three services to an SME but also provide a set number of hours per annum of advice and onsite support from HR experts to support the senior managers in the areas in which they specifically want advice. This kind of volume commitment to expertise usage then attracts discounted rates and is generally more economical than hiring the permanent HR resource.

Cost-efficient recruitment

Increasingly, recruitment companies are offering an 'outsource' proposition. This effectively means partnering with a recruitment specialist who will undertake all your recruitment requirements over the year. I emphasize the word 'all', because traditionally recruitment agencies were viewed purely as a 'contingency' source of candidates, when other, in-house-commissioned attraction methods failed to deliver the required candidates. These recruitment process outsource providers (RPOs) take responsibility for implanting a recruitment team who undertake *all* your recruitment, from the moment you identify a need to the day your new person starts. Because of the volume commitment you are making (ie because all your recruitment is done by the RPO), you can normally expect to receive extremely advantageous rates for this service and it can remove a large amount of the administrative burden of recruitment from your line managers.

Employee retention: improving organizational performance

As the war for talent rages on, Reed Consulting has launched a market-leading service to improve employee retention in the UK workplace. The service begins with the completion of a tool called RADAR, which can be used free of charge at our website, www.reedconsulting.co.uk. RADAR quantifies the cost of retention problems to an organization and how it compares with the organization's benchmarks (compared to other companies in the area, companies of comparable size or companies in the same industry). For one SME we worked with this year, RADAR calculated that its retention problems were costing it £2.25m per annum, which made it a business-critical issue to address.

Most SME senior managers, particularly those who own their own business, will acknowledge that the business is not just a business, it is personal. This could be because of the heart and soul they put into the original concept, or the sweat and tears, let alone hours, they have invested in getting the business off the ground, or the money they have at stake in the business. Because it is personal, people within the SME are often fearful to tell the truth about why people are moving on from the organization, since generally all the organization's practices have been influenced to some extent by the close-knit senior management team/owner. The independent provider undertakes a diagnostic intervention and gives top-level feedback directly to the board on what needs to change in the way the organization is operating, in order to improve its employee retention, which will bring significant commercial performance improvements and competitive edge. One Regional Development Agency recognized the improvement this intervention has been making to businesses and funded some of our work as part of its commitment to business improvement projects in its area. All the SMEs we have been working with thus far have already seen improvements in their retention levels, even the one in which the biggest cause of staff leaving was the management style of the owners themselves.

Conclusion

Whilst there is only scope to cover four of the latest advances in HR services that can support SMEs in gaining competitive advantage over their global competitors, this is a growing marketplace. More and more business owners recognize that, to compete, we have to work smarter in the United Kingdom, and this means, among other things, better, more focused people practices, which improve recruitment, engagement and retention of staff in a way that channels their energies into helping Britain's SMEs be the best in the world.

Reed Consulting is the HR consultancy and outsource services arm of the Reed family of companies. It has grown by over 100 per cent each year since its creation in 2002. Reed Consulting has over 450 Chartered Institute of Personnel and Development/British Psychological Society-qualified staff throughout the United Kingdom, making it one of the fastest-growing HR services companies in the United Kingdom. Reed Consulting helps small, medium-sized and large businesses to improve their commercial performance through results-driven people practice.

Laura Frith, BSc (Hons), MSc, CMC, MCIPD, CPsychol, is Managing Director of Reed Consulting. A certified management consultant with a first-class Master's degree in occupational psychology, Laura is also a chartered psychologist and has a broad range of expertise that she has applied in both the public and the private sector. Laura has worked with many organizations, including the Metropolitan Police Service, the BBC, PA Consulting, local government, Vodafone, Lloyds TSB and Arthur Andersen.

Complications and costs of employment law

It can be tough for small employers to keep on the right side of the law, but ignorance is no defence, says Mike Huss, an employment lawyer at Peninsula. Peninsula are a business partner of Corporate Risk Solutions at Alexander Forbes

Do you feel lucky? Do you feel really lucky? Do you feel at least 150 times lucky? For that is the number of pieces of legislation enacted by the Labour Government since coming to office in May 1997. So how many of those Acts, regulations, etc can you name? Start with the Data Protection Act 1998, the Working Time Regulations 1998, the Minimum Wage Act 1998…? Running into trouble? How about the Sex Discrimination (Gender Reassignment) Regulations 1999 or the Unfair Dismissal and Statement of Reasons for Dismissal (Variation of Qualifying Period) Order 1999?

The fact is that this Government has concentrated on giving additional rights to employees and workers, many of them under a generic description of 'family-friendly'. A right for an employee/worker is automatically an obligation for an employer. Government spokespeople are not defensive about this; they argue that the legislation is honouring manifesto promises for which they were elected.

It involves costs to obey the law and it involves costs to disobey the law. It cannot be good policy to rely on luck that you will not be caught – especially given the sheer amount of legislation, some of it with quite draconian penalties (how does prison grab you?). And, of course, whilst ignorance of the law might be bliss, it is not a defence!

Consequently, any employer must:

- be aware of the law;
- set up policies, documentation and systems to comply with the law;
- ensure that the policies and procedures are adhered to;
- ensure that those policies and procedures are updated whenever a flaw is identified or the law is changed or new laws introduced.

It is a simple fact that tribunals (and criminal cases involving health and safety breaches, sex or race harassment, data protection infringements, etc) are won in the workplace, not the tribunal room. As an old advocate, and much as it grieves me to say it, brilliance as an advocate is only likely to sway a very evenly balanced case. If you have not complied with the Statutory Disputes Resolution Procedures to the letter of the law, you've lost, and no argument can change that, although it might be possible to achieve a less than the maximum uplift to the award.

Clearly, keeping up to date is difficult. It is difficult for Peninsula, who specialize in this field; for in-house Personnel or HR departments it is more difficult, usually because people problems always seem to generate a higher priority; and for smaller employers, without dedicated specialists, it is impossible. But lack of knowledge of the law, or observance of it, is not a defence!

I shall return later to the issue of how to keep up to date, but what is it you have to keep up to date? The 'proper' answer to that is 'everything', but, given that it is so difficult to achieve, which are the critical areas that absolutely must be maintained?

Two basics you must have. *All* employers *must* issue a written statement of particulars of employment. Traditionally, employers have been a little lax in this regard – especially as there has never been a significant direct penalty for failing to do so. However, since the statutory disputes resolution procedures became law on 1 October 2004, not only has a direct penalty been introduced (not, it must be admitted, a terribly large one: two or four weeks' pay) but it is very unlikely that in the absence of such a written statement the employer will be able to demonstrate that the employee knew the disciplinary rules and procedures, or that the stages required by the statutory disputes resolution procedures, as well as those of the contract, have been followed. Failure makes it an automatically unfair dismissal, with any award(s) likely to be increased by up to 50 per cent! You *must* issue proper contracts.

Awards for unfair dismissal cannot exceed £58,400 for loss plus £8,700 for the Basic Award, giving a grand(!) total of £67,100 – plus possibly up to 50 per cent in addition for an automatically unfair dismissal, under statutory disputes, making in theory £100,650 a possible maximum. The reality is that very, very few come anywhere near this total.

Where the worrying figures and problems lie is in the area of discrimination. Awards for discrimination are calculated *on top of those for unfair dismissal*. They are unlimited (ie they are not capped), and come under two main headings: injury to feelings and aggravated damages. The awards are therefore normally higher. In addition, so are the costs; discrimination hearings invariably are listed for longer, and this automatically runs up witness time, costs and legal costs.

So, secondly, you *must* have an equal opportunities policy – an individual one for your organization. You need to ensure that:

- your policy is compliant in every respect;
- you have trained everyone in it during their induction (your 'trainers' must themselves be *properly* trained);
- that you enforce the policy if *anyone* transgresses;
- that you update it, if necessary, following any transgression and if the law changes.

This list is not an option; it is a necessity. If you can show, should a claim be made, that you have done everything possible to prevent discrimination or harassment, you may be able to prove you are not vicariously liable. If you can't – you won't!

You also should have considered how you are going to deal with age discrimination amongst all the others in your equal opportunities policy. Age is the biggest and potentially the most worrying of all. It covers every single employee/worker; race may only cover a few. Going forward, *every* employee/worker must be dismissed at retirement age. For those who reach 65 between 1 October 2006 and 1 April 2007 there are (complicated) transition provisions – but for those who are 65 in early October, and who have more than 12 years' service, you should already have dismissed them! The future is here now!

With over 150 new laws since May 1997 (plus those in existence before that), giving something like 85 separate jurisdictions (claims) that an employment tribunal can hear, getting it wrong will be very expensive.

You only have three ways to get it right:

- be lucky;
- employ someone in your organization to keep you up to date; or
- sign up with someone to keep you up to date (probably the only option for SMEs. SMEs have always, traditionally, used an outside accountant during the initial stages of growth. Health and safety, and people issues are now so complicated that the use of an outside consultancy is the only practical option).

Doing something right costs – but you do derive benefits from those costs. Doing nothing costs you more and you do not benefit at all!

Good luck!

Mike Huss is Senior Employment Law Consultant at Peninsula Business Services, the United Kingdom's leading provider of personnel, employment law and health and safety consultancy services. Peninsula works closely with the insurance broker Corporate Risk Solutions, a division of Alexander Forbes Risk Services Limited.

Lock in top performers

Retain talent and build long-term loyalty by encouraging a sense of proprietorship, says Andrew Broome, haysmacintyre

In today's highly competitive employment market it is vital to the success of your business that the key members of staff and business drivers are retained. Replacing key staff members is costly in terms not only of the direct costs such as recruitment agents' commissions but, more importantly, of the lost management time and disruption to the business that can often result. A business needs to use every tool at its disposal to retain talent.

What's the key? It's a balance between several aspects. There are the obvious things such as a competitive pay and benefits package; this may include a well-structured bonus scheme. Such schemes can be highly effective, and targeted to reward performance in certain areas.

Building long-term loyalty, however, takes more than this. The business needs not only to offer the opportunity for career progression, but to give people the opportunity to feel a sense of proprietorship about the businesses. This can be difficult to achieve, but where the right balance is struck the effects can be dramatic.

Offering shares in the business

The shares in many SMEs are frequently tightly held by the original founders and investors. Often there is a reluctance to open up the shareholder base for fear of loss of control over the shares, cash flow problems arising from the need to buy shares back from departing staff, arguments over valuation, lack of flexibility over profit extraction, etc.

Yet shares can provide an effective way of providing real value to an employee in a highly tax-efficient way, without any significant cash cost to the business. The right share scheme provides a mechanism to lock key employees into the company, give them that sense of ownership and align their long-term interests with those of the company.

In order to avoid the problems that can be associated with having a number of smaller shareholders, it is generally advisable in a private company to restrict the ability to exercise options and acquire shares to the sale of a controlling stake, or a listing, with the option lapsing if the employee leaves. This ensures that the day-to-day management and decision making is not unnecessarily complicated and that flexibility is retained over the extraction of profit from the business.

Any option scheme must fit with the long-term objectives of the business. There is little point in a scheme if there is no long-term intention to work towards a sale, or a listing, giving the option holder the prospect of realizing the value in his or her options. It is possible to create an internal market for the shares, but this is not a practical option for most companies.

Types of scheme

There are several types of scheme available. The three main schemes of interest to the SME sector will be the Company Share Option Plan (CSOP), the Unapproved Share Option scheme and the Enterprise Management Incentive scheme (EMI). It is important that professional advice be taken when setting up such schemes, and the comments below are just a summary of the main points.

With all these schemes there should be no tax liability for the employee or employer at the time the options are granted, any tax only becoming due on the exercise of the option, or later sale of the shares. Any gains realized under the CSOP and unapproved schemes will generally result in a 40 per cent tax charge for a higher-rate tax payer. Where the qualification criteria are met, the EMI scheme will be the scheme of choice.

Enterprise Management Incentive schemes

EMI schemes are specifically aimed at SMEs, allowing them to offer highly tax-efficient options to help retain and attract key staff. Both the company and the staff concerned will need to meet the qualification criteria. In summary, these are as follows:

■ Up to £100,000 worth of options, based on the value of the shares at grant, can be issued by a trading company, or holding company of a trading group, to employees working more than 25 hours per week, or, if less, 75% of their working time provided the employee does not have a greater than 30% interest in the company.
■ In aggregate, the company cannot have in issue more than £3m worth of options.
■ Most trades would qualify, though there are restrictions, for example on some property development and financial activities.

The EMI scheme's unique feature is that taper relief accrues from the date the option is granted – not the date it is exercised, as is the case with other schemes. After the option has been held for two years, the gain made will usually be taxed at an effective tax rate of 10 per cent.

Any number of performance criteria can be built into the scheme, though they must be capable of objective measurement. However, it is generally wise to avoid overcomplicating the scheme.

It is not necessary but it is advisable to agree the share value with HM Revenue & Customs before the options are granted. Options will usually be granted over a minority holding and therefore the valuation can be discounted to reflect this. The valuation will frequently be lower than the equivalent full valuation (discounts of up to 70–80 per cent of the 'full' value may be negotiated in appropriate cases), giving the opportunity to provide the employee with options with immediate potential value.

Options can be issued at any price over the nominal value of the share. The growth over and above the valuation at the date of grant will be treated as a capital gain. To the extent that the option price is below market value at the time of grant, a PAYE liability will arise.

Provided the options are in an unlisted company, a National Insurance liability will not normally arise. As with all option schemes, it is advisable to include provisions in the agreement for any tax payable by the employer to be reclaimable from the employee, avoiding what could otherwise be a potentially large employer's National Insurance exposure.

Share schemes, and the EMI scheme in particular, offer a tax-effective way to provide employees with an effective long-term incentive, locking them into the company and aligning their interests with the company's long-term aims, providing a useful tool to retain and reward staff.

Andrew Broome specializes in advising owner-managed, family and new entrepreneurial businesses on strategic, management and financial issues as well as dealing with corporate compliance and other related matters. Andrew's expertise covers a number of sectors including property development, investment and related businesses, professional services and consultancy businesses, but with a strong focus on internet and other IT based companies.

haysmacintyre, Chartered Accountants and tax advisers, comprises 23 partners and 130 staff based in Holborn, London. It provides high quality auditing and assurance, business and personal taxation, corporate finance, financial planning and other business support services.

Around 40% of the firm's business is within the corporate sector – small and medium sized enterprises many of which are within the property, media and entertainment, sports, motor trade and manufacturing sectors, 25% is for charitable and not for profit organizations and the remainder is for professional practices and private individuals.

haysmacintyre is a founding member of MSI, an international network of accountants and lawyers with over 200 firms in 90 countries.

haysmacintyre, Fairfax House, 15 Fulwood Place, London WC1V 6AY
Tel: 020 7969 5500; Fax: 020 7969 5600; e-mail: marketing@haysmacintyre.com; www.haysmacintyre.com

Flexible resourcing

Smaller companies can stay agile and versatile by engaging freelances, says John Thomas at the Professional Contractors Group

The word 'freelance' comes from the Middle Ages and literally means a mercenary soldier who is not attached to any master. His modern counterparts are far removed from their predecessors: they bring experience, knowledge and flexibility to a business world that is now based less on manufacturing and more on knowledge and service and needs to be able to react quickly to fast-changing markets.

Freelancing experienced a period of significant growth in the 1990s, but increased regulation and competition from abroad have slowed this growth since 2000. Without a legal definition, freelances inhabit the gap between external suppliers and employees. In the United Kingdom and elsewhere in the European Union, governments have sought to deal with this by legislating that freelances are more closely aligned with traditional employees.

This approach ignores the fact that most freelances have turned their backs on traditional employment models. Freelancing used to be the only option available to those who could not find permanent employment, but has now become the preferred way of working for the very best talent in all sectors, people endowed with precisely the skills, capabilities and attitudes most in demand from employers.

For many, the choice of freelancing as their preferred way of working is driven by lifestyle considerations: wanting more time for family, friends and hobbies; being able to work from home, perhaps; shunning corporate culture and politics; and rejecting the rigours of commuting.

PCG
PROFESSIONAL
CONTRACTORS
GROUP

The freelance workforce offers some of the smartest talent around

... and you'll find PCG members especially smart.

The Professional Contractors Group (PCG) is the not-for-profit trade association for freelance contractors and consultants in the UK. Our members work in a wide variety of sectors, including information technology, oil and gas, transport, engineering, finance and banking, management consultancy, marketing, media, telecommunications, construction and pharmaceuticals.

Freelancing has become the preferred way of working for the very best talent in all sectors, people endowed with precisely the skills, capabilities and attitudes most in demand from employers. Freelancers do not wish to be viewed as employees or "temps", nor do they hanker after the benefits and trappings of employment.

Our draft contracts, drawn up by experts in employment law and tax, can help you or your agency engage freelancers on the right terms and conditions, on a business-to-business basis.

Without the risks and responsibilities of an employment contract.

How large is the freelance workforce in the United Kingdom?

One UK worker in seven chooses to work for himself or herself, rather than for any fixed employer. Some are 'temps', and some have taken a career decision to operate as long-term freelances. There are an estimated 1 million people in this latter category. They include many of the country's most experienced and knowledgeable workers, and this highly skilled, highly mobile and highly flexible 21st-century workforce is growing – a trend that is likely to continue.

As the only one of its kind in the developed world, the United Kingdom's freelancing model represents one of the country's greatest economic assets. Derek Wreay, former chair of the Association of Technology Staffing Companies, says, 'A vibrant, highly skilled and committed freelance workforce is one of the cornerstones of UK plc's success. It is an area in which the UK leads in Europe, and this is a tribute to the competence of our freelancing community, and to the firms whose far-sightedness allows them to benefit from these freelances' world-class skills.'

Benefits of engaging freelances

Large corporations discovered the benefits of engaging freelance contractors for specific projects a long time ago. With a growing number of freelances, many of whom find some or all of their work through local networks and referrals rather than through agencies, it has become easier for smaller businesses to follow suit.

Small and medium-sized enterprises (SMEs) are in an ideal position to take advantage of the many skills and services offered by freelances, allowing their businesses to be agile and versatile in an increasingly competitive world, as well as leveraging the extensive industry contacts that freelances accumulate. As the burdens of employment legislation, which weigh disproportionately on the small business, become heavier, freelancing offers a pragmatic and flexible resourcing model to take on specific projects, help cope with peaks in demand, and provide valuable advice and expertise.

Making a strategic decision to deploy freelance talent gives businesses access to high-calibre professionals. Compared to larger, more traditional consultancies, freelances offer excellent value for money and a welcome focus on understanding and working in the client's business, rather than just executing their own internal processes. An independent freelance is only ever as good as his or her last assignment, and this motivation is a real driver for quality.

When meeting project deadlines is of paramount importance, engaging freelances can make the difference between success and failure. They usually have the experience, knowledge and expertise to be able to contribute and add value from the outset, and are free to focus solely on the task in hand, without being distracted by internal political considerations.

Utilizing freelance resources generally makes good sense for those businesses that:

- are subject to peaks and troughs in demand;
- have defined projects that need to be completed within set time-frames;
- are undergoing a transformation and require specialists to drive organizational change;
- experience difficulty in finding sufficient expertise, talent or knowledge in key areas of the organization;
- want access to better or more suitable skills, experience or contacts;
- need an injection of fresh thinking and creativity to increase productivity or profitability.

Headcount considerations aside, freelances offer a cost-effective deployment solution. Many operate from their own premises or homes, attending client sites only when necessary. Freelances are project focused, charging only for the time it takes or for performance of the agreed project. They generally charge hourly or daily rates based upon their skills, experience and expertise, and take care of their own tax and National Insurance payments, pensions, holiday pay and the like. Most freelances do not wish to be viewed as employees or 'temps', nor do they hanker after the benefits and trappings of employment.

Legal and contractual issues

Organizations wanting to take advantage of the flexibility, expertise and knowledge on offer from freelances need to understand some basic employment status and tax issues that influence contractual matters. Recent court cases serve to emphasize the risk of a relationship initially viewed as one of self-employment by all parties later being deemed to be one of employment, with the concomitant rights and costs issues. To avoid these risks, it is crucial that freelances be engaged on the right terms and conditions, through a business-to-business *contract for services*, rather than an employment-style *contract of service*. The contract for services must include:

- a substitution clause allowing the work to be performed by another person provided by the freelance business;
- a clause specifying that there is no 'mutuality of obligation' between the parties; in other words, there is 'no obligation, on the one hand, to work and, on the other, to remunerate';
- a clause stating that the freelance personnel will not be subject to supervision, direction or control as to the manner in which they render the agreed services.

The Professional Contractors Group (PCG), which is the not-for-profit trade association representing freelances in the United Kingdom, provides its members with draft contracts that have been vetted by experts in employment status, tax and commercial law. The benefit to an SME client of entering into such an agreement is that it removes all potential ambiguity about the employment status of the freelance contractor, eliminating any possibility of employment rights being claimed: holiday and sickness pay, redundancy and so forth. The termination clauses in these contracts typically allow the client to end the agreement with little or no notice.

The Professional Contractors Group (PCG) was formed in May 1999 to provide independent contractors and consultants with a representative voice in opposition to the original IR35 proposals. Since then, it has evolved from being a single-issue campaign group to being a fully fledged, not-for-profit professional body representing knowledge workers who choose to be self-employed.

PCG members work in a wide variety of sectors including oil and gas, engineering, information technology, finance, management consultancy, marketing, telecommunications, construction and pharmaceuticals.

For further information, see www.pcg.org.uk.

John Thomas had been working with PCG for two years when he was appointed Chief Executive Officer in January 2005. In a career spanning 30 years, 21 of which were at various divisions of ICL, John has undertaken a range of project management and programme director roles and projects, mostly in the IT sector. His activities have encompassed operational management, both in-house and outsourced, service-level management, the development of strategic alliances, board-level troubleshooting and sales and programme management.

e-mail: john.thomas@pcg.org.uk

Stretching performance

Ruth Spellman, Chief Executive of Investors in People UK, discusses how smaller companies can maximize the potential of their people in pursuit of organizational goals

There is little doubt that the small businesses of today can be the large companies of the future – if they invest in the development of the organization and the growth of the people who can take it forward. Yet some managers still maintain that there is no place for people development in this size of organization, that the effort outweighs the benefits, or that skills development is a 'nice to have' for companies with greater resources. But such views ignore the proven benefit that staff development delivers in terms of staff productivity and long-term business development.

The evidence of future benefits is compelling. Indeed, research shows that organizational changes made by companies with the Investors in People Standard, employing between 5 and 49 employees, are linked to increased profits of £303 per employee per year. So, where should employers start if they want to benefit from good people management practices?

One highly pressing issue – and one that is particularly pertinent to smaller businesses by definition – is that of the skills gap. Every small business is in the same situation, seeking to ensure that it can develop or attract the skills it needs tomorrow whilst gaining the most from the people on whose productivity it depends today. But it can be difficult to make time for long-term planning when day-to-day customer and supplier requirements demand immediate attention. In small businesses, without the resources or specialist expertise that larger companies can draw on, support from outside becomes even more important.

Another key issue is management skill. Research commissioned by Investors in People on management styles in the United Kingdom found that nearly a quarter of employees (24 per cent) feel that their line manager takes little or no account of their views or does not consult them when making decisions. Notably, managers working in organizations employing fewer than 250 staff were shown to be the worst culprits, with only 49 per cent of employees saying that their manager works with other staff when developing new plans or ideas, compared to 64 per cent in larger organizations (those with over 1,000 employees). In a small environment, lack of management experience can be felt keenly throughout the organization, affecting all aspects of its performance. Again, it's an area where specialist help can really improve the situation.

The Investors in People Standard is a tried and tested flexible framework that helps companies succeed and compete through improved people performance. To date, around 38,000 organizations have formally achieved the Standard. These organizations employ around a third of the UK workforce and range from companies employing anything from two people upwards, stretching across all sectors of the UK economy.

In essence, the Investors in People Standard provides a structure for organizations plotting the way ahead with a map to navigate them through change and ensure they bring their people with them. The Standard has always been valued as a tool that encourages organizations to continuously revise, refine and improve people development strategies in order to maximize the potential of their greatest asset – people – in support of organizational goals.

For those organizations that want to continually challenge themselves – to identify further areas for improvement even when they have achieved the Standard – Investors in People's Profile tool can help them progress. Profile, which was launched in 2002, contains four levels of good practice, of which achieving the Standard is only the first.

But to get started, there are some vital practical steps that smaller business managers can take to integrate workforce development into overall business planning:

- Take a step back and analyse your organizational goals in the context of the skills that your team will need to reach them. Analyse strengths and weaknesses, identify the gaps and put plans in place to address any areas of potential shortfall.
- Make sure development plans form a key part of each person's role. Stick to this commitment as your organization grows, so that all current employees and any candidate recruits can see that development is a key part of your offer to them. Training should also be viewed as an investment for the role that an individual will move on to do within an organization rather than just plugging a skills gap related to his or her current job.
- Identify and monitor employee potential within your organization. It's important to be able to think creatively about what an individual can offer in the longer term, given the right level of training and experience, and to plan how you can help him or her achieve that potential.
- Don't confuse ability with experience when seeking to fill vacancies. Talent is the crucial factor, and with the right support, employees can develop any specific skills needed for a particular role. Consider how your team members, whatever their role or prior experience, could play their part in providing the skills you are looking for. This is particularly relevant to people returning to the workforce after a break

or those who have decided to join an organization as a result of a career change. It's best to focus on transferable skills and to remain open-minded during the recruitment process.

■ Put robust succession planning processes into place to minimize the impact of any staff departures in future. Make sure you have the right systems in place from the start. This should involve training and mentoring to ensure that staff are ready to move up the organization should their managers decide to move on.

■ Don't be afraid to look outside the organization for new talent. If you can't develop the skills you need with your current employees, support your business plan by looking beyond the current organization.

We would encourage any small business that is looking for external expertise and advice in improving its people development to get in touch with Investors in People to find out how we can help them. If you're looking to stretch your organization and really put your people management practices to the test – and create the infrastructure you need to help your business grow – the Standard and Profile could be the tools you are looking for. It's all about unlocking the potential of your people, and seeing where they can take your business as a result.

For more information specifically tailored to small businesses, go to www.yourpeoplemanager.com. The site includes free practical advice to help employers manage their people more effectively, and covers topics ranging from recruitment to training and development. Further information is available at www.investorsinpeople.co.uk.

Recruiting in the new Europe

An army of talent is on its way from the new Europe, reports Rosemary Whibley at J S Hamilton Recruitment

Comparisons between Irish emigration to find employment in the 1970s and the flood of the brightest and the best currently leaving the Baltic States can undoubtedly be made. Similarities abound: depressed economies, well-educated young population, strong work ethic, family values, religion... the list goes on, and if these new EU members take advantage of the EU funding available to them, then surely their economies will grow at a rate to match the United Kingdom's Irish neighbour. Ireland has welcomed the wave of immigrants reaching its shores with a dedicated Polish TV channel and weekly supplements in Polish in an Irish daily newspaper. The influx of 400,000 has seen the population of Ireland swell by one-tenth since 2004.

It began as dawn broke on 1 May 2004 as the first in the new wave of immigrants began to arrive in the United Kingdom and Ireland. Coaches from all areas of the Czech Republic, Slovakia, Hungary and, especially, Poland arrived daily. (Table 5.6.1 gives population figures for the countries that joined the European Union at that time.) Shortly afterwards, the coaches were joined by economy air carriers, and the exodus seemed to have no end.

Just how many immigrants have come to Britain to work is difficult to ascertain with any great certainty. Some simply come for short-term contracts. Students looking for summer vacation positions swell the availability of casual labour across the country. The UK Home Office quotes the number of those registered with the Workers

Table 5.6.1 European enlargement, 2004: populations of countries joining

2004 entrants	Population (millions)	Percentage of total population
Cyprus (Greek)	0.64	0.9
Czech Republic	10.3	13.7
Estonia	1.5	2.0
Hungary	10.2	13.6
Latvia	2.5	3.3
Lithuania	3.7	4.9
Malta	0.39	0.5
Poland	38.6	51.3
Slovakia	5.4	7.2
Slovenia	2.0	2.7
Total	75.23	100

Registration Scheme as 345,000 (from 1 May 2004 to end 2005). However, many have not registered and work on a self-employed basis.

The UK Government greatly underestimated how many East Europeans would come to the United Kingdom, with a forecast that new workers would be attracted to the United Kingdom at a rate of 13,000 a year. In reality it is estimated that as many as 10,000 per month are leaving Poland. According to some sources, since 1 May 2004 about 2 million Poles have already headed westwards, the majority of them ending up in the United Kingdom and Ireland. It is also estimated that several hundred highly qualified specialists are leaving Poland daily.

Most analysts agree that the migrants from nations that joined the European Union in 2004 have boosted the UK economy by keeping interest rates down. The Ernst & Young Item Club, which uses the Treasury's model of the economy for its forecasts, said that the cost of borrowing would be 5 per cent instead of the current mark of 4.5 per cent without the arrival of more people willing to work.

The initial recruitment satisfied needs in parts of the economy experiencing labour shortages, and it has certainly helped to improve the quality of public services. The hospitality sector has greeted the new wave of labour with open arms. Hotels and restaurants found a source of talented, well-educated recruits with a strong work ethic and a vocation towards a career in the sector, seldom found in the local UK employment market.

Nursing homes have also benefited from trained staff coming from a culture where care and respect of the elderly is placed high on the agenda in the extended-family environment. The nursing home chains undertook campaigns across Poland to attract qualified nurses into this growing sector.

Polish nurses qualifying now are eligible to obtain full registration with regulatory bodies in both Ireland and the United Kingdom. English language skills have improved in this sector. Medical universities are now training nurses according to curricula complying with EU directives.

The largest contingent of labour has undoubtedly gone to the construction industry. Because of its current insatiable hunger, it has become nearly impossible to find any sizeable construction site in the United Kingdom or Ireland without its army of East European workers.

In the UK construction industry, output is expected to rise by almost 13 per cent over the next 3.5 years, boosted by a series of projects including construction for the 2012 Olympic Games. The Oxford Economic Forecasting group has elaborated a report on the Corporation of London order where it is clearly stated that there is going to be an increasing need for an estimated extra labour force of 50,000 qualified workers and engineers from Poland and other East and Central European countries to fill the deadlines for completion of new sports projects as well as the Olympic Village infrastructure in east London.

Further developments of the Thames Gateway corridor to the east of London, and port projects at Harwich, Shellhaven and Felixstowe are being undertaken, as are large-scale commercial developments and upgrades to transport developments at Victoria and King's Cross in central London. In addition, there is a £3.2 billion programme for social housing repair. These various projects lead sector analysts to forecast a need to recruit a further 348,000 workers by 2010. To meet this target we have to ensure that the buses and aircraft keep coming.

A move from mass labour to added value skills is in sight...

The above forecasts must lead to recognition that citizens from Bulgaria and Romania will need to be given the right to work in the United Kingdom if those countries join the European Union in 2007. The change that is occurring now is the realization by employers that you do not need to view applicants from the new EU members as a source of cheap labour. Rather, they form an extended pool of potential candidates with skills that not only match but often exceed those of counterparts in the local employment market.

The former Polish prime minister Kazimierz Marcinkiewicz said, 'We have a treasure that no other country in Europe has. This treasure is our young, well-educated, extremely ambitious and hard-working people.' Polish society is the youngest in Europe: 50 per cent of Poles are under 35 years old and more than 2 million are enrolled in university studies.

Engineering is a sector where East European candidates are very highly educated, not just to BSc level but extending their studies to MSc. In Poland the technical universities are currently in their boom years. Young secondary school graduates are more likely to choose various engineering courses at one of the 20 schools across the country. This compares well to what occurs in the United Kingdom, where only a fraction of those entering further education to study engineering actually finish the course. Every year there are several thousand fresh MSc and BSc holders eager to take up a challenge not only in the Polish but also in the EU labour market.

What were the applicant member states that negotiated entry in 2004 subject to national referenda?

First phase, 1 May 2004:

1) Cyprus   6) Lithuania
2) Czech Republic   7) Malta
3) Estonia   8) Poland
4) Hungary   9) Slovakia
5) Latvia   10) Slovenia

Second phase:

11) Romania
12) Bulgaria
13) Turkey
14) Croatia

Advantages and disadvantages of employing staff from the Baltic region

Advantages

- Well-educated, skilled workforce.
- Good training in their home country.
- Strong work ethic.
- Mobile workforce.
- Team players.
- Permanent or contract employment.
- Value for money.

Disadvantages

- Possible alienation of current workforce or subcontractors.
- Possible client prejudice against a foreign workforce.
- Language issues.
- Cultural differences.
- Possible longer induction.
- Support issues, eg providing accommodation.

Rosemary Whibley is Managing Director of J S Hamilton Recruitment Co. Ltd. Based in Westerham, Kent, in the United Kingdom, and Gdynia and Warsaw in Poland, J S Hamilton Recruitment has successfully placed in excess of 1,000 Polish candidates in the hospitality, healthcare and engineering sectors since 2004. The company is planning expansion in other areas of Poland, as well as Bulgaria, by the end of 2006.

6

Property and locations

SCOTLAND'S PREMIER CONFERENCE VENUE

- Over 100 venues
- Award winning architecture
- Full audio/visual equipment and specialist support
- First class catering and licensed facilities
- Delegate accommodation to suit all budgets

For full information visit the Conference & Visitor Services Office website at:

www.cvso.co.uk

Tel: +44 (0) 141 330 2263 / 3123
Fax: +44 (0) 141 330 2036   Email: sales@cvso.co.uk

UNIVERSITY
of
GLASGOW

Property challenges facing growing companies

Accommodating growth can give rise to numerous difficulties, warns Bradley Baker, head of Global Tenant Solutions at Knight Frank Newmark

The majority of occupiers understandably find it extremely difficult to predict their office requirements in terms of changes to headcount and amounts of space beyond two years, according to the recent British Council for Offices' Office Occupier's Survey conducted by MORI in association with Knight Frank Newmark, the Global Tenant Solutions division of Knight Frank LLP.

With many occupiers now entering a period of increased confidence and growth, the issue of expansion and how best to facilitate it is becoming increasingly important. Flexibility is key, and ideally occupiers should try to negotiate break clauses in their leases. However, as the market improves, the ability to negotiate these break clauses on shorter lease terms becomes increasingly difficult and places greater weight on the importance of these break clauses.

Landlords are often more flexible than perhaps they are given credit for and it is often a case of identifying the key drivers from the landlord's perspective in order to optimize the position from the occupier's point of view.

Escalating rents

With increased demand for offices, rental levels continue to rise, with some hot spots being particularly noticeable. Knight Frank tracks prime grade A rents across the City market and has seen headline levels increase by 10–20% during the course of 2006 from £46.50 per square foot at the end of 2005 which is a trend that is expected to continue in the short to medium term. This clearly illustrates the issues facing occupiers in central London. To compound the difficulty, at the same time as increasing rents, the net worth of incentive packages (i.e. rent-free periods being offered by landlords) is decreasing, thereby further pushing up the net effective rental levels.

As Figure 6.1.1 illustrates, there is a very strong correlation between prime City rents and the FTSE 100 index, which gives a clear indication as to future rental movements. One of the serious issues facing occupiers in a rising market is the concept of 'upward only' rent reviews every five years of the lease. If the review coincides with a spike in the rental market, the occupier can be left with a relatively high level of rent for the following five years regardless of market conditions during that five-year period. Therefore, it is important to focus on alternatives when negotiating transactions. An example would be to offer landlords fixed percentage increases for certain parts of the or lease throughout the term of the lease. This provides the occupier with the advantage of knowing the precise rental outgoing and is also attractive to landlords from an investment perspective.

Knight Frank Newmark undertakes forecasting for major markets throughout the world to assist occupiers in their decision-making process. Table 6.1.1 provides details of global office asking rents. This extract gives details of the top 20 cities (by cost).

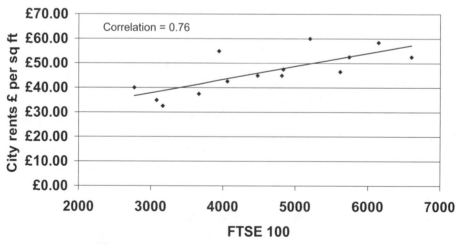

Source: Knight Frank/FTSE

Figure 6.1.1   City rents versus FTSE 100

You occupy.
Our minds©

With seven different buildings in the Farringdon Road area, plus a mix of tenures, Guardian Newspapers Limited saw a clear need for rationalisation. To achieve their challenging goals they decided to call in the experts, the Knight Frank Occupier Solutions Team.

Knight Frank Occupier Solutions is a dedicated group integrating the complete range of strategic consultancy, agency and professional skills for a uniquely focussed approach.

Our strategic review for GNL identified a number of options, among them a 'campus' approach or total relocation to a single facility.

Relocation was the preferred move. A single facility of 140,000 sq ft was acquired as a pre-let at Kings Cross. This was so successful it became Property Week and IAS/OAS's Transaction of the Year (Central London) 2005.

For the remaining portfolio, including two freeholds, GNL has continued to work closely with Knight Frank.

We think it's accurate to report that for GNL, calling in Knight Frank has been very good news indeed.

For all your occupier needs, contact: Bradley Baker 020 7861 1256.

You occupy. Our minds©

Knight Frank Newmark

Table 6.1.1 Global office asking rents

Market	Region	Rent (sq m/yr)	US $/sq m	GDP (£)/sq m	Rent (sq ft/yr)	US $/ sq ft	GDP (£)/sq ft
London, UK (West End)	Europe	1,259	1,500	861.12	116.96	139.38	80.00
Hong Kong	Asia Pacific	964	1,149	655.52	89.56	106.72	60.90
Tokyo, Japan	Asia Pacific	798	723	542.64	74.14	67.20	50.41
London, UK (City)	Europe	710	846	482.80	65.96	78.60	45.00
Paris, France	Europe	650	775	442.00	60.39	71.96	41.06
Moscow, Russia	Europe	600	715	408.00	55.74	66.42	37.90
Dublin, Ireland	Europe	540	643	367.20	50.17	59.78	34.11
Milan, Italy	Europe	475	566	323.00	44.13	52.58	30.01
New York, USA	North America	461	554	313.48	42.83	51.47	29.12
Manchester, UK	Europe	443	528	301.24	41.16	49.04	27.99
Edinburgh, UK	Europe	435	518	295.80	40.41	48.16	27.48
Birmingham, UK	Europe	435	518	295.80	40.41	48.16	27.48
Frankfurt, Germany	Europe	402	479	273.36	37.35	44.50	25.40
Mumbai, India	Asia Pacific	391	466	265.88	36.32	43.28	24.70
Bristol, UK	Europe	388	462	263.84	36.05	42.95	24.51
Glasgow, UK	Europe	364	434	247.52	33.82	40.30	23.00
Leeds, UK	Europe	364	434	247.52	33.82	40.30	23.00
Amsterdam, Netherlands	Europe	350	417	238.00	32.52	38.75	22.11
Munich, Germany	Europe	345	411	234.60	32.05	38.19	21.79
Shanghai, China	Asia Pacific	336	400	228.48	31.22	37.20	21.23

Source: Knight Frank, January 2006

'Village concept' versus one central building

Occupiers are frequently tempted to embark upon the 'village concept'. This involves an occupier that is expanding its business, growing out of one building and, as a result, acquiring another as close as possible. When the second building reaches capacity, it acquires another building that is also in close proximity, and this expansion continues. Whilst this approach can reduce disruption in the short term, it can also lead to significant issues in the long term. From an exit strategy point of view, it is important to avoid taking a series of leases that could prove problematic in later years. Therefore, common break clauses/lease expiries are essential in order to reduce costs when the time comes to eventually co-locate from a series of buildings. In the interim period the village concept can lead to significant escalation of costs due to duplication of resources, eg security, reception, etc, so the advantages and disadvantages need careful consideration.

A micro local view versus a regional macro-strategic view

As companies grow and acquire offices in different cities, the question of control and coordination arises. The larger the company becomes, the more it can benefit from a regional strategic view of the various offices contained within the portfolio. Therefore, it is important for occupiers to have the benefit of local market expertise interwoven with a more strategic, holistic approach. This ensures that a proper coordinated structure can be incorporated within an occupier's portfolio as it expands.

Information is key

Research into the various markets is absolutely essential. Occupiers need to have a knowledge as to the strength of the occupational market within which they are active. Knight Frank's Global Real Estate Markets annual review and forecast ranks major cities against 22 separate economic, demographic and property variables to determine the strength of the office market for 2006. The following are the strength rankings for the top 17 cities within Europe, as given by the Knight Frank review:

1. Dublin
2. Madrid
3. Moscow
4. London
5. Warsaw
6. Birmingham
7. Prague
8. Manchester
9. Bristol
10. Paris
11. Lisbon
12. Munich
13. Milan
14. Frankfurt
15. Brussels
16. Berlin
17. Amsterdam

Outsourcing/offshoring

In the same MORI poll as referred to above, one in six office occupiers could foresee circumstances in which their company would consider moving its headquarters or major operations outside the United Kingdom. Among office occupiers with global or European, Middle East and Asia (EMEA) space strategies, over a quarter could foresee their company moving its major operations or headquarters outside the United Kingdom. Of significance, among the telecoms/hi-tech companies surveyed, this figure rises to 50 per cent.

The main driver behind such a move is cost. Over a third of occupiers interviewed agreed that their organization will see greater outsourcing abroad or offshoring in the future (Figure 6.1.2). This increases to two-thirds among those occupiers with a current global EMEA office strategy, and even higher (70 per cent) among telecoms/hi-tech companies.

Q To what extent do you agree or disagree that in future your organization will see an increase in outsourcing abroad/off-shoring?

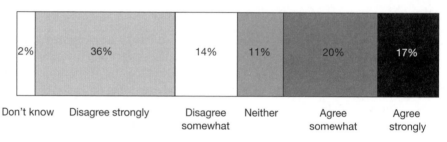

| 2% | 36% | 14% | 11% | 20% | 17% |

Don't know Disagree strongly Disagree somewhat Neither Agree somewhat Agree strongly

Figure 6.1.2 Proportion of companies considering outsourcing or off-shoring. Base: All respondents (100)

Summary

Growing companies face a number of challenges as they develop and expand – not only as regards predictions of their growth rate but how they accommodate their businesses in conjunction with such growth. To find the best solution, occupiers should ensure that they build in maximum flexibility to facilitate both expansion and concentration as far as possible.

Bradley Baker has spent the majority of his career in the City of London property market, advising both landlords and occupiers with a significant emphasis upon the latter. Bradley is now the Head of the Global Occupier team with responsibility for occupier transactions throughout the UK and Europe.

He has advised major occupiers on a number of significant transactions, including The *Guardian* on the acquisition of their new headquarters building in Kings Cross (150,000 sq ft), Swiss Re in the acquisition of their new tower building at 30 St Mary's Axe (540,000 sq ft) and Merrill Lynch of their new European Head Quarters Building at Newgate Street (560,000 sq ft). NB. The *Guardian* deal was awarded the Property Week/ O.A.S 'Transaction Of The Year' Award for 2005. Further details e-mail: bradley.baker@knightfrank.com or see the website www.knightfrank.com.

Relocation, relocation, relocation

With a raft of pros and cons to consider, not to mention significant associated costs, relocation is not something any business should enter into lightly. Graham Harrison, Head of Sector Development at the South West RDA, however, argues that, if properly considered, it can deliver significant results

Taking the plunge

Business is becoming increasingly mobile as improved communications and new technologies give companies greater choice as to where to base their operation. Thus, more and more companies are considering relocation. Ultimately, businesses will base their decision to locate and relocate to those areas that offer greatest potential for business growth and deliver the best potential route to markets.

One of the most common reasons for relocation is to be near to allied industries. The benefits are twofold. The first is that it brings companies closer to their respective markets. The aerospace industry is a classic example, attracting clusters of suppliers, however small, around a large manufacturer to be closer to market. The second reason is to be closer to research and to innovation. Forward-thinking and entrepreneurial businesses will want to exploit the latest technologies and innovations delivered through research with partner companies and academic institutions.

An available workforce is another influencing factor. Companies will look to locate to areas with a strong skills base, especially if they are setting up. If they are

"The South West has an independent spirit and fire in the belly. Quite frankly, if I were investing anywhere in the world today, it would be here."

TIM SMIT – CREATOR & CHIEF EXECUTIVE – EDEN PROJECT

SOUTH WEST ENGLAND BUSINESSES HAVE THE HIGHEST ONE-YEAR SURVIVAL RATES IN THE UK*
* Source: Small Business Service, DTI 2004

South West

SOUTHWESTENGLAND.CO.UK
WHERE BUSINESS COMES NATURALLY

relocating, finding an area with a strong skills match will also be crucial. Although less tangible, quality of life increasingly influences the location and relocation of businesses as work–life balance climbs the corporate agenda.

A record of established success of companies in the same or a similar sector within a particular location will also be important. For example, the South West has proved attractive to the ICT sector, as the decisions by Motorola and Intel to move to the region and their subsequent success have strengthened the region's appeal to other companies in the sector. Whether your company is a large multinational or an SME, the proof of the pudding is in the eating, and clear examples of success carry huge weight in the relocation decision-making process.

Careful consideration

The relocation process takes on average three to five years, from deciding to relocate to moving operation. It is consequently crucial to start thinking early and make decisions as part of a structured business plan. Companies should be considering which areas they want to move into as a business and where they see greatest opportunity for development, and then to decide how and whether relocation will support growth into those markets.

When deciding to relocate, companies should assess what types of business are already located within the area or region, whether business clusters offer a good match and whether suitable sites are available and at what cost. In addition to investigating opportunities for potential financial support for relocation it is also worth finding out whether venture capitalists are based in the area and, if so, whether your business might appeal to them. Relocation is no cheap option, and cost may in many cases prove prohibitive, so it is crucial to explore all opportunities for funding.

Current trends

Companies are becoming far more fluid as technology and changing business practices open up a growing choice of locations. Service industries have always been relatively footloose but in the past five years business mobility has increased in general. In the manufacturing industry in particular there has been a growing move away from large plants as technology has become smaller, becoming much more mobile in the process.

Meanwhile, the knowledge economy is taking on growing significance, as, following the Lambert Review of Business–University Collaboration, academic institutions and business forge closer links. The United Kingdom's science base ranks second only to that of the United States on the majority of indicators, and arguably outranks it on a per capita basis. The historical challenges of channelling research into commercial enterprise are increasingly surmountable, so that in 2004 alone, university spin-outs listed on the Alternative Investment Market were valued at £604 million.

This has had a significant impact on business location, leading to the formation of a growing number of clusters built around partnership between business and universities in addition to research partnerships between companies. Clusters have had a major

BUCKINGHAMSHIRE: THE FIVE STAR COUNTY
The Place of Choice

Buckinghamshire, the Five Star County – the Place of Choice – is full of opportunity. A slender county, 40 miles long, sweeping from the Thames to the west of London and halfway to Birmingham in the north. It is a mixture of woodlands, parklands and agricultural valleys, is prosperous and successful with an exciting mix of cultures, heritage and diverse communities.

The picturesque and historic market towns of Buckingham, Princes Risborough, Old Amersham and Beaconsfield add to its character and contrast with Aylesbury, the administrative centre of the County and High Wycombe both main centres of economic activity. It is home to a population of nearly half a million and is set to grow still further, Aylesbury Vale and Milton Keynes have been identified in the Sustainable Communities Plan as areas of growth. All these features combine to create a strong economic, social and environmental foundation on which to build a successful future.

Buckinghamshire's economy is presently worth around £5.6b and is one of the top ten business locations in Europe. It is home to many international companies such as GE Healthcare, Citrix, Pinewood and Shepperton Studios, Johnson and Johnson, McCormick, Martin Baker Aircraft, Ercol and Goodrich Power Systems, all having chosen to locate in the County because of its natural environment, education, quality housing, diverse workforce and access to motorways, airports, railways and low unemployment.

Situated in the centre of the Oxford to Cambridge (O2C) Arc a region of high technology growth, Buckinghamshire is set to take the advantages the growth will bring to its economy and attract the high value-added companies. Silverstone, the home of British motor sport, Stoke Mandeville Hospital with its world renowned Spinal Injuries Unit and Pinewood, the world famous centre for film-making are all world leaders in their own field.

The County is extremely proud of its high educational attainment through its grammar and upper schools and Buckinghamshire can boast the only private university in the country, the University of Buckingham, which majors on entrepreneurship and providing business solutions for growing companies.

There never has been a better time to invest in Buckinghamshire – make it your 'Place of Choice'.

For further information please contact:
Development Services
Room 813
Buckinghamshire County Council
County Hall
Walton Street, Aylesbury
Bucks HP20 1UY

Tel: 01296 382157
Fax: 01296-382060
Email: env-edt@buckscc.gov.uk
Website: www.buckscc.gov.uk

Buckinghamshire
the five star county

impact across a number of sectors, with cutting-edge research giving entrepreneurial firms an edge in an increasingly global economy.

The aerospace cluster

Of the 12 largest aerospace companies (by employees) in the United Kingdom, 9 have major facilities in the South West. The aerospace sector is founded not only on having global players at the cutting edge of commercial and military production but also on its enormous strength in research and development.

The University of Bristol has an outstanding reputation in aerospace research, linking closely with industrial partners developing research around fluid flow and aerodynamics, structures and materials, dynamics and control, and aero-mechanics. A strong group is also working on composite structures from novel fibres, and modelling and analytical techniques.

Into the future, the development of the Bristol Laboratories for Dynamic Engineering (BLADE) will provide world-class facilities to investigate how structures behave in unpredictable conditions. The new Composite Structures Development Centre, based at Airbus, is also expected to attract more than £100 million worth of R&D projects in the next five years alone.

Similar clusters have emerged in a number of other sectors across the South West, including marine science and technology in Plymouth and Devon and ICT clusters in Bristol and Bath, which have tapped into the international reputation of research at the cities universities.

More and more companies are also putting increased emphasis on the calibre of the business and living environment when making their choice of location. Senior decision makers, like employees, want to work and live in areas that can offer them not only an opportunity to grow their business but the best possible quality of life. A mild climate, ease of access to facilities, whether shopping centres, countryside or sandy beaches, is exerting a greater influence over business relocations than ever before.

The Met Office

In one of the United Kingdom's biggest corporate relocations in recent years, the Met Office moved from Bracknell into a purpose-designed new headquarters building and operations centre in Exeter, Devon. The move, as well as giving a new home to its 1,000 staff, has also enabled the Met Office to develop a massive new IT infrastructure, which will improve its services to businesses and government bodies throughout the United Kingdom and overseas.

The decision to move was based on the growing cost of working in multiple locations close to London and the associated problems of operational inefficiencies, retaining staff and dealing with congestion. The move to Exeter has put all the key components of the organization into a single, state-of-the-art new working environment.

A helping hand

A raft of support is available to help those companies prepared to take the plunge, make the right decision and avoid potential pitfalls. Regional Development Agencies across the country can help with advice about opportunities. There is support within regions through other partners, including the Business Link network and local authorities, which can help companies find the right location to meet their business needs.

The process requires thought and careful consideration but the rewards of moving closer to allied industries, to clusters and research or to a high-calibre working and living environment can be substantial, whether in terms of growing market share or of encouraging employee retention and recruitment. Relocation will not be right for all businesses, but for those for which it is, the benefits can be significant.

For further information on relocation, visit www.englandsrdas.com or www.businesslink.gov.uk.

Office hot spots

Regional office markets are emerging as a force in their own rights, says Catherine Penman, Head of Commercial Research at Knight Frank

Following a relatively low period of economic growth recorded in 2005, the prospects for the UK office market are far more positive in 2006 and beyond. The most recent UK report on services growth suggests that the sector has continued to accelerate during 2006 to date, which is an encouraging signal, particularly in the light of the poor growth witnessed from both the distribution and the retail sectors during the same time period.

Encouragingly, at the close of Q2 this year the service sector was showing annual growth of 30 per cent and thus continuing to demonstrate its importance as a driving force within the United Kingdom economy. Although the main business activity index has moderated slightly in recent months, the new business balance has continued to rise. Overall service activity in the United Kingdom remains encouraging and most indicators demonstrate that the sector remains in rude health.

The improvement within the service sector in the United Kingdom is becoming increasingly apparent in the performance of the office sector. Rental growth has improved consistently during 2006 to date to stand at 3.5 per cent over the 12 months to March 2006, which has further fuelled investor activity. Demand for investment product has not relented in 2006, as investment performance continues to improve. Office total returns over the year to August totalled 24.1 per cent, which was the strongest performance of the main property sectors and its highest level in over 10 years.

Office market prospects

The relatively subdued economic activity recorded in 2005, in contrast to the more positive figures recorded to date in 2006, inevitably impacted upon the regional office markets, with annual 2005 take-up levels remaining at similar levels to those recorded in 2004 in the larger regional cities, including Manchester, Leeds and Birmingham.

The smaller cities of Newcastle, Sheffield and Aberdeen witnessed notable uplifts in letting activity compared to 2004 and in line with their respective long-term averages, primarily due to a shortage of good-quality stock and active demand levels increasing in the latter part of 2005. This trend is expected to continue in 2006 across all the regional office centres, as occupiers become more positive about expansion plans for the medium term in line with an improving domestic economy and increasing realization of the potential that the regional markets have to offer.

In line with letting activity, rental levels rose most sharply in the smaller regional cities of Sheffield, Liverpool and Aberdeen. This was due in part to a lack of good-quality accommodation, which is becoming an increasingly common feature across many of the regional cities, coupled with a relatively low rental base. Rental growth is projected to continue within all the regional office centres over the next year, as detailed in Table 6.3.1, owing to the forecast of improved economic confidence and demand set to increase.

Indeed, Manchester and Birmingham have seen a considerable interest in potential occupiers in the first half of 2006, and prime rental levels are anticipated to reach £30.00 per square foot, a level comparable to that for a number of office markets in the South East.

Table 6.3.1 Prime office rental levels in UK cities, 2005 and 2006

City	Prime office rents per sq ft, Mid 2005	Prime office rents per sq ft, Mid 2006
Aberdeen	£20.00	£21.00
Edinburgh	£27.50	£28.00
Glasgow	£23.00	£25.00
Cardiff	£18.50	£20.00
Newcastle	£20.00	£22.00
Birmingham	£27.50	£30.00
Manchester	£28.00	£30.00
Sheffield	£18.00	£20.00
Leeds	£23.00	£25.00
Liverpool	£18.00	£20.00
Bristol	£24.50	£25.00
London	£80.00	£90.00
M25 (South East)	£31.00	£32.00

Cherwell M-40 Partnership –
Growing Business, Reaping Benefits

Travel from London on the M40, and in under an hour you'll be in Cherwell, north Oxfordshire. Straddling the Marylebone to New Street main line, Cherwell is the gateway between the South East and the Midlands. Many businesses have come to Cherwell to take advantage of this access to markets, including Kraft Foods, Prodrive, Brita Water Filters and Ascari. Alcoa, Vodafone, Hella, Faurecia…many businesses have recognised the advantages offered by the district.

Commercial property is available to suit a range of purposes and tastes – from period urban space to innovative modern business parks. Average rental rates are substantially lower than in many areas in the South-East.

Four top-rated business schools are nearby; Said and Brookes at Oxford, Coventry and Warwick to the north. Begbroke Science Park near Kidlington harnesses science and technology for the local economy. Four Innovation Centres are located across the district proving incubator space for high-tech start-ups. One centre includes a state-of-the-art biomedical diagnostic laboratory, and Cherwell now has more innovation centres than any district in the south-east.

Cherwell combines unspoilt countryside with bustling urban centres, providing a high standard of living. A network of honey-stoned villages offer the very best country living. Fancy a bit more bustle? Banbury has a lively town centre, with some of the best shopping in Oxfordshire, while Bicester Village's designer outlets attract shoppers from far and wide. House prices are strong, but the most affordable in Oxfordshire, making relocation appealing for key staff.

Perhaps the greatest asset in Cherwell is the Cherwell-M40 Investment Partnership, or CHIP. A collaborative effort between the District Council, commercial property providers, and business support bodies, CHIP provides information and support to relocating businesses, a collaboration that has proved very successful since starting in 1991. Cherwell certainly has to rank highly on any list of areas considered by a company looking to be in the south-east of England.

Contact

Find out more on how Cherwell can grow your business. Call Rob McKay, Economic Development Officer, on **01295 221860**, email **chip@cherwell-dc.gov.uk** or visit us at **www.cherwell-m40.co.uk**

Watch your business thrive.

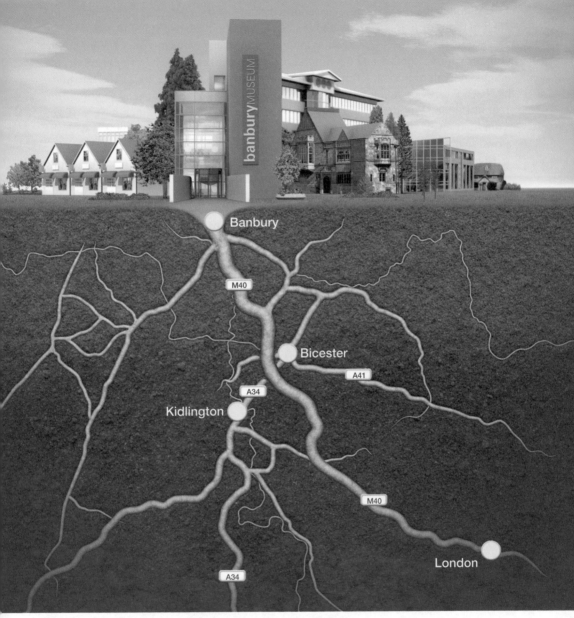

With London just over an hour away, Cherwell, North Oxfordshire is the perfect place to flourish. Quality of life, a thriving local economy, affordability and fantastic infrastructure – Cherwell has it all. So if you're looking to put down new roots, let us show you what's on offer.

Call Karen Matthews at the Cherwell-M40 Investment Partnership on +44 (0)1295 221863 or visit our website at www.cherwell-m40.co.uk

Although the majority of regional office centres witnessed an arguably unexciting 2005 in terms of letting activity and rental growth, their relative stability, aided by the absence of specific sectors targeting individual markets, compares very favourably to both the central London and the South East office markets, which have experienced a notable downturn in both letting activity and rental growth since 2001. The downturn has been partly due to a heavy reliance upon the Banking and Financial sector within central London and the IT sector within the South East, both of which have suffered from high levels of volatility and job losses over the past five years coupled with the slowdown recorded within the domestic economy.

During this period of decline, both markets have successfully widened the range of occupiers considering locating into their respective markets and consequently diversified their occupier profile, as illustrated in the pie chart shown in Figure 6.3.1, which details all the sectors actively requiring accommodation within the South East office market. The increasingly positive economic forecasts will also assist in the recovery of these markets.

Despite the projected recovery of the central London and South East office markets, over the past five years the regional centres have matured and are now firmly established as key office markets in their own right. In addition, the more expensive rental costs of the markets, where rents range from £60 to £85 per square foot in central London and £30 to £35 per square foot in the South East, have led a number of occupiers to consider relocating to the regional markets, which not only enjoy significantly lower rental levels but also in many cases benefit from an appropriately skilled labour supply with lower salary expectations, and a better quality of life for their staff, both of which are fast becoming the key considerations in any company's plans to move or expand its premises.

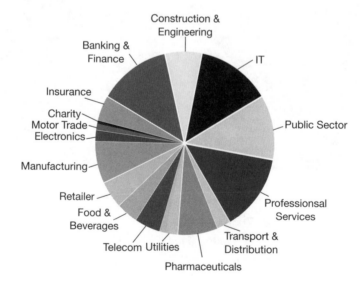

Figure 6.3.1 Office demand in the South East by sector, May 2006

Table 6.3.2 Prime office yields in UK cities, 2005 and 2006

City	Prime office yields, mid-2005	Prime office yields, mid-2006
Aberdeen	7.00%	6.00%
Edinburgh	5.75%	5.50%
Glasgow	6.00%	5.50%
Cardiff	6.25%	5.75%
Newcastle	6.25%	6.00%
Birmingham	6.00%	5.25%
Manchester	5.75%	5.75%
Sheffield	6.75%	5.75%
Leeds	6.25%	5.50%
Liverpool	6.50%	6.00%
Bristol	6.25%	5.50%
London	4.25%	4.00%
M25 (South East)	5.20%	4.75%

Investment market

In 2006 the weight of money targeting property has continued unabated, with all regional markets witnessing a hardening of yields over the past 12 months. This trend is forecast to continue over the next year.

Aberdeen and Sheffield saw the sharpest movement in yields in 2005, from 7.00 per cent to 6.00 per cent and from 6.75 per cent to 5.75 per cent respectively. Those cities continue to offer further potential yield reductions, with the average prime office yield in the larger regional markets standing at 5.50 per cent, which is expected to harden by 50 basis points to 5.00 per cent by 2006 year-end.

In summary, the outlook for the UK regional office markets is very positive. They are now firmly established as sustainable office centres in their own right and have had significant success in attracting a number of high-profile occupiers in recent years. For example, Manchester has successfully attracted Bank of New York and the Royal Bank of Scotland as a result of the substantial cost savings compared with other cities, coupled with the benefit of a plentiful and relatively loyal labour supply.

With encouraging economic prospects projected over the medium term, the future of the UK regional office markets is certainly rosy.

Knight Frank Research monitors office market activity in all the United Kingdom's principal centres and also tracks the performance of the majority of key global markets with a dedicated team focused on analysing the United Kingdom's office markets. The department annually produces over 40 published research titles, and its output enjoys an excellent reputation throughout the United Kingdom and the rest of the world.

Knight Frank's extensive market knowledge, via its network of 11 commercial UK regional offices and extensive in-house research databases, enables full and detailed analysis of the UK office market. ROMP (regional office market presentation) is the interactive tool created by Knight Frank that makes possible a detailed market comparison of all the key regional UK cities. Variables detailed include take-up, availability, vacancy rates, rental levels and prime yields. The website is updated quarterly to reflect the latest trends and issues affecting the regional office markets. Forecasts for rental levels for each of the cities are also contained within the website.

For more information, visit www.knightfrank.com/ROMP.

Property conversions

What do warehouses, wharves and watchtowers have in common, asks
Graham Elliott at haysmacintyre accountants

Your lateral thinking challenge is to tell me what the three Ws, warehouses, wharves
and watchtowers, have in common. Your clue is that watchtowers are a bit of a red
herring. They could be included, but there will be so few of them that they might as
well be ignored.

To put you out of your misery, the common factor is that all of them could
conceivably attract a special VAT regime. But that only applies when they are
transformed into something rather different – because warehouses, wharf buildings
and indeed watchtowers (or for that matter church towers) are sometimes converted
from their original function into residential accommodation. Society's need for these
types of building is diminishing over time, but the population is ever-increasing and
the need for housing follows suit. To encourage the recycling of existing buildings and
to keep the United Kingdom's built environment familiar and varied, the Government
has introduced a lower rate of VAT for the services provided in converting these
properties. This means that the construction services in question can be charged at a 5
per cent rate of VAT, rather than 17.5 per cent, which is less than a third of the usual
VAT cost. Whereas VAT applies to an extension of an existing house at 17.5 per cent,
the above-mentioned conversion works would only be charged at 5 per cent.

So it's good news for small businesses involved in renovating or investing in such
properties or for businesspeople looking to buy unusual (second) homes. The rule
that governs this says that the 5 per cent charge relates to works that create a different
number of 'single-household dwellings'. Thus, this includes alterations to what are
currently residential buildings as long as those alterations have the effect of creating
either an increase in the number of single-household dwellings, or (paradoxically) a

HILLALDAM COBURN LTD

Hillaldam Coburn Ltd has a heritage in manufacturing and development dating back almost one hundred years. From modest beginnings in South London, manufacturing trolley wheels, the company has grown to become a major supplier to the construction and building industries worldwide. Hillaldam Coburn consists of two divisions working from several UK sites. Coburn Sliding Systems is a leading supplier of sliding door gear and associated products.

Internationally, the company is renowned for its broad, high quality range of industrial and domestic sliding door gear. The door gear range is suited to the smallest of glass door cabinets to industrial steel and timber doors of 4000kg. Demand has seen the applications expand to include various sliding/folding systems for domestic as well as commercial and retail environments.

Evolution of the company's technical skill has lead it to offer additional products to the traditional door gear. A full range of bespoke movable walls is available giving a choice of finishes and acoustic rating for solving almost any room division problem. The latest edition to the impressive product sector is the Omega. Omega is a frameless glass movable wall, offering cutting edge technology by way of acoustic rating. Variations on the Omega theme give a totally weather proof option for external applications.

Technological and regulatory developments have also brought the company to offer a comprehensive range of automatic operators. These operators compliment the company's door gear technology perfectly, giving appropriate solutions to DDA automation requirements for both swing and sliding door scenario.

The business prides itself on its full technical advisory service as well as ex-stock product availability in most cases. Products are usually available 'off the shelf' from leading Builders Merchants and Architectural Ironmongers.

Trim Acoustic,s the second division of Hillaldam Coburn Ltd, similarly leads its field, but in the supply of sound reduction products for both home and commercial applications. Qualified Trim staff offer independent, impartial product advice for all domestic and industrial situations. Recommended solutions can be achieved from a broad range of leading brand products held in stock. Satisfaction of appropriate building regulations can be confirmed by the qualified sound testing unit based within the division.

Hillaldam Coburn Ltd is part of JBS Industries Ltd. This privately owned group of companies has a strong cross industry portfolio and includes Consort Ltd, Nico Manufacturing Ltd and Solair Ltd, established suppliers in their respective marketplaces.

EXPLORE SPACE

www.coburn.co.uk

Commercial
Retail
Hospitality & Leisure
Education
Residential & Social Housing
Healthcare

es@hillaldam.co.uk
20 8336 1515

Hillaldam Coburn
solutions in sound & space

decrease. But it also accordingly includes conversion of a non-residential building into one or more dwellings.

The lower rate applies only to services rendered, so it would not apply if a DIY converter purchased materials. These would be charged at 17.5 per cent. However, if he or she hires a VAT-registered contractor to incorporate those materials into the converted property, then all the services (including the materials value) are charged only at 5 per cent. These 'qualifying services' include work to the fabric of the premises, and carrying out works in the immediate site of the premises as long as these are in connection with the means of providing water, power, heat, waste disposal, drainage, security, and access in connection with the premises. It does not include certain items that are not 'building materials', and these usually consist of white goods, carpets and similar supplies. To this extent, the same restrictions as would apply to any housebuilder apply to the converter.

There are also special provisions for providing garages. As long as a garage is built at the same time as the conversion is being made, then the 5 per cent rate applies to the construction of the garage, and this even extends to converting a non-residential building into that garage.

The above applies irrespective of whether the building is listed (protected). But a further benefit can be gained where it is. In those circumstances, any of the works involved in the conversion which are also approved alterations can be zero-rated rather than charged at 5 per cent. This means that there can be a combination of charges at 5 per cent (the changes that did not need approval, or ongoing repair that is carried out at the same time as conversion) and 0 per cent.

Claiming the VAT

These reductions in the level of VAT chargeable on such works are a benefit in themselves, but the benefit can be enhanced significantly in any circumstances where it may be possible to sell or grant a lease in the property in a way that qualifies for the fullest possible relief. In this scenario, the person owning and carrying out the alterations will be a VAT-registered business, and it will intend, upon completion of the conversion, to sell the building, or grant a major interest (being a lease capable of exceeding 21 years). In that situation the business is deemed to have made a zero-rated supply for VAT purposes, because it is making a supply of (theoretically) new residential accommodation, just as it would have done if it were building and selling a new house. This allows the VAT that is incurred (whether at 17.5 per cent or 5 per cent) to be reclaimed in its VAT return. However, only VAT correctly charged at 17.5 per cent can be fully reclaimed, and it is therefore important for the developer to insist upon the 5 per cent rate of VAT being charged to him or her by contractors where that is appropriate.

The same rule applies for listed buildings that are also conversions, and, in exceptional circumstances, listed buildings that have been residential prior to alteration will also be zero-rated, but only if the transformation is very considerable in that particular instance.

DIY

A similar rule applies to so-called do-it-yourself housebuilders who buy a non-residential building and have it converted into a residential building, usually for their own occupation or that of their family. There are special rules that allow them also to reclaim the VAT that they have been charged by the contractors and other suppliers. Again they will need to insist upon the contractors applying the appropriate reduced rates where applicable, since only the reduced amount of VAT is ever refundable by HM Revenue & Customs. In the case of the DIY converter there are strict time limits and evidential requirements that must be adhered to. The DIY converter needs to obtain specific advice on these areas.

There are also some potentially confusing halfway houses. An old army barracks can be converted into single-household dwellings with the benefit of the 5 per cent rate on conversion works, but they will not be subject to the zero-rated supply of the grant of the interest by the developer, since they are fundamentally residential to start with.

So, a good deal of the United Kingdom's characterful built environment can be maintained on a VAT-efficient basis by being converted into residential use, and the prospective developer should always consider and take advice on these points as part of his or her initial feasibility study for such developments.

Graham leads the haysmacintyre indirect taxes unit, and specialises in Value Added Tax. Whilst covering all aspects of VAT, his main interests are in Real Estate and not for profit organizations

Graham leads the haysmacintyre indirect taxes unit, and specializes in VAT. Whilst covering all aspects of VAT, his main interests are real estate and not-for-profit organizations. Graham has worked in VAT since 1984, and became a professional adviser in Binder Hamlyn in 1988. He became a chartered tax adviser in 1995, and an MBA in 2000. He joined haysmacintyre in 1997, and was appointed a partner of the firm in 1998.

haysmacintyre, Chartered Accountants and tax advisers, comprises 23 partners and 130 staff based in Holborn, London. It provides high quality auditing and assurance, business and personal taxation, corporate finance, financial planning and other business support services. Around 40% of the firm's business is within the corporate sector – small and medium sized enterprises many of which are within the property, media and entertainment, sports, motor trade and manufacturing sectors, 25% is for charitable and not for profit organizations and the remainder is for professional practices and private individuals. haysmacintyre is a founding member of MSI, an international network of accountants and lawyers with over 200 firms in 90 countries.

haysmacintyre, Fairfax House, 15 Fulwood Place, London WC1V 6AY
Tel: 020 7969 5500; Fax: 020 7969 5600; E-mail: marketing@haysmacintyre.com;
www.haysmacintyre.com

Locate your *business* here...

The Isle of Man
Freedom to *flourish*

Isle of Man
Government
Reiltys Ellan Vannin

For further information:

[t] +44(0) 1624 687179

[e] development@gov.im

[w] www.gov.im/dti

With a first rate business environment, a world class telecommunications infrastructure, high bandwidth connections, a range of business support systems and government grants, the Isle of Man offers much more than low rates of tax.

Resident companies can benefit from being close to the UK and Europe, but at the same time have the huge advantage of being in an independent nation able to respond rapidly to the ever changing business environment.

When all these benefits are combined with an enviable quality of life, the Isle of Man provides everything you need to give you, and your business, the freedom to flourish.

Dti **Department of Trade & Industry**

The Isle of Man, North Lincolnshire and the North Midlands

Isle of Man

Passengers landing at the Isle of Man's Ronaldsway airport often report a strange phenomenon: when they set foot on to Manx soil, a feeling of relief sweeps over them. The quiet pace, the gentle air, the sense of space, glimpses of sheep nibbling grass and the glittering sea no doubt help reduce stress levels. But it's more than that. There's a sense of security and friendliness that permeates every level of life on the island – from the personal to the professional and political.

The island's economy is dependent on a solid and diverse economic base, and the Manx Government does everything possible to create a business-friendly environment. This approach translates into impressive statistics: the island is one of the world's most successful small economies and has enjoyed unbroken economic growth for the past 21 years (since 2000, the economy has expanded two and a half times as fast as that of the United Kingdom and three times as fast as that of Europe as a whole). Unemployment has been 1.5 per cent or less for the past six years. GDP per capita has risen from, in 1982, just 55 per cent of that of the United Kingdom to the present level of 107 per cent, and 130 per cent that of Europe.

The growth of the economy has also outstripped that of nearest offshore rivals Jersey and Guernsey, and that is set to continue. Future growth is spurred on by a new branding initiative that works under the slogan that on the island there is the 'freedom to flourish'.

There is extra freedom in its unique relationship with Europe. The island sits outside the European Union but, under Protocol 3 to the United Kingdom's treaty of accession, may trade freely with the European Union – the best of both worlds, some might say.

Tax and grants

Zero-rate corporate tax was introduced in April 2006 – as was a new £100,000 cap on personal tax for wealthy individuals. There is already no capital gains or inheritance tax. It is a bundle of incentives aimed at attracting high-net-worth individuals who will bring with them their inspiration and entrepreneurial spirit.

A government Financial Assistance Scheme provides yet more incentive for new and existing businesses. In this discretionary scheme, grants of up to 50 per cent are available for training costs and up to 40 per cent for several other areas, from the construction cost of a new building to marketing and capital equipment purchase.

Challenges

One of the strengths of the Isle of Man is its ability to respond swiftly and innovatively to the challenges thrown up by international regulation and changes to the global economy. Faced with EU concerns that offshore jurisdictions were havens for money laundering and implementing unfair tax regimes, the Government responded with stricter regulation through its Financial Supervision Commission. It also introduced an innovative zero per cent tax rate for all companies that satisfied EU requirements, creating a level playing field on tax in an acceptable, if somewhat unanticipated, manner!

The island is now regarded as having some of the most rigorous anti-money laundering regulation in the world, which, together with in excess of £1 billion in reserves and a legal requirement for government to budget for a surplus, has rewarded the Manx economy with an AAA rating by Standard & Poor's and Moody's. The Isle of Man has been named Best International Finance Services Centre by *International Investment* magazine every year since 2000.

With worldwide financial contacts, particularly with the City of London, and great local expertise in legal and financial matters, the island is a great place to float a company from. There are significantly more floats per capita on the London stock market from the island than there are from the United Kingdom.

Diversity

Recognizing that reliance on one area leads to vulnerability, the Government has been attracting businesses from non-financial sectors in recent years.

The shipping industry has grown impressively since the Marine Administration was established in 1984, and the island is now home to some of the industry's most prestigious companies – such as Döhle and Dorchester Maritime. The government is now repeating this concept in aviation with the creation of a Manx aircraft register.

The island has also been a prime location for shooting films since the Isle of Man Film Commission was established in 1995. Films don't just create some interesting diversions for locals (in summer 2004, Castletown was in the grip of the Second World War for *Island at War*, and a teenage spy in the recently released *Stormbreaker* was pursued along Port Erin beach); they bring in serious money too. The Film Commission will pay for 25 per cent of production costs so long as the film company spends 50 per cent of the shooting time on the island, and spends not less than 20 per cent of the actual filming budget locally. The investment pays off: nine productions shot in 2005 alone injected £10.1m into the local economy.

With its cutting-edge telecommunications infrastructure and tempting range of government grants and loans, e-business is booming on the island. Manx Telecom was one of the first companies in the world to offer broadband ADSL services, and the island was the test bed for Europe's first third-generation (3G) wireless system.

The island also boasts one of Europe's largest 'self-healing' optical fibre rings and the world's most advanced digital telephone exchanges. Its high-bandwidth connections to the United Kingdom and Ireland give it enough capacity to handle the equivalent of the transatlantic internet traffic between Britain and the United States 10 times over.

Companies that have recently moved here include massive bandwidth users such as online poker websites and payment service providers. These have been followed by their support sectors, such as software developers.

The Government is also ensuring that there will be enough local employees to meet the needs of e-business employers, and 75 per cent of school leavers have IT qualifications. All classrooms are wired for internet access, which is a first for an educational area in the British Isles.

Traditional manufacturing also features strongly, contributing 11 per cent of GDP. Focused mainly around high-tech manufacturing, the island provides essential components to the oil, gas and aerospace industries through firms such as Swagelok, Smiths Aerospace, Manx Engineering and Ronaldsway Aircraft Company.

Quality of life

A MORI poll (published in 2002) commissioned by the Government found that 93 per cent of residents are satisfied with the island as a place to live – one of the highest scores ever recorded by MORI. Commuting is hassle-free, the schools are all of a high standard (King William's College offers the International Baccalaureate), crime is low, and there's been substantial government investment in recent years, with a new state-of-the-art hospital, energy-from-waste facility and power station. The island boasts active vintage steam and electric railways, and there's also some of the most captivating scenery in the British Isles.

No wonder there's that touchdown phenomenon at Ronaldsway. While leaving the island is easy – a half-hour flight will bring you to a major airport in England and an onward flight to Europe – the real mystery is, why leave in the first place?

North Lincolnshire the natural choice

Finding the right business location and premises, in the right location, at the right price is not just easy; it's actually enjoyable in North Lincolnshire.

Purely in terms of its location alone, North Lincolnshire is a great place to be. The region occupies a central and strategic position in the UK. Travelling from North Lincolnshire to any destination in the UK or beyond is both easy and convenient. Thanks to investment in our excellent communications infrastructure.

Lower traffic levels, shorter commuting distances and faster journey times are the norm. The national motorway network and major cities of the North are close by and London is just 1 1/2 hours away on the train from Doncaster. International trade prospers in the area through Humberside International Airport, Doncaster Sheffield Robin Hood Airport and the Humber ports. The ports alone provide access to over 53 countries worldwide.

The business sectors most attracted to North Lincolnshire are food and drink, chemical, manufacturing, engineering and metals. For each there are proactive networking opportunities, existing supply chains, training, expertise, infrastructure, specialist support companies and experienced employees.

The local workforce has an excellent track record for industrial relations and productivity as well as a reputation for flexible working. The area boasts two excellent colleges with valuable links to the business community. Near by there are seven universities that offer R&D facilities and graduate recruitment opportunities.

More and more businesses recognise that when it comes to business support, readily available skills, and high levels of productivity, few regions in the UK work harder for their businesses. All in all, North Lincolnshire is the natural choice for relocating and expanding.

North Lincolnshire: the natural selection for evolving businesses.

We offer unrivalled transport links, a multi-skilled workforce, prime site locations and an outstanding quality of life. **All make a fertile growing environment for businesses.**

Find out how we can nurture your business call: **01724 297383** or www.northlincs.gov.uk/business

NORTH LINCOLNSHIRE COUNCIL

North Lincolnshire: the natural choice

North Lincolnshire is located centrally on the east coast of England, offering investors a prime-site location on the banks of the Humber Estuary. Businesses profit from the unparalleled access by road, air, rail and sea to over 370 million potential European customers – not forgetting the 40 million UK customers and suppliers within just a four-hour drive.

Investors highlight the first-class relocation support, high-quality serviced sites, together with skilled and adaptable employees as key reasons for their choice. This support makes North Lincolnshire the natural choice for business.

North Lincolnshire is largely agricultural and the pattern of settlements reflects this. There are attractive market towns surrounded by small villages. An important exception to this is the substantial urban and industrial centre of Scunthorpe, which is built around the steel industry. The town is surprisingly attractive, with substantial open spaces and parklands. It serves much of North Lincolnshire in terms of jobs, colleges, shopping and leisure facilities.

Business sectors

Traditionally, one of the area's major employers is Corus, the global steel producer. However, the economy is diverse, with a broad range of manufacturers and service industries. The area is particularly attractive to the chemical and food and drink sectors, because of the expertise, infrastructure and supply chains.

In excess of 50 UK public limited companies, 25 multinationals and 42 foreign-owned companies have chosen North Lincolnshire. ConocoPhillips, Kimberly Clark, Geest, ColepCCL, Clugston Construction and Deltron Emcon Ltd are just a few of the businesses to benefit from the strategic advantage of this attractive and forward-thinking business location.

Because of the traditions of steel making there is an abundance of skills in the metals and engineering sector, and convenient supply chains. New businesses benefit from the proximity and skills base of this large employer. Many of the companies operating within this sector utilize cutting-edge engineering and manufacturing techniques, and take a global lead in advancing the technology. Knowledge and innovation are nurtured through the nine world-class universities within the Yorkshire region, many of which are renowned throughout the world for their contribution to the pool of research knowledge in the metals field.

North Lincolnshire recognizes the importance of staying competitive, and packages of support and assistance are available to embrace innovative means to improve products and processes. These include some subsidized expertise and consultancy services, training and diagnostics for companies, as well as initiatives to promote work between universities, IT and engineering businesses.

Bulk chemicals are predominant in the area, owing to the accessibility of the ports and various feedstocks. Businesses also profit from access to five specialist research centres assisting with technical, product development and production issues. Amongst the sites available is a 2,000-acre greenfield site designated for chemical use, with direct access to the estuary. ConocoPhillips has already invested on the site, commissioning a flagship combined heat and power plant, one of the largest and most technologically advanced facilities of its kind in Europe. Jeff Tetlow of ConocoPhillips European Power says, 'There are few areas in the UK capable of sustaining a combined heat and power plant of this size, and the south Humber bank is one of them. We see this as an industrial infrastructure project, not just a power station, with the potential to stimulate industrial development and regeneration in the area. With the continued support and very positive business viewpoint of the local authorities I am confident this will be the case.'

Humber Chemical Focus is the focal point for the region's chemical and related industries, providing a source of expertise, information and support on all matters relating to the chemical industry. It is leading the development of the pioneering Competency Assessment and Training Centre – Humber (CATCH), which will undertake competency assessments and upskilling for the chemical and allied industries. It also has the potential to assist companies with emergency shutdown and response procedures, certification, and licensing.

The food and drink sector covers the whole food chain from agriculture to manufacturing, processing, packaging and retail distribution. The area is a promising and dynamic venue for the food and drink industry, with sophisticated distribution capacity, highly developed manufacturing systems and strong business networks. There is an exceptional level of support for the sector, including advice on food safety, new product development, quality management and legal compliance as well as training and development. A specialist research centre provides a pilot plant, state-of-the-art imaging facilities, and facilities for the cryogenic treatment of foods.

Nisa-Today's, the United Kingdom's biggest buying group for independent retail and wholesale companies, has recently completed a £30 million investment in a 625,000 square foot ambient warehouse on Normanby Enterprise Park in Scunthorpe. Dudley Ramsden of Nisa-Today's commented, 'This warehouse is a huge asset – not only to Nisa-Today's and its members, but also to the Scunthorpe economy. It really puts Scunthorpe on the map as an excellent location for a national distribution network and will hopefully attract more major players to the area.'

The local skilled workforce has an excellent track record for industrial relations and productivity, and a reputation for flexible working. Employees are well accustomed to a continuous environment of 365-day operations.

A number of proactive partnerships support business in the area. The Greater Economic Success Group (GES) is a pioneering partnership of education, the council and businesses in North Lincolnshire. Members share information and best practice, and access support, to improve their profitability, in turn strengthening the local economy. Elaine Neale of TSC Foods Ltd said, 'I firmly believe that the GES has helped in my continuing professional development as I have been exposed to many different companies and like-minded colleagues that have helped to stretch my imagination outside of the insular and incestuous world of food manufacturing. It has also helped the business immensely in a number of areas, such as introducing me to someone who has now enabled TSC Foods to attract a great deal of funding in training and development.'

Connectivity

The Humber ports handle in excess of 80 million tonnes of cargo a year. Deep-sea facilities allow the landing of cargoes 24 hours a day. Fast overnight crossings mean hauliers can drive into the heart of mainland Europe within their time allowance. There is a rail freight facility within the dock area, linking to the main lines, and the local rail freight terminal for the Channel Tunnel is only 32 kilometres away, allowing excellent rail access to Europe. The transport of petrochemicals, coal and steel is the biggest market for rail freight, and suppliers are well accustomed to handling chemical products both bulk and speciality. Humberside Airport and the nearby Doncaster Sheffield Robin Hood Airport offer international business travel and expanding freight services. The M180 runs through the centre of the area and leads directly to the M18, M1, A1 and M62 motorways connecting to the rest of the United Kingdom.

What all this means is that locating your business in the area has the potential to give you a competitive edge in a demanding global market.

Sites and commercial property

The right infrastructure for business is a priority. Greenfield and brownfield land are available with plot sizes ranging from less than 1 acre (0.405 hectare) up to 150 acres (60.7 hectares), with all land in council ownership being fully serviced. Premises and land are available at a highly competitive cost compared with other regions in the United Kingdom.

The council's Economic Development Team offers a tailored search highlighting land and property in both the public and the private sector. The service is free of charge and confidential, and matches your specific land or property requirements to local availability on North Lincolnshire's up-to-date database.

Training and education

Training and education opportunities go hand in hand with the availability of a flexible workforce. North Lincolnshire boasts two colleges recognized nationally as centres of excellence, between them enrolling more than 9,000 students each year. The colleges are proactive in their approach to working with the local business community. North Lindsey College is recognized as a centre of excellence, and a major provider of professional training and business support services in the area.

Within a one-hour drive there are seven universities offering extensive research and development facilities and excellent graduate recruitment opportunities.

Financial support

The council business advisers act as a signpost for local and national grants or funds that may be available to investors. Within certain parts of North Lincolnshire, companies may be eligible for Selective Finance for Investment – a discretionary capital grant designed for businesses of all sizes that are looking to invest but need financial help to go ahead.

A variety of 'top-up' loan finance is also available to enable businesses to facilitate projects, as is equity finance through UK Steel Enterprise and other providers, including 3i and Yorkshire Company Services.

Added value

We offer an experienced professional team who will work with you on a free and confidential basis. Tailored investor proposals are available; these can include an overview of the area, demographics, comparative technical data and supply chain information. In partnership with the Learning and Skills Council and Job Centre Plus, we can also put together tailor-made recruitment and training packages as well as workplace trials.

The support offered by the Economic Development Team and its partners can save inward investors to North Lincolnshire significant expense and valuable management time.

Quality of life

North Lincolnshire is blessed with more than its fair share of delightful picturesque villages and traditional market towns – welcoming communities full of character, with a wide range of excellent services right on your doorstep. Whatever you like to do for fun and relaxation, you can live life to the full. Whether you are the active and sporty type or prefer to take life at a more relaxed pace, there is so much to see and do. There's a wide choice of superb private golf courses and sailing opportunities. Forest Pines has greens to rival some of the finest in the country, including a quality health and fitness club and spa to relax.

Standards of education in the area are amongst some of the best in the country. Government inspector reports demonstrate the high standards that are being achieved, from pre-school and primary, to secondary schools and colleges.

More and more people and businesses are recognizing that when it comes to business support, readily available skills and high levels of productivity, few regions in the United Kingdom work harder for their businesses. All in all, North

Middle of the UK? Absolutely.
Middle of the Road? Definitely not.

5 million population within an hour's drive | House prices are 34% less than the national average
15 universities and FE colleges in the surrounding areas producing 140,000 skilled individuals a year
Major rail, road and air services on the doorstep | Large rural areas including historic Sherwood Forest
Over £1 billion investment in site development and business capacity | 12 Business Innovation Centres

Here in North Nottinghamshire and North Derbyshire
we are anything but middle of the road. Rich in
historical and cultural assets, we are one of the
most evolving areas of the Midlands. From our
proud roots in traditional industries such as coal and
textiles, we are reinventing ourselves as a modern
21st century economy.

If you are looking for quality of life, a central location
and a large employee base, why not come and
see what the area has to offer. We are
already home to some of the UK's best business
performers – we'd like you to join them.

If you are looking to relocate, set up a new operation
or expand your business, please contact us and let
us welcome you to the North Midlands.

Tel: **01623 811223**
Email: enquiries@alliancenorthmidlands.co.uk
www.alliancenorthmidlands.co.uk

Alliance
NORTH
MIDLANDS
energy, industry, connectivity

Lincolnshire offers an unmatched quality of life and is the natural choice for relocating and expanding.

For further information, please contact the Economic Development Team (tel: +44 (0)1724 297383) or visit www.northlincs.gov.uk/business.

The changing face of England's North Midlands

Not for decades has the future looked as bright as it now does for north Derbyshire and north Nottinghamshire, an area that had suffered for years from the decline of its traditional industrial sectors. Momentum has been gathering pace to bring new prosperity to England's North Midlands, which was previously known worldwide for its coalmining, textiles and engineering industries.

The time has never been better for aspiring firms looking for a new business location to consider the merits of this area, which is situated right at the heart of England adjacent to major provincial cities and is serviced by a superb network of road, rail and air connections.

The North Midlands area of north Nottinghamshire and north Derbyshire lies at the centre of the country. Extending from the northern edges of Nottingham and Derby to the southern edges of Sheffield and Doncaster and from the Lincolnshire Wolds in the east to the Peak District in the west, the North Midlands has at its heart the world-famous Sherwood Forest.

The principal commercial hubs of the North Midlands are the urban centres of Chesterfield and Mansfield, both of which have around 100,000 populations, and the sizeable towns of Newark, Worksop and Retford. The M1 motorway and A1 run through the patch, as well as two mainline north–south railway lines. Motorway links to the North West/Yorkshire/West Midlands regions and to the Humber/east coast ports are excellent via the M1, M62 and M18. Airports at Nottingham East Midlands and Robin Hood Doncaster/Sheffield provide direct business and freight connections to international destinations.

Many high-quality and diverse property options, a plentiful, loyal and adaptable workforce combined with a mature business support network, access to financial incentives, together with being a great place to live are some of the benefits businesses can enjoy. In addition, there is a strong partnership of local bodies which has a common aim of welcoming and supporting a new, high-quality business culture. This partnership is also putting in place the vital supporting infrastructure to provide local people with the chance to take advantage of the opportunities that modern business in the 21st century provides.

Coordinating and contributing funding towards much of this activity is one of the principal tasks of the Alliance Sub-regional Strategic Partnership (SSP), which is charged with delivering the Regional Economic Strategy in the area on behalf of the East Midlands Development Agency. Established only in 2003, the Alliance SSP has already invested well over £25m in projects in its priority activities: economic infrastructure, employment and skills, and enterprise and innovation. These are considered to be the key themes that have to be addressed to transform the economic performance of the North Midlands region over the medium term.

The focus of the Alliance SSP's investments is on quality and diversity. With unemployment rates now below the UK average, the emphasis has changed from trying to attract any type of job to one of attracting employers that may create fewer, but higher-quality, jobs. Creating the economic environment in which entrepreneurship and enterprise can flourish, providing support for those businesses and assisting local people acquire the skills to secure employment with these businesses is the central theme of the Alliance SSP's efforts to bring about a transforming step change in the economic performance of the North Midlands.

Some of the current major initiatives under way being developed by both the public and the private sector demonstrate how the face of the North Midlands area of north Nottinghamshire and north Derbyshire has changed dramatically over recent times. Not only are large brownfield sites being reclaimed and brought back into productive use, but also new sites and premises in well-accessed locations are seeing strong demand from a range of new and expanding businesses.

If you are considering a new location for a start-up or expanding business, then you should visit www.alliancenorthmidlands.co.uk, where you will find further information to help you make an informed decision.

Key current projects in the North Midlands

Markham Vale, Bolsover/Chesterfield

Markham Vale is a 200-acre (80-hectare) former coalfield site subject to a £50m reclamation project by Derbyshire County Council. Future development of the site will be carried out by Henry Boot Developments Ltd. The site straddles the M1 motorway and will benefit from a dedicated J29a junction, construction of which was scheduled to begin in spring 2006. Freehold/leasehold plots are to become available for B1, 2, 8 projects from autumn 2006.
Contact: Matt Taylor, Derbyshire County Council (tel: 01629 580000 x5402); Vivienne Clements, Henry Boot Developments Ltd (tel: 0114 2555444)

Chesterfield

Major regeneration of the southern and eastern edge of the town is taking place, to provide large new commercial opportunities for mixed-use developments.
Contact: Jim Moore, Chesterfield Borough Council (tel: 01246 345255)

Bevercotes

Located adjacent to the A1 between Retford and Newark, the 200-acre (80-hectare) former Bevercotes colliery site has been purchased by Gladman Developments Ltd to construct almost 300,000 square metres of warehouse and

distribution space in four big sheds (outline sizes of 20,000, 60,000, 70,000 and 120,000 square metres). This site is ideal for businesses wanting A1 access in the centre of England, with Robin Hood Airport and the Humber ports within easy distance.
Contact: Mike Sowerby, Gladman Developments Ltd (tel: 01260 288800)

Space 27

Space 27 is a brand-new £30m development by Innov@te Property on the well-established and high-quality Sherwood Business Park adjacent to M1 J27, which provides easy access to Derby and Nottingham as well as connections to the rest of the United Kingdom. The stunning campus-style development has been constructed to BREEAM 'Excellent' standards and provides almost 12,000 square metres of fully flexible office/workshop facilities.
Contact: Jonathon Bishop, HEB (Agents) (tel: 0115 950 6611); Mark Proctor, Innov@te Property (tel: 01623 729300)

Mansfield and Ashfield

A number of development sites are to become available along the route of a new 15-kilometre relief road that bisects the two towns (which together have a population of over 200,000) and improves M1–A1 links. The sites will be within 5 miles of M1 J28 and are suitable for a range of commercial uses. In addition, Wilson Bowden plc is shortly to begin development of its 200-acre (80-hectare) Castlewood site, which lies immediately adjacent to M1 J28. A range of units for B1, 2 and 8 uses are expected (contact Fisher Hargreaves Proctor, the agents; see below). These new developments will add to the already significant investments made in the area over recent years, which are transforming the commercial base away from the traditional manufacturing industries of the past.
Contact: Tom Rawsterne, Nottinghamshire County Council (tel: 0115 9773790); John Proctor, Fisher Hargreaves Proctor (Agents) (tel: 0115 8411130); Mark Lynam, Ashfield District Council (tel: 01623 457172); Stephen Jackson, Mansfield District Council (tel: 01623 463463)

Business Innovation Centres

One of the primary objectives of the North Midlands area is to encourage the start-up of quality businesses operating in innovative technologies and/or the 'knowledge economy'. A number of high-quality Business Innovation Centres (BICs) have been set up over recent years to offer accommodation and expert support appropriate for start-up and small, growing firms. All BICs are listed below, with relevant contact details for current vacancy updates:

Dunston Innovation Centre, Chesterfield
Richard Taylor   01246 267700

Tapton Innovation Centre, Chesterfield	
Westthorpe Innovation Centre, near Chesterfield	
Alison Flint	0114 2180604
Coney Green Business Centre, near Chesterfield	
Frank Jones	01246 252300
Environment Centre, Markham Vale, Chesterfield	
Trudi Novakovic	01246 826000
The Turbine, Worksop	
Paul Mallatratt	01909 512100
Edwinstowe House, Edwinstowe, Notts	
Linda Shepherd	01623 827931
The E-Centre, Sherwood Energy Village, Ollerton	
Stan Crawford	01623 860222
Newark Business Innovation Centre, Newark	
Mike Robinson	01636 655258
Mansfield i-Centre (Phases 1 and 2), Mansfield	
Bob Scott	01623 600600

Major recent investments/developments

Sportsworld International Ltd

Sportsworld International Ltd is a major UK sports clothing/goods retailer in the process of moving its headquarters and national distribution centre from Dunstable to Shirebrook, a small ex-mining town outside Mansfield. A 65-acre (26-hectare) plot was purchased from the East Midlands Regional Development Agency, which had reclaimed the former colliery site, and a 1 million plus square foot warehouse and office complex constructed. It is anticipated that over 1,000 new jobs will be directly created in a range of activities. This will also have a significantly positive impact in creating many local indirect jobs in the town. A partnership of local support agencies has been working with the company to ensure that as many local people as possible are helped to access the positions that become available.

B&Q/Excel Logistics

Over 1,000 new jobs are being recruited at a major new distribution centre near Worksop, north Nottinghamshire, for B&Q which will be run by Excel. The former Manton colliery site had been reclaimed by the East Midlands Development Agency and a large plot purchased for a 1 million square foot distribution unit, which will also house training and merchandising facilities. This will add to the already strong logistics and distribution presence in the town, where major companies like Wilkinsons Hardware, Prolog Logistics, Greencore (formerly Hazlewood Foods) and Peppers Distribution are located.

Sherwood Energy Village

Sherwood Energy Village is a unique development of the former Ollerton Colliery in Nottinghamshire, where the local community created a social enterprise company to develop the site along environmentally sustainable lines. The development was recognized in 2005, with the Government awarding it the accolade of 'The Most Enterprising Community in Britain'. The site will be for B1, 2 and 8 use alongside residential housing and retail space. The E-Centre has been specifically constructed for new small businesses operating in the energy and environmental technologies field. High-quality building, energy use and environmental standards are being set for all occupiers.

The development has attracted so much interest that, currently, little land remains unallocated. Center Parcs, the major holiday company, has recently relocated its HQ facility to the site. The way in which the community planned the model for the business structure has attracted widespread interest from communities across the United Kingdom and Europe looking to replicate it.
Contact: Stan Crawford, Sherwood Energy Village (tel: 01623 860222)

Newark

DSG plc, the Dixons retail group, is rationalizing its UK distribution network from 17 warehouses down to 2. Demonstrating the strategic advantage of the town, one of these will be at Newark adjacent to the A1, where an existing 750,000 square foot unit will be doubled in size. The town is also to see the development of one of Gazeley Properties' 'G-Park' distribution centres, which are being established across the United Kingdom. Work has started on a 40-acre (16-hectare) site on the edge of town, close to the A1. With superb East Coast main line rail connections to both London and the North, Newark also sits within commuting distance of Nottingham, Peterborough, Doncaster, Lincoln and Leicester.
Contact: Mike Robinson, Newark and Sherwood District Council (tel: 01636 650000)

Robin Hood Airport Doncaster Sheffield

The United Kingdom's largest new full-service airport for 40 years was opened in April 2005 at the former RAF Finningley near Doncaster. The site was purchased by Peel Group, owners and operators of Liverpool John Lennon and Teesside Airports, and developed in record time. Its first year of operations has seen over 800,000 passengers fly to over 35 European destinations, and summer 2006 will see transatlantic flights to the United States, Mexico and the Dominican Republic commence. Over 500 local people now work at the airport, and expansion of operations will see this figure rise. Plans are being worked on to expand the huge freight and cargo potential; to develop new routes to exploit in-bound tourism links, eg the Pilgrim Fathers heritage on the doorstep of the

Robin Hood Airport Doncaster Sheffield

Domestic wind turbines produced by Eclectic Energy Ltd

airport; and to exploit the 65-acre (26-hectare) business park on-site, where a number of occupier/developers have already signed up. The operators' ambitions to see Robin Hood Airport become the airport of choice for the northern and eastern part of England will bring a huge economic boost to the North Midlands area and beyond.

Contact: www.robinhoodairport.co.uk

Eclectic Energy Ltd

Established six years ago, Eclectic Energy Ltd is a small family business operating out of Edwinstowe House, a complex of managed offices and workshops located in the small village of Edwinstowe in the heart of Sherwood Forest.

Eclectic Energy's principal products are small wind turbines that have a number of applications in domestic, agricultural and leisure settings. Having taken advice from a number of organizations, including the on-site advisers, Eclectic is concentrating on production and promotion of its StealthGen 400-watt domestic turbine, which, in optimum conditions, can produce around 25 per cent of a typical family's electricity.

Exhibiting at the All-Energy Show, Aberdeen, in May 2006 alongside Alliance North Midlands, Eclectic's turbine was the star of the show, attracting phenomenal interest from prospective purchasers, both domestic and trade, as well as attracting the attention of major companies looking to bolster their 'green' credentials.

The challenge for the North Midlands now is to help the company increase production to take advantage of this interest and to ensure that the company and its supply chain of subcontractors remain and grow in the area.

7

Cash flow and working capital

The Quest for Cash
by Andrew Myall

From the moment we are conceived we start consuming cash. Child-friendly, stimulatingly-decorated nurseries, schooling and even the clothing on our backs all cost money. Later in life, when our entrepreneurial spirits show themselves, the demand for cash increases and as with any start-up business the demand always seems to be greater than the amount of cash available. Once personal cash is committed, and we have auctioned most of our saleable body parts on eBay in the hope of raising more money, we look at other avenues hoping that they will be more fruitful.

When considering external finance you should always tread with caution as there are many loan sharks and pitfalls to avoid. This is especially prudent when looking at Business Angel Funding as there are companies who will demand due diligence fees upfront without actually having any cash to invest in the first place. Despite this on my *Quest for Cash* I was heartened to find many legitimate government-supported schemes. There is also grant money in addition to UK based Business Angel Organisations with more cash than companies to invest into.

Soft Loans

If someone told you that you could get a 250k soft loan (that's an *unsecured* loan for us mere mortals e.g. a loan that requires no personal guarantees or charges over your house) for your start up business, you might dismiss it as something not entirely legitimate or something that requires you to relinquish you first born child and a large part of your enterprise. Not only is this option of funding legitimate, it's actually a scheme that's been in operation for over ten years and is supported by the Department of Trade and Industry. It's unsecured lending (really the sexiest sort there is) and really does bridge the equity gap for eligible companies, so why is it when I speak to many budding young (or not so young) entrepreneurs they have never heard of it?

'The Small Firms Loan Guarantee is a DTI-supported scheme that affords start-up companies and businesses under four years old the opportunity to obtain unsecured funding where a conventional loan is not possible due to lack of security.'

Entrepreneurs are sadly not the only people kept in the dark. I have found that many of the primary lenders (on a local level) are poorly briefed on the guidelines of the scheme thus making the whole process of gaining these funds a tad confusing to say the least.

'The DTI-supported scheme offers unsecured lending from £15-250k for eligible businesses. A full business plan and three years worth of cash projections are required. Up to 75% of the loan is guaranteed by the DTI, the other 25% is secured on the tangible assets of the business.'

Sound advice for this type of lending prior to any money exchanging hands is absolutely essential.

How can we help?

On my *Quest for Cash* I did not want other entrepreneurs and SME to fall into the same pitfalls as me thus I founded my own business **www.IBAdvisor.co.uk** that provides business support and a facilitator for Venture Funding. We have over eight years of 'real world' experience, give honest sound advice. We provide templates for the business plan and guide you through every step of the process.

We also have Business Opportunities for anyone looking to become an IBA (Independent Business Advisor) who would like to work under the guidance and support of our umbrella.

Call the Business Advice Bureau (SE) Ltd on **0800 019 8552**

DTI Small Firm Loan Guarantee
'Unsecured Lending to 250k'

Is your company eligible?

FREE PHONE
0800 019 8552

Over 8 Years of Experience

Other Services

Business Planning
Unsecured Finance
DTI Grants
Financial Planning
Business Support
Franchising
AIM Intermediary
Business Angels

IBA is a Brand of the Business Advice Bureau SE Ltd
01276 804 540

'Unsecured' Lending supported by the DTI

- For clients that wish to start a company
- An established business looking to expand (under 5 years)

Your Personal Security..........

- The DTI will cover up to 75% (on business failure)
- The Bank secures 25% on Business Assets
- Up to 100% Risk Free to you

A loan that bridges the equity GAP.........

- 3-10 Year Term
- A 12 Months Repayment Holiday
- Loans between £15k and £250k

How to apply..........

- A Business Plan & 3yr Cash Projections.

We develop the business plan with you and assist in every step of the process.

Your success is our success.

www.IBAdvisor.co.uk   info@IBAdvisor.co.uk

Reviewing the efficiency of your business

If you had a dripping tap at home, you would get it fixed, but many businesses drip profits away for years and never even know about it, let alone do anything about it. Do areas of your business need some repairs and maintenance? Fiona Rook of My Business Centre suggests places to look

This isn't the sexy side of business; this doesn't drive sales or create a wow-factor advertising campaign. This is all about checking that your housekeeping is in order and that your back office is working effectively. It may not be sexy, but it can save you huge amounts of time and money, and that should be enough incentive for you to take some time out and look at how efficiently your business is running. This chapter focuses on three areas generic to all businesses:

- streamlining your processes;
- keeping your assets and liabilities well maintained;
- using benchmarking and budgets.

Streamline your processes

As businesses grow, processes tend to be bolted together as new functions are added. This normally leads either to duplication and over-complication, which can be costly in both time and resources; or, potentially worse, to gaps in communication.

Do any of these exist in your business?

■ reports produced that no one really reads;
■ information being circulated that no one uses;
■ multiple departments keying in the same data;
■ departments using different versions of the same data (that probably don't agree);
■ hours being spent getting information that you think should take minutes;
■ breakdown in communications between departments.

If you know that your business is in a bit of a muddle, then sit down with a blank piece of paper and redesign your business processes based on the functions that exist now and the planned growth areas. Communicate to your staff why you are planning changes and get their input too. Spending time in the planning stage will reap rewards on implementation.

To find out how streamlined your processes are, you need to follow information flows through your business. You may be amazed at the number of dead ends and circuitous routes that exist.

Start with a phone call from a potential new customer:

1. Who takes the call?
2. Who takes on responsibility to turn that enquiry into a sale?
3. How do price and contract terms get negotiated and who authorizes this?
4. If timelines are agreed with the customer, are these agreed upfront by the people expected to meet them?
5. How do other departments, eg production, finance, get to know that an order has been placed?
6. How are the details communicated?
7. How is the work planned, components ordered, etc?
8. Who checks that the order has been sent and that the customer is satisfied?
9. How is customer satisfaction/dissatisfaction communicated and who issues actions?
10. How does the customer get invoiced?
11. How does the receipt of funds get monitored?
12. How do the sale, purchase and stock movement get recorded into the accounts?

At each stage you need to follow each outflow of information, so if a sales order is raised that has three copies, then follow each one.

If the answer to the above is that you do it all yourself, then:

■ What happens when you are not there?
■ As the business grows, you won't be able to do it all yourself, so start delegating and free up your time to focus on growth.

Once you have cleaned up one process, start on another. Usually, once you have started on one then you start to see inefficiencies in other departments, and the process cascades throughout the organization.

Reviewing your processes can be a hard thing to do as people get used to current ways of working and think therefore that the present way is the best way. In fact, it is just the way that they are most comfortable with. Sometimes you need to bring in 'fresh eyes' to help, but there is no reason why you and your management team cannot review your processes yourselves.

As yours is a growing business, you need to make sure that work carried out is necessary and optimizes the time spent. Spending time focusing on growth rather than unnecessary paperwork is time well spent.

Make use of your balance sheet

You are probably familiar with using your profit and loss to report your business, but to use your balance sheet to control your business?

Control your assets and liabilities

Fixed assets

You should have a register of all your fixed assets and be able to identify each asset on the register. Stickers with serial numbers are useful for plant and machinery items, registration numbers for vehicles, etc. Check that you know the whereabouts of everything that has been bought and do regular checks (at least annually) to ensure that the list is updated if assets become obsolete or broken, and follow up any that mysteriously go missing.

Rather than the register just being a control sheet, consider whether it can be used to help the business. By adding a bit more data you may be able to schedule maintenance from it or to note compliance testing dates.

Stock

Stock control is often an issue and has to be controlled at an early stage for businesses to work efficiently. Holding too much stock has a negative impact on your cash flow and may also incur high storage costs; getting the stock mix wrong or not holding enough stock can lead to downtime caused by missing parts, or lost sales as customers are forced to look elsewhere.

Stock levels can often be reduced if your suppliers can guarantee deliveries with a shorter lead time. Talk to current and potential suppliers to find out what is possible. Check how your stock levels compare to your competitors'. If they manage with less, find out how.

Every manager knows that pilfering is money walking out of the door but would you know if it was happening to you?

Debtors

Can your debtor days be reduced by either prompt collection or reduced terms? Getting the funds into your bank account means that interest is being earned and you have funds to invest in other areas. If some of your customers are abusing your payment terms, perhaps credit control need to make more frequent contact to chase payments, or could you charge interest on late payments?

Charging interest is often a difficult issue, as it tends to be fairly detrimental to client relationships, but discounts for early payments are generally acceptable and have VAT advantages. Compare your debtor days to your competitors' and to your industry standards.

Also check that you have controls in place to stop customers ordering above their limits. This is easy in the beginning when companies are small, as everyone knows what is going on, but as businesses grow, the controls that worked informally before can be lost. Set limits for each customer and put in an approval process for customers that wish to exceed their limit.

How much does it cost you to raise an invoice and to collect and bank the funds? You may not have worked this out before, but it is a great indicator of how efficiently your sales ledger team and credit control are working. Think through all the costs, including labour, equipment costs, paper, telephone, bank charges and postage, and then see whether there are areas where savings can be made without reducing the service. There are benchmarks for the cost of sales ledger and credit control costs per invoice. Check how yours matches up and then see if it can be improved.

How is the information collated? Can it be more streamlined/automated? Can invoices be e-mailed rather than posted? Can customers be encouraged to pay electronically and therefore save process time and reduce bank charges?

Bank and loans

First check that you are getting the best service that your bank offers, and at the best rates. Ask your bank to review your tariff charges and to see whether it can offer you a better tariff structure or simply a reduction in rates. It never hurts to ask. Does your bank offer other services that may be beneficial to you – higher interest rate accounts for instance, or conversion of an overdraft to a loan?

Look at other options for both your bank and your loan facilities. Other institutions will gladly provide a quote, but do weigh up all the pros and cons and try to get references from current customers. There is no point in saving a few pennies but finding yourself with someone who will not support you in the future. A good relationship with these bodies is essential to grow your business; they must believe in both you and your business.

Creditors

Have you negotiated the best terms with your suppliers, or could your terms be extended to improve your cash flow? Again, compare your creditor days with your competitors' and your industry benchmark.

How much does it cost you to process an invoice and to make the payment? Adopt the same procedure as for debtors and find out how efficient your purchase ledger function is compared to industry benchmarks. Think through all the costs, including labour, equipment costs, paper, telephone, bank charges and postage, and then see whether there are areas where savings can be made without reducing the service.

How is the information collated? Could it be more streamlined/automated? Could invoices be received by e-mail? Is your authorization process cumbersome? Could you pay electronically and therefore save process time and reduce bank charges?

Whilst you are looking at your creditors it may be a good time to see if you can negotiate any price reductions. Determine your annual spend per item and then start at the top and shop around for better value or ask your current suppliers for a more competitive price. Also, ascertain how much you spend with each of your biggest suppliers. Are you using the purchasing power that you have? They may offer you a preferred customer discount.

Benchmarking and budgets

'If you're not keeping score, you're just practising.'

Benchmarking

How efficient are you compared to others in your industry? What margins do others achieve? If similar businesses are achieving a higher gross margin then you could save thousands by emulating their practices.

How much do your contemporaries spend on labour, on overheads, etc., what debtor's terms do they offer and how much credit do they manage to negotiate? Decide where you can realistically position your business in the short term and long term. Decide what will need to be changed to achieve the top results and plan accordingly.

It can be difficult to do accurate benchmarking, as no business is quite like yours, but there is a wealth of competitor information out there on which you can base your targets. Many business advisers offer a benchmarking service that takes data from thousands of companies' accounts and can be filtered by industry. Check how the filters are set up, though, as you may find yourself compared to the corner shop and an international conglomerate!

If this route is too expensive then there is a lot of information on the internet, although you do have to be selective. You can also download company accounts from the Companies House website. There is a small charge, but the information on your direct competitors may be invaluable for understanding your marketplace and for setting your own goals.

Also, try your industry bodies. They will know the industry standards and can probably direct you to other sources specific to your industry.

Budgets

The complexity of budgets can range from the back of the proverbial fag packet to bound documents several inches thick. You need to decide what works best for your business and how the budget will be used.

Everybody works harder when trying to achieve a goal, so having a budget or target in place that people feel a part of will in itself drive efficiencies. The difficulty is twofold:

1) setting the right target in the first place;
2) getting people to feel a part of it.

The tried and tested method to achieve both of these (at the same time) is to get everyone involved in setting the budget in the first place. Simple; but then the best solutions often are.

Senior management need to communicate the top-level goals for the business, eg:

■ We want overall sales to increase by 20%.
■ We want to cover a wider geographical area and attract new sectors.
■ We need to improve our gross margin by 5%.
■ Our overheads must only increase by 10%.

The process will need to be coordinated and steered, but each area should be instrumental in agreeing its own targets.

When done properly, a budget will motivate a team to achieve, and will give a sense of satisfaction when the goals are met.

In conclusion

For start-ups, this area may not be as important, as the controllers are usually the owners and will generally be aware of every transaction and every detail. Also, the processes have just been designed so they are running as efficiently as possible at present. However, two key things happen as a business starts to grow:

1. New functions are bolted on to the existing structure. This can lead to complicated processes with much duplication and production of irrelevant information, or processes that circumvent your internal control procedures.
2. The knowledge base becomes diluted as tasks are delegated, as do the ownership of costs and the drive to keep costs down. Other factors take over, such as job security, ease of working, peer relationships, etc. It is, after all, much easier to spend someone else's money than your own.

As a business grows, significant benefits can be achieved from taking time to check that the basic structure of the business is running as efficiently as possible, thereby ensuring that the resources are fully utilized and focus can be maintained on growth.

My Business Centre offers a comprehensive service to growing businesses across all industry sectors. We offer full consultancy and business advisory support, along with a complete accounts and tax service, including book-keeping, management accounts, VAT and payroll as well as year-end accounts and tax returns.

For more information about My Business Centre and the ways we can help your business, please contact Fiona Rook (tel: 01837 851676; e-mail: fiona@mybusinesscentre.co.uk) or visit www.mybuscen.co.uk.

Make this your toughest decision of the day.

Graydon UK offers a number of recognised specialist services in commercial credit risk management, credit reports and credit application processing. These services enable you to manage your commercial risk and maximise business opportunities, by providing instant access to over 68 million credit reports covering businesses in more than 130 countries. Each of our packages provides specialist information in different areas of credit control, yet they all deliver the same single positive outcome - complete peace of mind and confidence in your workplace. So the tough decisions you make on a day-to-day basis should get much, much, easier. For further info call Graydon on 020 8515 1410 or visit www.graydon.co.uk

Minding your business. **GRAYDON**

Slow payments

Before celebrating a major order, first check the payment terms, warns Martin Williams, Managing Director of Graydon UK, otherwise cash could run dry

For growing companies, the priority is usually chasing sales and driving up revenues. Credit management is rarely given much consideration when a major new order is won. Instead, the reaction is one of gratitude, excitement and relief. But it is worth pausing for a moment and asking about payment terms, explaining why, in servicing the order, it is important for invoices to be settled strictly on time. Forgetting to spell this out at the beginning is a sure way to start to put pressure on cash flow.

Take the instance of a new small design consultancy that won an order to redesign perfume bottles and skin cream jars for a cosmetics manufacturer. Because this deal was going to account for 75 per cent of sales revenue for three months, work for some other clients was postponed and delayed. Five months after accepting the initial deal and starting work on the job, the consultancy had to make one of its designers redundant simply because the manufacturer was not sticking to its credit terms and had paid only one monthly invoice out of four. Cash, in simple terms, had dried up. A range of credit control actions taken at the appropriate times could have prevented such a situation ever occurring.

Unfortunately, this is an all too common problem for smaller companies working with larger corporates. They should always ask themselves whether they have the infrastructure to handle the order, as well as being aware of the dangers of putting all their eggs in one basket and relying too heavily on one major customer that may not pay on time.

The cost of running a credit check has fallen significantly in the past 20 years. A report that would once have cost £35 can now be bought online for under £10. Most of the 4 million companies in the United Kingdom are covered. Yet only 40,000–50,000 regularly check the credit histories of their customers. The rest seem to be happy to win the business and ignore potential trouble with their cash flow until it hits them.

Most growing companies cannot afford a full-time credit manager to chase their bills, so here are 10 ways to improve cash collection:

1. *Sign your customer up.* Ensure that your company has a signed contract with the customer that clearly states your payment terms. These terms should also be clearly described on your application forms and the invoices you subsequently send out. Be sure the customer knows what the credit terms are, whether you offer discounts for prompt payments or bulk purchases, whether additional costs are payable (eg VAT or carriage costs) and whether you charge interest on overdue accounts (all businesses are legally entitled to do this).

2. *Do a credit check.* Buy a credit report from a recognized credit reference agency, especially one that collects trade payment information on how large companies pay their bills, eg Graydon, Experian, Dun & Bradstreet. Don't rely totally on the taking up of two references given to you by the potential client. They may be cultivated! Don't be taken in either by a great-looking set of accounts to determine whether you will get paid on time; a healthy-looking balance sheet might mean that your potential customer is very proficient in getting its suppliers to finance its business! Set a credit limit for each new client, and don't allow customers to exceed limits without your permission. After all, they are set for a good reason, as you have assessed the creditworthiness of the customer and how much your business can afford to wait for (or lose, should the worst occur).

3. *Is a purchase order required?* As part of their internal control procedures, large companies often require signed purchase orders before paying invoices. Ask the manager or department placing the order whether they need to raise an internal purchase order covering the value of the order, and, if they do, whether they have done so. Ask for a copy of the purchase order. (Note that some large companies require invoices from suppliers to quote the purchase order number before they are paid.)

4. *Avoid excuses.* Prevent excuses for delayed payment. After dispatching goods, ensure that your customer has received them and that there are no problems with quantity or quality.

5. *Send statements.* Send statements at different times in the month regarding your invoices. Sometimes this tactic can provoke questions, particularly when original invoices have been lost, not received, or mislaid.

6. *Check on expected pay date.* Confirm with your client when your bill is expected to be paid, remembering to ask whether the client has specific cheque run dates.

7. *Use the telephone to chase.* If payment is delayed, chase your money by telephone rather than letter. Some experts in this field say that the telephone method can be 80% more effective! Always prioritize your cash collection activity, making sure you chase the oldest and largest debts first. Be friendly but firm when speaking with your customer, and don't forget to remind the customer that you charge interest on all late payments.

8. *Maximize your bargaining power.* Maximize your leverage. Try to establish how valuable the product you're selling is to your client. It may be a vital component in a manufacturing process, especially if it has been developed to the client's own specifications.
9. *Monitor your risk portfolio.* Keep abreast of news that may affect the creditworthiness of your key clients. Put their names on a low-cost monitoring service with a credit reference agency (Graydon's service is called CreditWatch). There is nothing worse than being the last to know when something has happened to one of your key customers.
10. *Develop a 'friend'.* Try to establish a personal rapport with one or two people in your client's Accounts department. The personal touch never fails!

The message could not be clearer. If SMEs follow this advice, they will find that cash flow difficulties will ease. This course of action will be far better than doing nothing about slow payments from large organizations (apparently, half of small businesses continue to suffer slow payments in silence for fear of losing 'valuable accounts'). Or do the extreme opposite: that is, close the account. One thing is certain: large companies are not going to change their payment habits overnight. It is time for SMEs to take positive action for themselves.

For more information, contact Graydon UK Limited (www.graydon.co.uk), the Federation of Small Businesses (http://www.fsb.org.uk/) or The Better Payment Practice Group (http://www.payontime.co.uk/).

Martin Williams has spent the past 30 years in the credit information industry. For the first nine years, he held a number of management positions with Dun & Bradstreet UK, but was transferred in 1984 to Dun & Bradstreet Europe, as part of a high-level team employed to help Dun & Bradstreet companies in Europe to computerize their operations. In 1987 Martin moved to Graydon, which is now one of the top five players in the United Kingdom. Since 1989 Martin has been a board director of Graydon UK and became Managing Director in 2001. Martin is currently the President of Eurogate, a network of European credit information agencies of which Graydon is a part. He has also been a member of the Institute of Credit Management in the United Kingdom since 1991, and is a regular presenter and speaker at credit management forums in the United Kingdom.

Graydon UK Limited is one of the leading database information providers specializing in credit risk management. The company helps clients reduce the uncertainty of commercial risk by providing a high-quality package of credit scoring, credit rating and credit risk management services. Graydon provides access to credit information and reports on more than 68 million companies in more than 130 countries worldwide. The Graydon group is owned by Atradius, Coface and Euler Hermes, three of Europe's leading credit insurance organizations.

For additional information, go to www.graydon.co.uk.

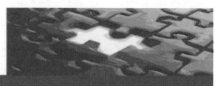

Banking relationships for smaller companies

*How should you manage your bank manager? Stewart Dickey, a director
of the British Bankers' Association, gives his view*

The UK economy depends on the entrepreneur and on small businesses. Of course, its
real strength depends on growth, and it is important for the health of the SME sector
that businesses are encouraged to grow and expand.

There is no doubt that all organizations associated with government, and other
stakeholders such as small business representative organizations, the press and
banks, are supportive of the Small Business Service's stated vision of helping the
United Kingdom become the best place in the world to start and grow a business. It
seems that all these stakeholders recognize the importance of encouraging a spirit of
entrepreneurship in the country. However, whilst many such commentators are nicely
established in salaried jobs with a decent pension to look forward to, there is no doubt
the self-employed person is the subject of much nervous admiration. There is so much
encouragement and advice around for small business owners that it is disappointing
that many surveys of the business scene suggest that ignorance and lack of confidence
still abound.

The appeal of 'running your own business' remains as attractive as ever, and it is
encouraging that many people are prepared to start up in business. British Bankers'
Association figures show that during 2005, 515,000 small businesses established first
banking relationships. Quite a staggering figure, but unfortunately many will fall by
the wayside in their journey to grow their business. This number of new businesses
means that bankers, advisers and suppliers to the small business community are facing

untold opportunities to help develop businesses and, of course, by doing so grow their own businesses.

The current banking market for small businesses is very competitive: many businesses will close, and customers increasingly switch their banking allegiance. Because of this, a manager needs to replenish about 20 per cent of his or her portfolio in a year just to stand still. So, if a small business customer is showing signs of successfully growing the business, that customer is going to be loved by his or her bank manager. Good bankers want to expand their own business and they actually enjoy moving out of their comfort zone. By supporting their customers they will be able to share in the excitement and ups and downs of the customers' business life.

Working with your bank

If your business is growing, you will need to work with your bank manager. Maintain a good relationship with him or her and keep an eye on the operation of your bank account so that when you ask for additional funds your manager will know the strong points about your business and will be able to assess your application to your satisfaction. In other words, in any relationship with a bank manager make sure the management aspect is mutual.

How to manage your bank manager

- Talk to your relationship manager. Do what the relationship manager's title implies: build up a relationship with him or her.
- Get the relationship manager to come out and see you and your business; keep him or her interested in what you are doing.
- Avoid surprising or disappointing your banker; if you have an overdraft limit, stick to it. If you are suddenly going to draw a large amount of money that is not in keeping with the way you normally operate your account, explain to your manager what you are doing.
- Keep an eye on your bank account (which is easy with internet banking) and don't issue cheques if you haven't got any money on your account to cover them. If you think you are going to go over your overdraft limit, call your manager and discuss why, and if possible arrange an increase.
- If you discussed a business plan with your manager, keep an eye on it, and if things are turning out differently, go and discuss the new circumstances with your manager.
- If your business is beginning to struggle, the last thing you should do is avoid your manager. Go and discuss the problems you are aware of and the solutions you have identified.
- Don't just rely on your banker for advice; discuss your business with other advisers such as your accountant. Make use of the many business help sites on the internet such as the Government Business Link (http://www.businesslink.gov.uk).

When you are looking for additional assistance to help you grow, prepare your business plan carefully and don't forget to state how you plan to repay your debt.

The more money you want to borrow, the more the bank may be interested in the security you can offer. Do you have friends or relatives who may be prepared to guarantee some or all of the debt?

■ The Small Firms Loan Guarantee Scheme has recently been relaunched and may be suitable for those who cannot offer the appropriate security (http://www. businesslink.gov.uk/bdotg/action/detail?r.s=sl&type=RESOURCES&itemId=1074 447105). To qualify, businesses must be under five years old and have a turnover of less than £5.6m.

Negotiate with your bank manager

Negotiate with your banker; if your business is successful, the manager needs you as much as you need him or her. Have a close look at the charges you are paying; see if there is any way to reduce them. Could you reduce the amount of cash you handle, for example?

When managing your bank manager, keep an eye on other offerings from competing banks. Surveys have shown that it could actually benefit you if you stay with your bank for a period of time because you get to know each other better. However, if you find the relationship is becoming unsatisfactory, be prepared to talk to other banks. Have a look at the website http://www.bba.org.uk/bba/jsp/polopoly.jsp?d=142&a=225, which gives details of the accounts and services offered to businesses by most of the banks in the United Kingdom.

If you have a broker you trust, you may find that he or she will be able help you find a sympathetic banker who is prepared to get involved in your business and go along with your plans.

Remember that banks have to comply with the Business Banking Code when transferring accounts. The process should be relatively painless.

The bankers I speak to on a regular basis tell me the competition for SME business has never been fiercer. Banks are looking for your business and now may be a good time to consider your options. If you want to grow your business, read this handbook, take advice and manage your bank manager.

Stewart Dickey is the policy director responsible for small business banking issues at the British Bankers' Association, a trade association representing approximately 200 banks operating in the UK. More information for small and medium enterprises can be found on the BBA website: www.bba.org.uk.

Challenges for tax planning in the growth cycle

Raising money? Developing products? Spending capital? Incentivizing staff? Making an acquisition? All these growth activities have significant tax implications that can hold back profitability, says David Mansell at Mazars

You are incredibly busy – managing conflicting deadlines and juggling your business and personal lives. Your focus is to grow the business profitably. Are you sometimes tempted to ignore the tax issues and leave them to your accountant to sort out at the end of the year? In the scheme of things, is tax really important?

Yes, it is. Tax will impact on virtually every decision you make. For example:

■ What can I give my manager to make him or her stay for the long term?
■ How can I find the extra cash to develop my product?
■ Where can I find some extra working capital?
■ It would make sense to set up a manufacturing/service centre abroad. What will that do to my affairs in the United Kingdom?
■ I have found a great business to bolt on to mine that would really add value. How do I structure the acquisition?

In the scope of this chapter it is not possible to cover everything you may need to know, so I have highlighted five key areas:

■ raising additional finance;
■ product development;
■ capital spend;
■ staff retention and incentives;
■ acquisitions.

Raising additional finance

When raising funds, essentially you have two choices: 1) loans; and 2) equity.

Loans

The position on loan finance is relatively clear: there is no tax relief on capital repayments but tax relief is available on interest costs. One point to bear in mind is that tax relief is also available on the costs of raising loan finance (eg the bank arrangement fee) even if these are capitalized in your accounts.

Equity

The commercial implications of issuing new equity can be great but, looking just at the tax impact, can you structure your business to make it more attractive to new investors?

There are essentially three classes of investor and potential reliefs to benefit them:

■ Individuals → Enterprise Investment Relief (EIS);
■ Companies Corporate → Venturing Relief (CVS);
■ Venture Capital Trusts (VCTs) → requirement to invest in a qualifying company.

Provided certain conditions are met:

■ EIS provides income tax relief at 20% on the amount subscribed up to £400,000, it gives the ability to defer capital gains on the total amount subscribed and it provides for exemption from capital gains tax on sale.
■ CVS provides corporation tax relief on the amount subscribed and the ability to defer the gain on any disposal of the CVS shares into the next CVS investment.

The qualifying conditions are broadly similar and relate to the trade carried on; the quantum of non-trading activity (capped at 20 per cent) and gross assets being less than £8 million after the issue of new shares.

Product development

The key relief in the area of product development is research and development relief. This provides for tax relief on, broadly, relevant salaries and consumables at 125 per cent or 150 per cent of spend, depending on the number of employees and whether or not your company is large by Companies Act definitions. It additionally provides for capital allowances at 100 per cent on relevant equipment.

To see whether your product creation and/or development would qualify, you should look at the DTI and HMRC websites: links may be found at www.hmrc.gov. uk/randd/qualify.htm.

Capital spend

It is important to review capital spend to see what capital allowances are available:

- 100% on green technology – see www.eca.gov.uk (should your product be registered?);
- 50% or 40% first-year allowances for certain businesses on plant and machinery;
- 25% on plant, fixtures, cars (capped at £3,000 pa);
- 6% on plant with a life in excess of 25 years;
- 4% on industrial buildings.

You will appreciate that it is important to review properly the nature of the spend to maximize tax relief.

If plant and the like are to be leased, the key areas to consider are whether the leases will be:

- finance leases, where the lessee takes on the risks and rewards of ownership that provide for tax relief on interest costs and depreciation;
- operating leases with a life in excess of five years – tax position as above;
- other operating leases – tax relief on lease costs (capped for cars with a value in excess of £12,000).

Staff retention and incentives

Staff retention and incentives is a huge area and this chapter cannot cover all issues, so I have concentrated on two: share incentives, and tax-effective payments and benefits.

Share incentives

Approved share schemes can offer your employees a guaranteed right to subscribe for shares in your company at an agreed future date at today's price. You can link the right to, among others, continuing employment, performance, or sale/flotation of the company. The last of these can give employees a share in ultimate value with no cash commitment up front and no entitlement if they leave before the event but, in the meantime, no shareholder rights and all with a potential 10 per cent tax charge.

There are various types of share scheme offering different benefits, with different qualification criteria. You should look at the rules in detail before making any decision.

Tax-effective payments and benefits

Set out below is a brief (and by no means comprehensive) list of some tax-favoured payments:

- mileage allowances for business miles in private cars: 40p per mile for the first 10,000 miles, thereafter 25p;
- provision of workplace parking;
- incidental overnight expenses, eg telephone, newspapers, etc up to £5 per night;
- works transport facilities;
- employer-provided cycles and safety helmets;
- late-night transport home;
- annual party – up to £150 per head;
- childcare vouchers – increased to £55 per week in the most recent Budget;
- mobile phones – now limited to one per employee, and extended to cover vouchers in the Budget;
- reimbursement of removal costs up to £8,000;
- pension contributions;
- provision of uniforms or protective clothing;
- canteen facilities open to all staff at a particular site.

Acquisitions

Shares versus assets

For you, the key question on any acquisition is shares or assets. For buyers, assets offer more advantages: no acceptance of history, tax relief on plant, goodwill, etc. For sellers, a sale of shares normally provides a tax charge at 10 per cent whereas a sale of assets out of a company gives rise to an additional tax charge in the company before any personal realization of proceeds. This can only be resolved by negotiation.

Structuring for the future

The Substantial Shareholdings Exemption provides (very simplistically) for an exemption from tax on the disposal of a subsidiary out of a trading group. Because of this relief it is now sensible at least to consider a group structure for acquisitions to provide the possibility of relief on a future sale of part of the business, as shown in Figure 7.4.1.

The structure provides additional opportunities, including the ability to provide transparent reward structures in each company, easy separation and recharge as

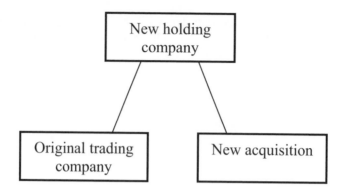

Figure 7.4.1   Group structure for acquisitions

required of main board costs, and some corporate protection in the event of one business failing. It is a relatively simple process to establish the structure but does require a formal clearance from HM Revenue & Customs.

In conclusion

In any growing business, decisions have to be made, and made quickly. However, the impact of tax on decision making may be substantial and should not be ignored. If you are not absolutely sure of the tax impact on any decision, ask a specialist.

David Mansell is a tax partner in Mazars' Nottingham office. He has extensive experience of providing tax compliance and planning advice to companies at all stages of growth and to their directors. Unusually for a tax partner, David began his career with a clearing bank, where he worked for twelve years, in a range of managerial roles. He then trained with KPMG prior to joining BDO Stoy Hayward as a Senior Manager in their tax department. David specialises in advising on complex tax issues, including tax efficient deal structuring, group reorganizations, employee incentivization and transfer pricing.

Mazars acts for some of the fastest-growing entrepreneurial companies in the UK, offering a complete range of accountancy and business advisory services including: audit and assurance, tax advisory and compliance, corporate recovery and insolvency, consulting, forensic and investigations, corporate finance and financial services for private individuals.

Tel: 0115 943 5363
e-mail: david.mansell@mazars.co.uk
www.mazars.co.uk

Treasury risks

Interest rates, exchange rates, commodity prices, energy prices? All these have the potential to produce shocks, warns Paul Gamba of the Treasury Solutions Group at The Royal Bank of Scotland

To what extent should growing businesses be concerned about treasury risk management? Managing the risk generated by volatile foreign exchange rates and taking as much uncertainty as possible out of interest rate management may look like the territory solely occupied by the United Kingdom's larger businesses. However, for the growing business it will be increasingly important as it progresses with its own development strategy.

Across our entire customer base, we encourage businesses of all sizes to take a longer-term view of economic events and consider the potential for the unexpected to happen – such as the rise in oil-related fuel costs. The actual impact of market events on the bottom line will of course be variable, and naturally driven to a large extent by the size of the exposures the business has, such as the total extent of borrowing or the level of currency purchased and/or sold each year from international activities.

At some stage the business will get to a level where the potential impact of movements in areas such as interest and exchange rates becomes a problem, something that the entrepreneur or business manager feels is a big enough issue to want to investigate how it can be controlled. In The Royal Bank of Scotland (RBS) we normally start having these conversations with customers who have total medium- or long-term borrowing of £500,000-plus or who have currency volumes of at least £500,000 per year.

Most businesses confronting these issues will tend to associate financial markets risk management with foreign exchange and interest rates, which remain extremely important and will account for the bulk of our risk management activity. However, we see our involvement with businesses as an increasingly broader proposition. From our teams based in six key locations across Britain, we provide risk management services covering a wide range of issues that could affect our customers, such as commodity, inflation and credit risk.

For the growing business, most often the initial contact we have with its managers will be their first experience of investigating treasury management techniques. Now this can sound horribly complex and, if not handled correctly, can turn customers away from investigating how they control their key financial risks. Certainly some of the jargon and language used in the financial markets can act as a deterrent, so we take a different approach.

Our approach is to focus on customers and the real financial variables that drive their business and assess, with them, a range of potential solutions to the challenges they could face. For example, customers may be concerned about increased input costs, possibly energy or raw material related, and come to us for ideas on how the underlying commodity price can be controlled within parameters that are important to them, such as key budget rates. Others will be coming to us with their budgeted foreign exchange rates for the year and will be looking to protect either cost or revenue streams against these critical levels. Others will want to make sure that, despite an apparently benign interest rate outlook, they manage the risk of interest rates rising, as they are borrowing over a much longer-term horizon.

In all of these cases the key for us is to deliver a timely and appropriate solution, and that comes from clearly understanding the client's needs. So, for the growing business, what are the important issues to concentrate on? Interest rates, exchange rates, commodity prices, energy prices? The answer is that the important ones are those that have an underlying potentially sizeable impact on the financial health of the business.

For growing businesses, typically borrowing to fund an ambitious growth plan, clearly the level of interest rates will be a key variable, and a real consideration should be to identify the level of interest rates that place profitability or the planned financial outcome for the business at risk. For us, a considered and detailed conversation around why this is important to the business and the constraints it has to work within is the starting point to creating a range of potential solutions.

The same can be said for businesses looking to grow by entering new overseas markets. Often businesses in this position see the potential additional overseas markets as great opportunities without considering the additional risks they will be facing. That's fine if you can persuade overseas customers to pay you in sterling or get agreement from suppliers to take sterling from you, but that isn't always possible and you will more likely be faced with an income or cost base that has an indeterminate value. A discussion around why that is important to the people driving and growing the business is the starting point for creating solutions.

No doubt you can spot a trend here. The discussion around what is important to the business and the potential financial impact that the growth strategy can have is absolutely key. Without that level of engagement and discussion of the real issues confronting the business, providers of financial solutions are merely pulling pre-packaged 'products' off the shelf. Some may fit and some may not. You could get lucky.

For us, getting to the bottom of the potential issues a growing business may face is the starting point to creating solutions. There are plenty of financial products out there. However, the really talented risk manager will do a large amount of listening and questioning before blending a range of instruments together that create a range of solutions. The next stage is to discuss these in detail with the customer to find the preferred solution.

Paul Gamba is Director of Business Strategy at The Royal Bank of Scotland Treasury Solutions Group. The Treasury Solutions Group is part of the RBS Global Banking & Markets division and provides businesses in the UK with a broad based financial markets risk management services.

Paul joined RBS in 1984 as a graduate trainee and has worked in several locations throughout the UK in both Corporate & Commercial Banking, Marketing and Treasury Solutions businesses. He first became involved in treasury related business in London in 1990 and is now based in Edinburgh where he forms part of the management team for the Treasury Solutions Group.

Contact details:
Tel: 0131 525 2020
e-mail: paul.gamba@rbos.com

For further information please contact your local RBS UK Treasury Solutions Group team:

London and South East Commercial
135 Bishopsgate
London EC2M 3UR
Tel: 020 7085 1415

London Corporate
135 Bishopsgate
London EC2M 3UR
Tel: 020 7085 1370

Midlands
5th Floor
2 St Philips Place
Birmingham B3 2RB
Tel: 0121 233 5244

North West
6th Floor
1 Spinningfields Square
Manchester M3 3AP
Tel: 0161 941 0500

South and South West
3rd Floor
Phase II, Trinity Quay
Avon Street
Bristol BS2 0YY
0117 940 3233

Yorkshire and North East
Whitehall II
3rd Floor
2 Whitehall Quay
Leeds LS1 4HR
Tel: 0113 397 2510

Scotland
Gemini House
24–25 St Andrew Square
Edinburgh EH2 1AF
Tel: 0131 525 2046

Or visit us at www.rbsmarkets.com.

Energy contracts

What are the options for buying energy in the face of rising prices and market volatility, asks Dr Sebastian Eyre at John Hall Associates, the energy market analyst

Rising commodity prices and increased market volatility mean that the days when buyers could simply tender on the basis of a fixed price are long gone. Energy procurement has undergone a quiet revolution over the past couple of years as buyers can no longer exploit falling prices. Effective buying now requires an increasingly sophisticated knowledge of the marketplace.

Buyers are now exposed to a number of increasingly complex markets, which means that purchasing decisions cannot be made on a simple unit cost basis alone. There are a number of supplier offerings that essentially trade off budgetary certainty against price. This chapter outlines the factors driving the market and then considers the types of contract available in the industrial and commercial retail market. I argue that today's buyers now have to consider and adjust their risk aversion profiles accordingly.

Increases in commodity prices

Over the course of the past year, *energy* as an issue moved up the boardroom agenda, given that UK industrial and commercial consumers witnessed substantially higher energy costs in real terms. This was due in part to the marked increase in the global energy complex. Oil prices rose significantly, owing to the highest rate of demand growth in nearly 30 years, to average some $61.78 so far in 2006, representing an increase of 22 per cent on the 2005 average. Meanwhile, coal prices have increased

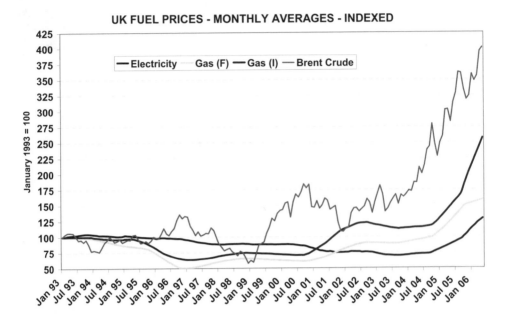

Figure 7.6.1 Trends in UK fuel prices

marginally from 2005, averaging $61.23/tonne so far this year. In July 2006, Brent prices topped $76 per barrel.

The increase in global energy prices led local markets in the United Kingdom to rise. The operation of the Bacton–Zeebrugge interconnector has led to the re-establishment of an oil–gas price link in the UK market, since gas on the Continent is priced using formulae linked to oil price movements. These markets were also affected by perceptions of issues on security of supply and environmental constraints as a result of new European legislation. Accordingly, the wholesale gas price for a 12-month supply contract from October 2006 increased by 37 per cent compared to 2005, to average 64.07 pence per therm (ppt) so far this year. Meanwhile, rising gas-fired generation input costs helped the UK wholesale electricity price for a year's supply from October 2006 to rise approximately 30 per cent when compared to 2005 average prices, to average £54.27/MWh in trading so far this year.

With hindsight, we know the markets were following an underlying upward trend, and the rational move would have been to settle supply contracts well before the October start date. Although John Hall Associates (JHA) advised buyers to do exactly that, many buyers vacillated in the belief, now seen to be unfortunate, that prices would ease before the end of the summer. This serves to illustrate just how complex the interaction of market drivers and the importance in having a strategy can be.

Complex and volatile energy markets

The burden of increased energy costs for industrial and commercial consumers results from the interaction between a set of various market drivers. Clearly, in the UK gas market, unexpected weather, seasonality and North Sea production levels define the underlying supply and demand conditions.

However, placed in the strategic context of declining indigenous production, an understanding of price movements is further complicated by the interplay between gas storage levels, the operation of the interconnector pipeline between Bacton and Zeebrugge, and the importation of liquefied natural gas (LNG). In addition, consumers are troubled by the general lack of market transparency and asymmetrical provision of market data. Moreover, just as the United Kingdom is moving towards becoming a net importer of gas, the Government has developed energy policies to reduce carbon emissions that will have had a fundamental impact on the United Kingdom's generation mix and demand for gas, and hence market prices.

An understanding of the market must involve an awareness of the interaction between three sets of factors:

■ the underlying industrial economics of the industry (supply and demand);
■ interplay between world energy markets and geopolitical events;
■ commodity trading activity.

It is worth noting that data for the underlying economics of the industry are difficult to obtain but relatively easy to model. For example, details of field maintenance in the North Sea may be commercially sensitive, but if they were available then it would aid the understanding of the resulting change in the supply–demand balance.

Market-driven explanations are easy to understand but can be difficult to predict. For example, a new record high of 70.00 ppt was set in the NBP prompt market in January 2004 when forecasts of very cold weather were compounded by news that withdrawals from the offshore Rough storage facility had been temporarily curtailed.

Meanwhile, geopolitical events are well reported but it is harder to gauge their impact on the market, and the duration of impact. For example, there was a degree of uncertainty over how much oil Iraq would produce during 2004. It was thought that, given infrastructure constraints, production would stabilize in the region of around 2.5 million b/d. For much of the year, however, the country's insurgency meant that production and exports subsequently remained intermittent. This in itself was not enough to seriously impact on oil prices. However, when placed in the context of a surge in global demand and the uncertainty over dwindling OPEC spare capacity, it did.

In addition, although there was no major attack against a Saudi installation, market fears served to underline a belief that regional insecurity added a premium of several dollars to a barrel of oil.

Prices have increased substantially

The combination of the industrial economic base, political economy and the resultant trading activity conspired to push energy prices to new highs. In the United Kingdom the largest cost component of any industrial energy buyer's bill is the cost of the commodity, ie the gas or power itself. As a consequence, industrial and commercial end-user gas and power prices rose substantially in 2005/06.

An analysis of fixed-price contracts for industrial and commercial consumer prices reveals that interruptible (sites with consumption in excess of 200,000 therms per annum) contract prices rose compared to June 2005. At that time, the weighted average price paid was 33.31 ppt. By June 2006 the weighted average price of gas for contracts had risen to 58.63 ppt. This represents an increase of 76 per cent.

For sites with firm gas consumption in excess of 25,000 therms per annum, the weighted average price of gas in June 2006 rose to 56.13 ppt compared to 45.52 ppt the same time a year earlier. This is an increase of 23.3 per cent. Meanwhile, when sites with consumption of less than 25,000 therms a year are considered, the weighted average price of delivered gas rose from 51.23 ppt in June 2005 to 65.88 ppt in June 2006. This represents an increase of 28.6 per cent. Given that gas forms approximately 40 per cent of the United Kingdom's generation portfolio, this in part led the price that industrial and commercial consumers paid for their power to rise too. Once again this was based on the increase in wholesale electricity prices.

According to the JHA electricity portfolio, for sites with maximum demand of over 1 MW, the delivered price increased from 3.82 p/kWh in May 2005 to 5.37 p/kWh in May 2006, representing an increase of 40.6 per cent. In the smaller 100 kW-plus market, the delivered price paid by industrial and commercial consumers rose from 4.55 p/kWh in May 2005 to 5.84 p/kWh in May 2006. This is an increase of 28.4 per cent. The 100kW-plus sector has tended to have a fairly constant rate of increase over the past couple of years whereas the higher rate of increase in the 1MW-plus sector can be seen partially as a correction to the sector previously increasing at lower rates than the 100kW-plus sector.

Risk management and financial tools

Price volatility in the energy commodity markets has spurred industrial and commercial buyers to consider managing their risk by contracting for shorter periods of delivery or employing financial tools. The traditional option of fixing a price for a year means that the buyer only has one chance of making the correct decision. Inherent in this decision is a perception of the risk associated with the combination of the industrial economic base, political economics and the resultant trading activity at the time of settling the price. This increases the likelihood that the decision will be made at the wrong time. However, flexible procurement options offer the buyer the chance to mitigate this risk by contracting for supply over shorter delivery periods. This allows the consumer to stay closer to the market and make decisions which reflect market reality.

Indexation

Indexed options include contracting over a variety of delivery periods such as on the day of consumption (within-day), the day before (day-ahead) or the month before (month-ahead). However, different indices are affected by different market drivers. Within-day and day-ahead indices are flexible, reflecting the reality of the supply–demand balance. They also happen to be the most volatile, with significant daily price swings. Over the longer term, however, they do provide a better performance than an index covering a longer period. The month-ahead index is more likely to be affected by more seasonal perceptions of supply and demand. Meanwhile, seasonal and quarterly prices may be influenced by the price of related energy commodities such as oil.

Alternatively, a combination of flexible pricing options known as a matrix may be employed. This allows the purchaser to buy gas by splitting the volume for a certain period of consumption into 'tranches' and buying over time. However, this is the most complex and time-consuming of options.

In the power market too, owing to the unprecedented increases in prices there has been a growing trend towards indexation. A number of large industrial and commercial customers are opting to arrange a more flexible option with their supplier. The possibilities include monthly purchasing, quarterly purchasing and purchasing on an indexed basis, although suppliers have been willing to consider a variety of options that buyers have put to them.

Hedging

Financial hedging tools may be used in conjunction with indexed pricing contracts to trade risk against budgetary certainty. A number of standard financial tools are on offer from a range of providers, including banks and suppliers' trading arms. There are a number of pricing arrangements a buyer could choose, including swaps, caps, collars and costless collars.

A swap price is calculated by an average of the futures prices for the period of the swap. The seller pays the buyer the difference when the market is above the swap price and the buyer pays seller the difference when the market is below the swap price. The swap gives protection against adverse market movements, but no benefit from beneficial market movements.

An alternative form of this type of shared risk agreement is the use of caps and collars. These are similar tools in that they allow the price to float against an index, but, in contrast to a swap price, are arranged within pre-agreed limits. A cap provides an upper limit that the price may not exceed and a collar provides a lower limit to which the price will not fall. With a cap, the benefit of lower market prices is achieved and the risk of high prices is limited to the value placed on the cap. With a collar there is a benefit of limiting exposure to risk and at lower cost than a cap; however, the benefit of lower prices is also limited.

An option provides the buyer with a right, but not an obligation, to buy a specific volume at a pre-agreed price on or before a specific date. The seller is obliged to fulfil the price if the buyer exercises that right. The strike price and time period unexpired influence the price of the option. An option provides a known maximum price for a period of time. If during the intervening period the price falls, the lower price can be taken.

Exceptions

However, indexation or financial tools are not available to all types of consumer. Conversely, businesses or public-sector organizations with multi-site supply contracts and low individual consumption generally favour, or indeed have no option but to take, a fixed price contract. They are more likely to be risk averse, preferring the certainty that a fixed price offers.

In these situations the strategy surrounding the timing of contract settlement becomes important. To mitigate risk, consumers should be prepared to act on a timely basis. This involves ensuring that tender information is as accurate as possible. By looking further ahead when contracting their gas and electricity supplies they are more likely to encounter a greater number of windows of opportunity. With this in mind, tenders should be in the market as soon as possible with a view to settling at any time. For example, on a historical basis the best electricity wholesale price for October 2005 was in December 2003, when it reached £23.90/MWh. The best wholesale gas price for October 2005 was in October 2003, when the price was 22.33 ppt, though in practice many consumers are unable to buy this far ahead.

For some, though, price is not the only issue, and these consumers may weight a competitive offer against the level of service they can expect to receive. In some instances, staying with the incumbent supplier has been the preferred option. Buyers with multi-site business may prefer to stay with their incumbent rather than run the risk of problems relating to administration or registration, despite losing the chance of making savings.

Diesel

Diesel prices in the United Kingdom are closely linked to prices traded in the North-West European regional market, which is based around the hub of Amsterdam–Rotterdam–Antwerp, commonly known as 'ARA'. The North-West European (NWE) region forms just one part of an interconnected system of regional markets and should be viewed in the context of what happens globally. Prices largely move in relation to crude oil prices as well as being influenced by the underlying refining economics, geopolitics and trading opportunities.

The monthly average diesel price during June 2006 was 78.32 pence per litre (ppl), a decrease on the May average of 79.01 ppl of 0.9 per cent. Twelve months ago the average price was 73.05 ppl. The recent increase in crude oil prices will eventually filter through to the UK bulk market, with the likelihood that prices will rise above 80.00 ppl.

Procurement is normally made on a lagged basis whereby the unit price for a future delivery period – for example, the next five working days (otherwise known as a weekly-lagged formula) – is set by averaging daily prices as quoted by a price information provider such as Platts or Argus over a previous number of days. The price structure includes three elements: the cost of the commodity, the duty and the margin. The buyer is unable to do much about the first two elements, so options available to buyers simply reflect their ability to influence the margin, ie the cost of delivery. A customer's ability to influence the margin will vary depending on the geographic location of the site in relation to the terminal, as well as on its ability or otherwise to accept loads over 30,000 litres.

Large logistics companies may also have the ability to procure a proportion of their consumption by paying the spot price, which can reduce the margin. This gives them the flexibility to take advantage of more favourable market conditions, although this does require a certain level of market intelligence. For smaller buyers, fuel cards are more appropriate, though their utility can be limited by the geographical distribution of participating garage chains.

Conclusion

In summary, rising energy prices and increased market volatility have led to a change in buyer behaviour, which now requires a sophisticated knowledge of the marketplace. Energy as an issue has moved up the boardroom agenda, given that buyers are witnessing higher energy costs in real terms due to the marked increase in the global energy complex. With hindsight, the rational decision would have been to settle supply contracts early last year. Many buyers unfortunately adopted a reactive strategy rather than a proactive one.

The burden of increased energy costs results from the interaction between a set of various market drivers. An understanding of these is underpinned by the awareness of the impact that the combination of industrial economics, political economy and trading activity has.

Price volatility has spurred buyers to consider managing their risk by contracting for shorter periods of delivery or employing financial tools. The traditional option of fixing a price for a year means that the buyer only has one chance of making the correct decision. This increases the likelihood that the decision will be wrong.

Flexibility offers the buyer the chance to mitigate risk by contracting for shorter delivery periods, which are governed by a more manageable set of market drivers. However, different indices are driven by different drivers that reflect differing levels of volatility. Financial hedging tools may be used in conjunction with indexed pricing contracts to trade risk against budgetary certainty.

However, indexation or financial tools are not available to all types of consumer. Indeed, because of their needs they may favour, or have no option but to take, a fixed price contract. In these situations the strategy surrounding the timing of contract settlement becomes important. To mitigate risk, consumers should be prepared to act on a timely basis.

The market is increasingly complex, which leads to a need for greater understanding of it, leading to an understanding of risk aversion. A number of tools can be employed, with differing trade-offs. These have to be matched with an individual customers risk profile. Ultimately the best course of action is to seek advice.

John Hall Associates has been specializing in energy market analysis and energy audits since 1973. For further information, please contact Dr Sebastian Eyre or Damien Cox, 9 Piries Place, Horsham RH12 1EH (tel: + 44 (0)1403 269430; e-mail: info@jha.co.uk; website: www.jha.co.uk).

The Esso fuel card: driving down fuel costs for your business

Introduction

For many businesses, especially small and medium-sized companies, fuel is one of the most significant expenses. Cost control is an essential part of running a successful business, and fuel cards can assist a business with precise monitoring and management of fuel costs.

Today, some companies still use outdated methods of paying for fuel, such as pay and reclaim. Asking employees and drivers to pay for their fuel, obtain (and not lose) receipts and reclaim the expenses puts unnecessary pressure on both the drivers and the company administrators or transport managers. In addition to being a laborious method of paying for fuel, this makes it very difficult for a business to monitor and control fuel expenditure. Using a company credit card is little better. Apart from providing a credit period, this method presents the same problems and lack of control as paying with cash.

Fuel card benefits

Esso Card has evolved over many years by working with our customers to develop a business tool to deliver powerful benefits that can really make a difference. The benefits of the Esso fuel card are numerous:

- They offer a convenient and cashless method of payment.
- They reduce administration and provide valuable time saving with accounting.
- Fuel card operators can provide vital management information that can be used to monitor and help control fleet costs.

Driving Down Fuel Costs for
Your Business with Esso

For many businesses, fuel is one of the most significant expenses. Cost control is an essential part of running a successful business and an Esso fuel card can help by providing precise monitoring and control.

Benefits

Esso Card offers a convenient and cashless method of payment. Esso Card reduces administration and provides valuable time saving with accounting. The Esso Card can provide vital management information to help monitor and control fleet costs. The cards themselves can be tailored to the individual's needs of your business and drivers.

Coverage

Esso Card provides you access to a national network of around 950 service stations, or 1,850 with the extended network card (with Shell). Esso's motorway service stations make up 30% of the motorway network (or 45% with the extended network).

Network Investment

Over the last 2 years, Esso have undertaken a multi-million pound investment programme in a revolutionary new convenience retailing and cafe brand – 'On the Run'.

'On the Run' addresses the needs of today's consumer. It is 'Fast, Fresh & Friendly' combining, an enhanced convenience store with a cafe/bakery style offering with an extensive range of hot and cold food with an easy access and quick fuel sales offering. 'On the Run' sites are very competitively priced sites due to their location and local markets.

e-Business

Esso Card's new e-business service makes managing your fleet so much easier. It puts all your account details at your fingertips, so you can access everything online in seconds, whenever and wherever it suits you. The new service allows you to:

- View transactions within 24 hours
- View new and historic invoices
- Faster card management, ie. New and replacement cards, cancellation, etc
- Access to fleet management reports and summaries

Customer Care

A friendly and efficient after sales and account management service is available to make sure that all your fuel card needs are met.

To find out how your business would benefit from Esso Card please contact:
Freephone number: **0800 626 672**
e-mail: **essocardsales.uk@exxonmobil.com**
or visit our website at **www.essocard.com**

Relief for fleet drivers

Receipts? Expenses claims?
The remedy is a phone call away
Freephone 0800 626 672

We're drivers too.

■ The cards can be tailored to the company's requirements, helping to prevent driver misuse of the card.

Cost savings

As already mentioned, controlling fuel costs is paramount to companies of all sizes. Dependent on a company's annual fuel spend, Esso Card can offer competitive pricing and credit terms to enable the fleet manager to keep a tight control on the company's costs and cash flow.

Online invoicing and administration

An Esso fuel card does not just benefit the on-the-road employees. For the company fleet manager or the owner of the business, the Esso fuel card can take away the headache of administering fleet fuel costs and make the process easier and more efficient.

Once up and running, Esso Card will provide a single VAT invoice or multiple invoicing and payment points that can be used to track fleet costs. Alternatively, customers can elect to register for the new Esso Card e-business service. By putting all your fleet account details at your fingertips, Esso Card e-business allows you to access everything you need in seconds online, whenever and wherever it suits you. The service allows you:

■ to view transactions within 24 hours;
■ to view new and historic invoices;
■ faster card management, ie when ordering new and replacement cards, cancelling, etc;
■ access to fleet management reports and summaries, enabling you to analyse your costs and spending patterns, of both invoiced and un-invoiced transactions.

Having access to un-invoiced transactions has many benefits for fleet managers, especially businesses that use contract drivers on a short-term basis. Moreover, being able to view transactions within 24 hours allows you to monitor fuel spend even more closely.

Fleet management reports

Esso Card's fleet management reports can be a vital aid in keeping tighter control on your budgets. Now freely available as part of our e-business service, the following are the most commonly used:

- MKII Transactions Extract is produced from your invoiced transactions and enables the 'electronic' reconciliation of your invoice. This extract can be downloaded for both UK and international transactions.
- Volume summary shows the volume and invoiced amount for the period and is broken down by cost centre, invoice date and product.
- Invoice summary provides a breakdown of purchases by cost centre showing volume and invoiced value for each grade of fuel or non-fuel product.

All fleet management reports can be downloaded and/or printed.

Security

Esso fuel cards can be driver name or vehicle registration specific and can be restricted to the purchase of one type of fuel, specific additional vehicle products, shop goods or car wash.

A card hot-listing service can help ensure that your business has optimum control over any potential card fraud. Replacements for lost or stolen cards can be supplied quickly, to keep your drivers on the road. Additional safety features include the ability to restrict the number of card transactions in a day and towards the end of 2006, PIN cards will be introduced.

For company employees on the road, an Esso fuel card can make life that little bit easier. With a nationwide network of conveniently located service stations, a driver can have the peace of mind of being able to refuel without worry.

Coverage

With Esso Card you and your drivers have access to a national network of around 950 service stations, or, with the extended network card (with Shell), up to 2,000 service stations. Esso's motorway service stations make up 30 per cent of the motorway network (or 45 per cent of the extended network).

Service station investment

Over the past two years, Esso has undertaken a multi-million-pound investment programme in a revolutionary new convenience retailing and café brand: 'On the Run'. 'On the Run' recognizes evolving lifestyles and addresses the needs of today's consumer. It is 'fast, fresh and friendly', combining an enhanced convenience store with a café/bakery-style offering with an extensive range of hot and cold food, easy access and quick fuel sales. Moreover, our 'On the Run' sites are competitively priced.

Convenience store offering including café and bakery

The stores are more spacious and comfortable, with more facilities, including hot food with café-style seating or standing areas in some of the large sites, as well as ATMs and toilet facilities. The product range will be tailored to suit the needs of our customers and their lifestyles, and many outlets will also sell wine and beer.

Hot and cold food for all tastes are prepared: hot pizza slices, juicy breakfast rolls and a cosmopolitan selection of fresh sandwiches and salads, combined with an extensive range of coffee and tea. Customers can take time out to eat on-site or take the food away and enjoy it on their journey.

International Esso card

Our European Esso Card is available to customers to use across continental Europe, giving access to approximately 8,000 Esso service stations across 19 countries, many of which include specialist facilities for commercial vehicles and trucks. Furthermore, there is the option to extend this to 17,000 service stations through Shell sites and other affiliated service stations, across 24 countries.

Tolls

Access to the Continent brings with it payments for road taxes, tolls and tunnels. Dealing with toll payments can be a tedious and time-consuming process. Motorway, bridge and tunnel toll barriers cause additional paperwork, administration and extra payments. However, Esso Card can facilitate the handling for you, easing payment and avoiding delays.

Through our recommended agent, you have access to one single contact for toll cards in Europe and the convenience of settling all fees/charges via your Esso Card payments. You will receive clear invoices but you don't have to deal with additional bank transfers and payments.

With the toll card option, payment for motorways in France, Austria and Germany can be charged to your Esso Card account, avoiding the need for your drivers to carry cash and reclaim expenses.

VAT recovery

Filing for international value added tax recovery can be a time-consuming and arduous task. Your fleet drivers travel all over Europe making purchases of fuel or other goods and services. VAT normally applies to all of those purchases and can be as high as 21 per cent. Reclaiming the VAT makes good business sense but involves a substantial amount of multilingual administrative work and, sometimes, many months of delay before the claim is processed. Esso Card has set up an arrangement with a specialist VAT recovery agency that covers 17 countries across Europe:

Austria	Ireland	Slovakia
Belgium	Italy	Spain
Czech Republic	Luxembourg	Switzerland
France	Norway	The Netherlands
Germany	Poland	United Kingdom
Hungary	Portugal	

The agency will work with you directly and act to recover VAT on your behalf, whenever and wherever you are eligible.

Other products and value added services

Furthermore, the Esso fuel card can be used to purchase additional product options, such as:

- Car wash – make sure your fleet always looks clean and presentable. A well-presented fleet is a great advertisement for a professional business.
- Lubricants – using high-quality Esso or Mobil lubricants contributes towards lower fuel consumption and longer engine life.
- Vehicle accessories – giving your drivers the flexibility to purchase a wide range of accessories, including most of those essential items for their safety on the roads, from light bulbs and fuses to batteries and windscreen wipers.

Account management and what some of our customers have to say

Just as important, a friendly and efficient after-sales and account management service is available to make sure that all your fuel card needs are met.

EBB Paper delivers paper to printers and stationers throughout the Midlands and South of England. Philip Bourne says, 'We work in a very competitive industry and keeping costs under control is of paramount importance to us. We are staying with Esso, using Esso stations as our main choice, but also use Shell on the same card as a handy backup... We enjoy a good rapport with the Esso Card Centre staff, who have been extremely helpful to us whenever we call.'

Likewise, Alan Warner of BSW Heating has been a card customer since 1988. 'During that time we have been approached by other fuel suppliers wishing to obtain our business and it is a testament to the excellent service we enjoy from Esso that we remain a loyal and satisfied Esso customer.'

Finally, the Esso Card offers a straightforward and easy application process that ensures you receive your cards quickly, usually within seven working days of your application acceptance.

You can apply online at www.essocard.co.uk or Freephone 0800 626672 and speak to a friendly Esso Card representative.

Fuel cards

Fuel cards create an accounting trail that allow you to keep your fuel costs down to a minimum, argues Alyson Bawa at JetCard

If you are in business, you wouldn't dream of sending your drivers out on the road without a spare tyre or back-up in case of a breakdown. By sending them out without a fuel card, you are missing out on the most important part of today's business toolkit!

The EC Advocate General's decision in 2004 to ask the European Court to declare the United Kingdom in violation of the 6th VAT Directive could mean that many UK businesses will face an increase in their fuel costs, as they will be unable to reclaim input VAT. Currently, many UK businesses allow employees to purchase fuel and then the business reclaims the VAT on the fuel at 17.5 per cent.

The Directive states that VAT can only be reclaimed if the transaction is between two parties that are registered for VAT. If UK law is amended as a result of any ruling, employers could only continue to reclaim VAT on fuel transactions if the transaction is directly with a supplier. This could only be achieved via a fuel card or a company credit card that allows for billing to be made in the name of the employer.

So maybe getting a fuel card now is the answer. Fuel cards put you in the driving seat when it comes to controlling cost and saving money on your fuel and fuel-related purchases. You decide what your drivers can buy and where they can buy it – only at outlets where you know they will get value for money.

Fuel and related purchases are some of the largest parts of your budget, and fuel cards give you an accounting trail to help you run your business as efficiently as possible. They are accepted across the various networks, with some being cross-accepted, which would aim to give you more sites to call in at whilst out on the road.

So how do fuel cards work? They operate as charge cards for purchases of fuel as well as lubricants, car washing and shop goods. You can choose which of these product groups you want your drivers to be able to purchase. If you decide not to include shop goods, for example, your drivers cannot add confectionery or snacks to your fuel bill.

You are invoiced either weekly or monthly, depending on the card you choose. In the majority of cases the invoice you receive will be a VAT-approved document, making your VAT reclaim simple. The invoice will show vehicle registration number, mileage, outlet used and price of fuel. The format of the invoice differs between different cards but the majority give this information. The cards can be either driver or vehicle specific, allowing you the freedom to allocate cards as dictated by the needs of your business.

Most fuel cards offer the following, but you need to check whether there is a cost for them or not:

Online services

Technology is always striving to provide you with the efficiency that today's businesses demand and to support this with high levels of customer and information services. In order to achieve these goals there is a constant drive for more internet-based services that provide real solutions and add benefit to you as fuel card customers.

Fuel card administrators offer many services, such as the ability to order new cards or place lost cards on stop, but there are additional services that some customers may not be aware of. The two main services that are growing in popularity with fuel card customers are the e-bill and web fuel services. What are these services?

E-bill

An e-bill is effectively an electronic invoice and is a free service that is easy to set up on any computer. The benefits to you for using the e-bill service are as follows:

■ You will receive your invoice earlier.
■ Your invoice goes directly to the relevant person or department.
■ An e-bill reduces paperwork and filing.
■ Your e-bill can be stored electronically, printed or forwarded to others.
■ E-billing is approved by the relevant VAT regulatory bodies.
■ You can contact your fuel card supplier directly from your e-bill with any queries.
■ An e-bill is a more environmentally friendly method of receiving your invoice.

Web fuels

Web fuels is a service that allows you to view and download transactions for your company's vehicles directly from the main database and is username and password protected so that only you or selected members of your staff can have access to this service. The transactions are updated on a daily basis, and for transactions that took place on any given day, the data will be available for viewing or downloading by approximately 2.00 pm on the following working day.

With some fuel card providers the transaction data are stored in web fuels for two years and you can perform a search across all or specified vehicles in your fleet from any start and finish date during this two-year period. In addition, you can also view or download a complete list of your cards and their individual details, including: 1) vehicle registration/driver name embossed on the cards; and 2) individual card expiry date.

It could not be simpler to register online for this service, and the information provided could be a real benefit for your business.

Other services

Other services may include:

■ Card insurance.
■ Fuel card 'Guard' service, which is centred around concerns regarding possible frauds that could have a significant effect on your business. By paying a small monthly premium per card for this service, customers gain peace of mind when it comes to the security of their fuel cards.
■ Some fuel card providers offer an automated site locator service, which provides information on sites where you can use your fuel card. This service is available 24/7 whether you are in the office or on the road looking for the nearest site *en route*. Some locator services inform you whether the sites are suitable for HGV vehicles, which types of fuel they supply, including LPG, or whether the site is fully automated, for which you may require a PIN number. This is the easiest form of site location and is current. The problem with atlases or hard-copy site locators is that they usually go out of date quite quickly.

So, how do you choose the right one for your business?

If your drivers have the ability to choose the filling station they use, it is doubtful they will look for the cheapest. Most of the time it will be the nearest outlet when the red light comes on, or where they can collect vouchers, mugs or something similar. Back to route planning as a necessity! Choosing a national unbranded fuel card will not stop this, I'm afraid!

However, it sometimes comes down to good fuel management on the part of your driver. If you choose a branded fuel card of a low-priced oil company then your drivers cannot use an outlet charging a higher price. This may mean that they have to plan their fuelling in a more controlled manner but you can save money in the long run.

What are the other benefits to a fuel card? Some cards offer discounts on vehicle-related products such as tyre and exhaust repair, national breakdown recovery and windscreen replacement. Payments for these services are made via the fuel card, so you still receive only one fuel card invoice. This again reduces administration as well as ensuring that a good price is paid for these services and your drivers are not overcharged.

Last but definitely not least is the saving on time and reduced administration for your company. A fuel card can reduce your annual expenditure by 15–18 per cent by cutting down administration, eliminating fraudulent or incorrect claims from your drivers and simplifying VAT reclaim.

This figure is reached by the following:

- 4% fraudulent claims – such as the odd sandwich being paid for as petrol;
- 3% incorrect claims – losing petrol receipts, etc;
- 6% purchasing cheaper petrol/company participation in loyalty scheme;
- 2%–6% saving in administration costs.

So, in summary, if you have a fuel card, look into other cards to make sure you are still using the one best suited to your needs. If you do not have one, now may be the time to start looking!

Further information at www.jetcard.co.uk.

What is JetCard?

JetCard is a business charge card that allows you to take control of your fuel costs. Not only do you receive one monthly VAT approved invoice, giving you up to 6 weeks interest free credit, but you also determine the products that your drivers can purchase. You decide whether your cards are vehicle or driver specific and there are no minimum volume requirements. No card charges or monthly fees either!

With JetCard you know that your drivers are using the network that suits you and not just the local site to their house that may be charging a couple of pence more per litre. It may not be much each time but it can add up over a year – and you are paying for it!

On-line access to your account is available for you to look at for your current and historical data, order additional/replacement cards or stop cards if necessary. You can also choose whether to receive your invoice on-line or in hard copy.

JetCard is accepted nationwide at approx 800 outlets, including JetCards new extended network. This means that wherever you are in the country you can purchase your fuel on JetCard. For more details of the additional sites please ring 08457 44 40 44.

JetCard Benefits

AA National Breakdown Recovery
Sign up with one of Europe's largest uniformed patrol forces and get up to 35% discount with JetCard. You will receive Roadside Assistance, Home Start, Relay and Relay Plus.

Jet Car Valeting and Lubricants
As a JetCard customer you automatically receive 10% discount, off invoice, on your car valeting and lubricant purchases at all Jet outlets.

Site Locator Service
JetCard operates an automated telephone service 24/7 for you or your drivers to use either in the office or on the road. If you are away from your local site, wherever you are in the country you will be able to locate your nearest Jet outlet.

Workshop Payments*
JetCard can be used to pay for repairs, services and MOTs when you use Jet workshops or garages for your car maintenance. This means less invoices to receive, less paperwork and less payments coming out of your bank. It can all be done on your one monthly direct debit.

JetXtra
This gives all the employees of a JetCard account holder, the opportunity to register with us and get preferred pricing on a wide range of products and services. You can get up to 60% discount on high street prices on items from kettles to computers, holidays to cars. All at no cost to you in either administration or money!

*At participating sites only.

Apply On-line Now at **www.jetcard.co.uk** or call **08457 444044** and start saving you and your company both time and money.

"JetCard helped me take control"
of my rapidly expanding business

 the national fuel card for local business

What is JetCard?

JetCard is a business charge card that allows you to take control of your fuel costs. Not only do you receive one monthly VAT-approved invoice, giving you up to 6 weeks' interest-free credit, but you also determine the products that your drivers can purchase. You decide whether your cards are vehicle or driver specific and there are no minimum volume requirements. No card charges or monthly fees either!

With JetCard you know that your drivers are using the network that suits you and not just the site local to their house, which may be charging a couple of pence more per litre. It may not be much each time but it can add up over a year – and you are paying for it!

Online access to your account is available for you to look at for your current and historical data, order additional/replacement cards or stop cards if necessary. You can also choose whether to receive your invoice online or as hard copy.

JetCard is accepted nationwide at over 800 outlets, including JetCard's new, extended network. This means that wherever you are in the country you can purchase your fuel on JetCard. For more details of the additional sites, please ring 08457 44 40 44.

JetCard benefits

AA national breakdown recovery

Sign up with one of Europe's largest uniformed patrol forces and get up to 35 per cent discount with JetCard. You will receive Roadside Assistance, Home Start, Relay and Relay Plus.

JetCard valeting and lubricants

As a JetCard customer you automatically receive 10 per cent discount, off invoice, on your car valeting and lubricant purchases at all Jet outlets.

Site locator service

JetCard operates an automated telephone service 24/7 for you or your drivers to use either in the office or on the road. If you are away from your local site, wherever you are in the country you will be able to locate your nearest Jet outlet.

Workshop payments (at participating sites only)

JetCard can be used to pay for repairs, services and MOTs when you use Jet workshops or garages for your car maintenance. This means fewer invoices to receive, less paperwork and fewer payments coming out of your bank. It can all be done on your one monthly direct debit.

JetXtra

JetXtra gives all the employees of a JetCard account holder the opportunity to register with us and get preferred pricing on a wide range of products and services. You can get up to 60 per cent discount on high street prices on items from kettles to computers, holidays to cars. All at no cost to you in either administration or money!

Apply online now at www.jetcard.co.uk or call 08457 444044 and start saving you and your company both time and money.

8

Business technology and systems

The current trends in business travel are not sustainable. Can companies affect change?

Business travel today is both expensive and increasingly inefficient. Congested roads, rising fuel costs and a growing awareness of the impact on the environment are prompting businesses to look again at their travel arrangements. With continuing delays for businesses, this adds up to wasted hours travelling to and from meetings. A business trip for a two hour meeting typically entails spending six hours out of the office – time that can be used to boost productivity in the workplace as well as a better work-life balance. It also results in higher fuel bills and running costs for company cars. The RAC Foundation estimates that congestion costs the economy £20bn a year.

Videoconferencing in the work place has steadily increased over the last few years as businesses have become more aware of its benefits. The new generation of video conferencing systems uses the latest technological developments to improve quality and lower cost. The move to running video conferences over IP networks gives systems access to more bandwidth, improving audio and picture quality.

But it is not just large, multinational companies that can build a business case for visual communications as a way of reducing the need for face-to-face meetings.

Careful review of the company's travel budget will show that a video conference can be a viable alternative to many meetings, even allowing for the up-front cost of the equipment, installation, consulting and training.

Businesses also have an obligation, to assess and reduce the environmental impact of their operations. Travel is a significant contributor to pollution as well as congestion on the roads.

Transport accounts for one third of all UK energy use, and the Government expects CO_2 emissions to increase by as much as 30 per cent in the next five years. Even a relatively small reduction in the number of business flights or car journeys will have a quick and positive impact on a company's "environmental footprint".

Visual meeting technology gives businesses, and as importantly, employees, a choice. There will always be occasions when a face-to-face meeting is essential. But at other times, a well-planned video conference will do the job just as well, with less inconvenience and cost.

Managed well, it can reduce the need for journeys, saving companies costs and time, as well as easing some of the environmental consequences of business travel.

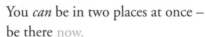

You *can* be in two places at once –
be there now.

In the current climate of uncertainty companies are aware of the need to consider alternatives to business travel, but what choice do they have?

Signalling the arrival of a new era in visual communication, TANDBERG High Definition videoconferencing will change the way people communicate. To outpace the competition, organisations must increase the speed and accuracy of information. With high-definition video in offices and meeting rooms, distributed teams can communicate with a clarity and frequency never before possible — it is as productive as sitting across the same desk.

Contact First Connections specialist in video conferencing consultancy and installation to find out more

Freephone 0800 096 6396 Email: info@firstconnections.co.uk www.firstconnections.co.uk

The Federation Against Software Theft (The Federation)

Federation Against Software Theft

The world's first anti-piracy organisation is still working to protect the intellectual property rights of its members 21 years since its inception.

The Federation is unique in that it works not only with the industry itself but also with end-users to counteract the spread of illegal use and copying.

Through their activities over £5.5m of software has been purchased during the last five years.

Software publishers, resellers, distributors and all those in the industry who join The Federation enjoy benefits which include;

- **Copyright enforcement on behalf of publisher members**
- **Internet enforcement**
- **Up to date legal information on related areas**
- **Legal workshops/seminars**
- **Entries on three websites**
- **Use of the Federation's logo**

End-Users can work toward the FAST Standard for Software Compliance, a private standard developed in collaboration with the BSi.

For more information please contact:

Anne Mead

Federation Against Software Theft

York House
18 York Road
Maidenhead
Berkshire SL6 1SF

Tel: +44 (0)1628 622121

Fax: +44 (0)1628 760338

www.fast.org.uk

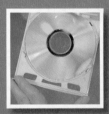

Making your way through the software asset management minefield

Chris Minchin, Membership Manager at FAST Corporate Services, discusses why software asset management should be a priority for businesses

The two main reasons why companies should look to manage their software assets are compliance and cash. Indeed, avoiding a jail sentence or a hefty fine is often the reason that most companies make software licensing compliance a priority. Yet a survey conducted by FAST Corporate Services found that 41 per cent of UK businesses could also be wasting thousands of pounds through over-licensing their software and not having measures in place to manage applications on the network.

Every business knows exactly how many company cars it owns, yet many do not have an accurate picture of how many PCs or software licences they have. Businesses need to recognize the fact that this area is just as valuable as fleet vehicles and other more tangible assets. Software licences are often regarded as intangible assets, unlike other items owned by the business.

Not only will undertaking an audit ensure that all software present on company PCs and other hardware such as personal digital assistants (PDAs) is licensed and legal, but having greater visibility of what is on the system could result in redeployment of software assets and cash channelled into other areas of the business.

Money down the drain

FAST's own experience suggests that when most companies conduct a software audit they discover they are actually over-licensed, sometimes by as much as 5–10 per cent. The main reason for over-licensing is that most companies simply do not know how many licences they actually require and therefore spend years over-buying licences that do not coincide with the needs of the business, just to avoid operating illegally. This process can then snowball and result in organizations having a huge surplus of licences that they do not use or need.

Businesses need to implement the correct procurement procedures and controls in order to avoid overspending and to remain in charge of their software assets. Carefully reading licence terms and conditions before purchasing can save a business money, as, for instance, some publishers may state that for every 10 licences you get 1 free, so a business of 50 employees would only need to buy 45 licences.

Over-licensing occurs because many IT managers deploy a standard suite of software across the whole organization even to employees who do not require certain packages, simply because it is easier to support and should make light work of any software licensing concerns. However, in many organizations the end-user will alter the standard desktop by personalizing it in some way, to the point that there is often no consistency amongst users and therefore it is no easier to support.

Some companies provide access to all software applications regardless of whether each individual needs them. For example, the accounts department is unlikely ever to use PowerPoint; likewise, a company director will not use the marketing team's design software. In these cases, redundant software should be uninstalled to avoid wasting money on over-licensing. If a business purchases a licence for every desktop and half of the business does not use a particular package then it is automatically throwing money down the drain.

Software that sits on the shelf because it is inappropriate, unusable or there is a lack of knowledge regarding its use is the most expensive, as the licence remains unused. Licences can also be made redundant when users leave the company or move to a different department. In some cases PCs may have been retired, yet the organization may still be paying support fees for the software that ran on those machines. This means that many companies are paying for maintenance on software that isn't needed any more. In fact, it can cost as much as 20 per cent of the purchase price to maintain software each year, so if you don't use it, uninstall it and store it. The product can always be reinstated if it is required in the future.

Legal compliance

Whilst the business benefits of effective software asset management are often anchored around a drive to save money, the threat of facing a jail sentence for not having licences in place should also set alarm bells ringing. Most people wouldn't watch TV or drive without a licence – so why are so many businesses, from large corporates to SMEs, using software without one? The answer in the majority of cases is ignorance. But, as software publishers crack down on piracy, businesses would do well to remember that ignorance is no defence in a court of law. Many company directors are still unaware that they face uncapped fines and up to 10 years' imprisonment for software theft, as stated in the Copyright Designs and Patents Act 1988 (section 107). Even when a case is not pursued in court, an out-of-court settlement could damage a company's reputation, not to mention its bottom line.

Improving asset management can therefore be a relatively simple process and can result in huge cost savings and legal compliance.

Setting boundaries

The first step towards improving the management of assets is to ensure that the appropriate policies and procedures are implemented so that employees know what they can and can't do. Just as there is no point in mopping up a flood when the taps are still running, doing a software audit is pointless without first telling staff what they may and may not do.

Ensuring that all staff know the business risks involved and the consequences they face if found not to be adhering to company policy is vital to facilitate software licensing compliance. Every member of staff should sign a document to say that they have read and understood the policies and procedures that have been put in place. Users should be made aware of new policies and procedures, and this can be done via posters, newsletters and noticeboards. A disciplinary process should also provide reinforcement, and should be followed if staff are found to be contravening the new policies and procedures.

Getting your house in order

The audit process needn't be a daunting task, and once in place will pay dividends for the organization. The process will provide a record of all software assets to find out exactly what is already installed and, more importantly, what is actually used.

The audit process can either be done using an electronic network auditing tool or via a manual walk-round audit. There are advantages and disadvantages to both, and it may also depend upon the size of the organization and how many PCs it owns.

Collecting data via an electronic tool is much quicker, but it is practically impossible to obtain all the information required for the audit. Information on the user – name, department, physical location, etc – as well as details of stand-alone PCs or laptops that may be off-site cannot be collected via an electronic audit. A physical walk-round is very time-consuming, but ensures that these details are not left out of the audit. It also takes into account peripherals such as printers, plasma screens, scanners and external modems.

Ensuring compliance

The third step in the process is reconciliation of the audited assets with relevant software licences, to ensure that the organization is correctly licensed. An asset register should be devised, listing the unique asset number identified during the audit process with the licence number. Many software publishers allow invoices to be used as proof of licence purchase, so it is worth reconciling software to invoice numbers as back-up.

The organization should then ensure it has the correct number of licences. This is likely to involve purchasing licences for software that is under-licensed and deleting any unlicensed software that is not needed.

Ongoing management

The last and perhaps most difficult task is ongoing management of the compliance programme. Policies and procedures should be reviewed frequently and updated as necessary, with regular communication sent out to all staff to remind them of their existence. A full audit should be carried out at least once a year as well as an interim audit every quarter of between 5 and 10 per cent of the organization's PCs. This will ensure that the organization is as compliant as it can be.

Although the process seems simple, and many businesses audit their own software, they do so without the experience and expertise of carrying out an effective asset management project, and may find themselves with useless, outdated information –wasting both time and money. For these reasons, many companies seek the advice of experts who can run the audit and reconciliation on their behalf – leaving the companies to get on with running the business and be safe in the knowledge they are legally compliant and won't be wasting money.

Six-point guide to software asset management

- All software is copyrighted material and must be licensed correctly. You never own the software, regardless of how much you pay; you are only buying the right to use it.
- Licence agreements are often printed on single sheets of paper that may or may not come with the boxed software. It is important to keep them in a safe environment, such as a fireproof safe, as they can often be the only proof of the organization's right to use the software.
- If a licence agreement genuinely cannot be found, the receipted invoice can often be accepted as proof of purchase. It is therefore advisable to reconcile the invoices as well as licence agreements with software installed on your system.
- Shareware, freeware, games, screensavers, fonts, music, video and pictures are all copyrighted materials and should be treated in the same way as any other software, with careful consideration of the licence details.
- Policies should include obtaining authorization from the appropriate person before downloading or installing anything on to computers.

- Businesses cannot always afford the wide range of technology on the market for controlling computer use. Often a cost-effective way to begin to address this issue is with robust policies that help the users to understand the implications of incorrect computer use.

For further information on these and other software licensing issues, please contact FAST Corporate Services on 01628 622 121 or go to www.fastcorporateservices.com.

E How to Profit from the Internet

Many companies spend thousands of pounds on a website and get very little back on their investment. Why is this? Unfortunately many web design companies just want to sell a website, get paid and then move on to the next job. What they don't realise or maybe don't care is that in order for a website to offer a good ROI (return on investment) it must be promoted properly in order to obtain good rankings in Google, MSN, Yahoo and Ask etc. There is no point in having a great looking website if no one can find it. Search Engine Optimisation (SEO) is now a whole industry by itself and it's unfair to expect a client to be able to work through this minefield on their own as well as run a business.

In my experience most web design companies fail to even do the very basics like add meaningful titles, descriptions, keyword tags let alone build links, do keyword research, add ALT tags, good content, headings and numerous other things. Just a little help and advice from their side could get the client off to good start. It doesn't cost anything except time but its something that would be a valuable service to the client.

In my opinion any web design company that doesn't automatically add the basic optimisation techniques into any new website is failing in their duty to the client. My company always offer three months free SEO with any new site which includes link building, keyword research, monthly reporting, content optimisation and on going advice about the ever changing search engines algorithms.

Whenever you next think about spending your hard earned money on a new website make sure that your web design company offers at least these basic optimisation services and you might find that your website starts to make you money rather than cost you money.

Author: **Rob Lawley (WSI Internet Solutions)**
Tel: **01789 471541**
Fax: **01789 881105**
Mobile: **07966 075469**
Email: **bob@wsiprimesitesolutions.co.uk**
Web: **http://www.wsiprimesitesolutions.co.uk**

Types of offshoring engagement models

Offshore relationships are becoming more long term, says Rajiv Dey, Senior Vice President and Head of Business Development, NIIT SmartServe

One of the most critical decisions that will be faced with an offshoring operation is to decide on the type of engagement model to have with the offshore service provider. Often this is dictated by the business model and strategy of the client organization. There are various options and hybrid models that have emerged as experience of offshoring has matured over time.

Clients look for offshore partners for various reasons. Among these are cost savings, greater efficiency, higher productivity, flexibility and scalability, the need to overcome shortage of labour and skills, and improved time to market. Another factor that is increasingly being considered is that offshore origins such as India and China are booming economies with a large and increasingly affluent middle-class consumer base, and Western clients have started looking at these as important emerging markets for their products and services.

When offshoring first started, clients viewed an offshore vendor as an arm's-length supplier, and contracts were created to reflect this. So, most contracts were of short-term duration with stringent service level agreements (SLAs) and performance metrics around which bonus and penalty clauses were built. However, today there is a growing realization that Western companies need to engage with offshore origins on a more sustainable medium- to long-term basis as they start to rely on the offshore vendor to create long-term value and competitive advantage for the client. The offshore vendor has now been transformed into a long-term strategic partner, and the contract forms need to reflect this long-term relationship. The offshore partner has also become a launching pad for the client to enter the lucrative, fast-growing consumer markets of these offshore origins.

For these reasons, different engagement models have emerged for offshore relationships:

- *Captives.* A captive is a wholly owned subsidiary set up by a Western company in the offshore location. Typically used by banks, insurance companies and financial services, captives are used when security and confidentiality are of paramount importance and where there is a high level of governance and regulatory compliance. The use of a captive also indicates a long-term strategic commitment to that origin and so it is good for long-term investment. Setting up a captive requires an existing footprint in the market.

  The disadvantages are that you cannot backtrack easily, as the company would have invested significant capital in the subsidiary and the workforce would be directly employed by the company, leading to long-term employee commitments.
- *Joint ventures.* Joint ventures retain the spirit of a long-term engagement but provide more flexibility than a captive. A joint venture leverages the expertise of the local partner in the origin and is useful to set up operations and get going quickly and without risk, particularly when the client has no footprint in that market and is not attuned to local nuances and business practices.
- *Arm's-length third-party vendor.* The offshore vendor may be looked at as an arm's-length supplier and not a strategic partner. This is the quickest route to market. The contracts involved are relatively shorter term and the client can pull out and exit the relationship quickly and painlessly. This model affords the greatest flexibility and transparent costings, and SLAs can be strictly enforced by means of penalty clauses. The downside is that the client has very little operational control, and risks relating to data security and regulatory compliance are highest in this model.

Each of these three basic models has its relative benefits and disadvantages, and I have tried to summarize these across some key variables in Table 8.2.1.

Value creation: hybrid models

As Western companies have started perceiving offshoring as a value creation opportunity as opposed to a supply and cost side opportunity, some interesting models have emerged:

Build, operate and transfer

Build, operate and transfer is a hybrid model where a Western client with no footprint in the origin uses the offshore vendor to set up the initial operation as an arm's-length vendor with an option to buy out the operation once it has stabilized. This delivers the full benefits of speed of entry and flexibility, and leverages local expertise, with

Table 8.2.1 Analysis of sourcing model options: the offshoring objective determines the solution

Factor	Third Party	Joint Venture	Captive
Security/data privacy	•	••	•••
Operational control	•	••	•••
Regulatory/governance	•	••	•••
Value creation	•	••	•••
Speed of exit	•••	••	•
Fixed cost → variable	•••	••	•
Risk sharing	•••	••	•
Flexibility/scalability	•••	••	•
Cost advantage	•••	•	••
Cost transparency	•••	•	••
Metric driven	•••	•	••
Time to market	•••	•	••

Note: three bullets indicates greatest suitability, one bullet least, with two being intermediate.

no market entry risk. Once a successful operation has been set up, the client retains the option to buy out the operation and develop the long-term value potential of the business.

Captives going to market

Western clients sensing the value creation potential of offshore captives have set up successful operations and then divested their holdings at a substantial premium to allow the captive to take on business from other clients looking for offshore partners whilst continuing to service the requirements of the original owner. Both parties have benefited by this: the original owners have reaped a reward for the value they created and the divested captive has become free to pursue a wider range of opportunities in the market and operate as a profitable independent business. The divested captive has a significant competitive advantage, owing to the fact that it has experience of running core processes, which would normally have been considered too critical or sensitive to outsource to an arm's-length vendor.

Venture capital-funded projects

The immense scope for global sourcing has attracted the interest of venture capitalists, who have provided the financial resources to entrepreneurial technocrats to set up new projects in this space. The primary strategy of these venture projects is to create value for shareholders and key employees by taking the company to the stock market in a relatively short span of time after setting up a successful operation.

Latest trends

Just as Western companies have tried to leverage the cost and skill advantages of low-cost economies by setting up captives, joint ventures and third-party vendors to improve productivity, lower costs and launch into offshore markets, so have offshore vendors started contributing to Western economies by setting up onshore and near-shore operations in order to compete with the multinational outsourcers. This has enabled offshore service providers to have a front-end presence in the client markets and blend offshore services with a strong local presence, resulting in the creation of additional employment in the Western economies. Recently there have been some large TUPE deals where the offshore vendors have taken over the entire workforce of a company or division in the United Kingdom. Some offshore vendors now offer a multi-locational, multilingual comprehensive solution to multinational clients operating across the globe, coupling a strong offshore delivery with onshore and near-shore local market presence.

Conclusions

Globalization is truly a two-way trade. The ultimate success of organizations in the future will depend on how effectively they create and implement strategies that harness the cost structure and intellectual capital that resides in low-cost economies to create a lasting competitive advantage. The internet and broadband connectivity have flattened the world to a point where traditional geographical boundaries are no longer a barrier to trade and services, allowing companies to engage with the most efficient and productive sources for products and services delivery across the globe. Successful offshore engagement models will be the differentiator between the winners and the losers in the new business order.

NIIT is a leading global IT and BPO services and solutions provider serving customers within the banking, insurance, manufacturing, retail, technology, telecommunications, transportation and travel industries. Established in 1981 and spanning 19 countries across Europe, Asia Pacific and India, it has been working with global corporations for over two decades.

Rajiv Dey joined NIIT soon after its business process outsourcing (BPO) business was set up and has played a major role in building the UK business for NIIT SmartServe. Projects currently running at NIIT SmartServe include closed books, life insurance processing, FSA regulatory compliance, consumer lifestyle surveys, B2B directory cleanse, telesales, customer service and inbound call handling across many industry verticals.

Video conferencing

Reduce travel? Accelerate decisions? Control projects? John Cooper of JKC Information Technology reviews the point at which video conferencing can pay its way in smaller companies

What is video conferencing?

Video conferencing in its simplest form is the use of visual and audio technology to enable people in different locations to communicate, as if they were in the same room, through the use of cameras, monitors or screens. Participants in such a meeting can also share documents, spreadsheets and images, depending upon the quality of the network links and the equipment used.

Types of video conferencing

There are three main types of system.

Desktop

This form of video conferencing has recently enjoyed rapid growth and is designed for use by individuals, as a small screen on the desk is used. It is now possible to display images for up to eight other conference participants, using high-quality video, excellent voice communication and integrated document and application sharing. This form of video conferencing is also available on laptops, which provide a mobile communication platform.

Figure 8.3.1   Visual Nexus desktop system

Figure 8.3.2   Polycom VSX 7000 set-top unit

J K C Information Technology Limited

JKC is a specialist video and audio conferencing business. Established for more than 8 years, we have experience within the company from the early years of commercial video conferencing, gained from working within IBM. This experience has been used to develop our team, who will take the time to understand your needs before recommending a solution.

If you wish to experience video conferencing before purchasing then we have extensive demonstration facilities at our disposal.

Our satisfied customers come from all sectors. They include UK national and international businesses, small and medium-sized enterprises, local authorities, H.M.Police, education and the National Health Service.

Whatever the size of your business, whether you work from home or a large office, we have a conferencing solution that could be of benefit to you. This could be to improve the efficiency of internal communication within your business, with external suppliers and customers, or as a means of delivering training. It also has a value as a means of enabling you to stay in touch with your family when you are away from home.

From laptop to boardroom, whatever your requirement, JKC will work with you to ensure you have the right solution for your needs. This will provide you with the potential to maximise your return on the investment. The rest is up to you!

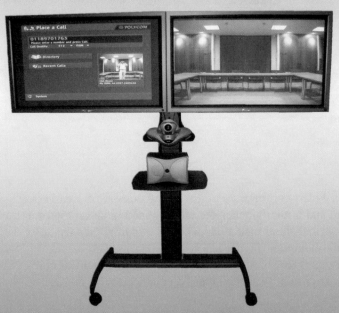

Figure 8.3.3   Roll-about unit

Set-top

Set-top systems are compact video conferencing units. They consist of a camera, which can pan, tilt and zoom, and a microphone, and are designed to sit on top of a monitor. For added flexible use in different locations within a building, they can also be used on a purpose-built roll-about unit (Figure 8.3.3).

These systems are usually used for small groups of people. They provide a high-quality visual and audio meeting facility, which can be enhanced with the use of additional presentation equipment.

Integrated

Integrated systems are video conferencing systems that are generally built into larger rooms, such as boardrooms and conference rooms (Figure 8.3.4). They are a highly professional communication facility and can provide a variety of presentation displays, depending on the equipment used. Typically they are used for groups of 10 or more people.

All of these different types of video conferencing units and systems can link to each other, to provide a variety of mediums through which people can communicate, either within an organization or externally.

Figure 8.3.4   Integrated system

What you should consider

When you are beginning your search for the right video conferencing solution, then as with all investment decisions, a carefully thought through process will ensure that an informed choice is made. The following paragraphs are intended as a 'walk-through' thought process guide to enable a decision to be reached as to whether video conferencing would add value to your activities.

The first set of questions is designed to get you thinking about your environment and how you may wish to use video conferencing to your advantage:

■ How do you want to use the equipment and who do you want to call?
■ How many offices do you want to call and how many locations will participate in a meeting at any one time?
■ How many people do you expect to participate in the video conferences in each location?
■ What type of room will the video conferencing unit be located in? Consider size, lighting, availability of power points and connection available to the internet or ISDN lines.
■ What is the most appropriate type of system for each location?

Justification of investment in video conferencing

Here detailed thought is required on how video conferencing will be used in your business, how it will fit in with your communication processes and who will champion its use. The majority of businesses that invest in video conferencing will experience cost savings. The more it is used, the more rapidly the breakeven point will be achieved. It is therefore important that business owners and managers encourage and champion its use to ensure early acceptance of the technology. Its effective use is to complement other business tools, not to be used instead of them. For example, there will always be a place for face-to-face meetings or use of the telephone. However, it is the extent to which these other business tools are used relative to video conferencing that will determine payback time.

How can payback be assessed?

The following list is designed to provide you with some thoughts on how efficiency savings may be calculated within a business through the use of video conferencing. It is not designed to be exhaustive, and indeed you may well come up with specific uses that are not on the list but are relevant to your business.

Video conferencing can:

- reduce travel costs;
- accelerate decision making;
- provide enhanced control of projects;
- improve use of executive time;
- provide cost-effective training to remote locations;
- be used as a medium to conduct interviews;
- reinforce close relationships with suppliers, clients and remote staff;
- save note taking at meetings, as a full record can be recorded on to a DVD;
- provide you with the capability to respond to a communication need immediately.

Beginning your search

The process so far should have enabled you to consider the uses to which video conferencing can effectively be applied to your business, the size of the audience in each location and the value that may accrue with its deployment. You are now ready to venture out and seek advice on the right type of equipment for your business requirements.

Armed with the knowledge of the anticipated cost savings that you expect to accrue from the deployment of video conferencing and the value of any competitive advantage that can be gained, you will be well placed when pricing is discussed. When you are provided with a price, including any installation cost and additional warranty, calculate whether the payback period is acceptable. A decision can then be made, based upon the return on the investment, whether the price is acceptable or negotiations need to continue.

Choosing a supplier

Once you have used sound business reasoning to invest in video conferencing, it is vital that a competent supplier be used to advise, install the equipment and provide training and support if you are to gain full business advantage. Some questions to consider are:

- How long have they been in business?
- What experience do they have?
- What does their client portfolio look like and can I speak to any of the clients?
- Are they prepared to take the time to understand my business needs?
- Can they provide demonstration facilities?

The result

With a reputable supplier who takes the time to find out your needs and provides you with the appropriate solution, your business will be able to enjoy the benefits of video conferencing. A carefully thought through video conferencing solution, supported by management, will provide early payback and competitive advantage.

John Cooper has worked in video conferencing for more than 15 years. Originally his specialization in this area was with IBM, until he left them to start up his own company, JKC Information Technology Limited.

Formed more than eight years ago, JKC Information Technology Limited specializes in video, audio and data conferencing. The company has extensive experience in the conferencing market, not just with businesses but also through work carried out in the education sector, councils, police and the NHS.

For more information contact John Cooper on:

Tel: 01794 390050
e-mail: johncooper@jkcit.co.uk

Or visit the company website, www.jkcit.co.uk.

Imagine a business that has access to all the latest technology, all of the time. Where whatever's needed, whether it's 20 laptops for a training room, plasma screens in an exhibition, a colour laser printer for a project or a full back projection unit with PA system at a conference – where just about any technology needed could be called in at a moments notice.

It won't surprise you to know that there are companies who enjoy these facilities right now. Huge multinationals have the budgets which make this kind of thing possible; the oil companies, car manufacturers, supermarket giants, IT companies… oh, I almost forgot, your company does too!

All the equipment you are ever likely to need can be rented, and what's more, it can be rented on a "by the job" basis, so if you only need it for a day, you only rent it for a day. Specialists like Hire Intelligence hold fleets of equipment to furnish your company with whatever's needed by the day, week, month or year.

The beauty of the system is that it allows you the freedom to use exactly the right equipment for the job in hand. If you're exhibiting at a show alongside your larger competitors, you needn't look like the poor relation because you have access to all the greatest AV equipment just like they do. You just have to give it back afterwards.

Even big organisations use Hire Intelligence because they realise the benefits of having just the right equipment at just the right time. No depreciation, no running or maintenance costs, no obsolescence, and they can change, add to or dispose of equipment they're using whenever they like.

While some liken IT & AV rental to car hire, Hire Intelligence have pushed the boundaries of the industry by offering full technical services too. From installing all the equipment to providing on-site support and even project management, a single phone call and you have one of the UK's best equipped IT and AV facilities on hand to make your project or event a brilliant success.

Hire Intelligence UK can be contacted on **0845 600 7272**.

Be Smart.
Hire Intelligence.

Plasma screens, desktop PCs, tablet PCs, Laptops, Digital Cameras, Servers, Apple Macs, PA Systems, Lecterns, video conferencing systems, audio mixing desks, TV Combo Units.... and much, much more.

When you need to rent top quality IT & AV equipment, just Hire Intelligence.

When you need to make an impact at an exhibition, enthral an audience with your presentation or bring in a stack of extra computer power for your office, it pays to rent from Hire Intelligence.

With a network of branches across the country, rental periods from a single day to a year, a services portfolio which ranges from simply delivering the boxes to your door right through to full technical project management, Hire Intelligence are the only partner you need to make a success of any business event, large or small.

Next time, don't just rent it. Hire Intelligence.

9

Managing the growing organization

PKF

Accountants &
business advisers

fresh thinking

Using management information

Without focused, accurate and timely management information, running a business is like trying to fly a plane without instruments, says Craig Goodwin at Mazars

Management information (MI) is critical to managing business performance. As you read through this handbook there are countless occasions where the authors describe a key fact about the organization and the behaviours that this should drive. In this age of information overload it is tempting to think that the plethora of reports available from business systems mean that growing businesses have got all the bases covered from an information perspective. However, experience suggests that whilst information can be extracted more easily from systems than in the past, the step to creating meaningful management information is often lacking. In this chapter I highlight some of the key factors to consider when developing a management information system.

What to measure?

Too often the reports produced in the name of MI are actually a reflection of what can be extracted from the systems, rather than being coordinated and focused on the measures that are most important for the business. Any analysis of what to measure should always start from the strategic goals of the business. Businesses of all sizes must develop a clear strategic plan. The plan will identify the strengths of the organization and the opportunities that these strengths can generate in its chosen market. In short, the strategic plan will focus on the two key questions of 'Where are we now?' and 'Where do we want to be?'

The link between this strategic plan and the ongoing management of the business can then be measured using a 'balanced scorecard' approach to MI. The balanced scorecard is a performance measurement system that has its origins in the work carried out by Kaplan and Norton in the early to mid-1990s. Whilst the term has been used, and perhaps abused, in business management since then, applications of the concept to SMEs have proved to be fairly limited in number. Nevertheless, the balanced scorecard is every bit as applicable for SMEs as it is for large corporates.

At the highest level, the key performance indicators (KPIs) that support the strategic plan are what should be measured, and these should be coordinated into a balanced scorecard.

Surely management accounts tell me all I need to know?

Unfortunately, it is not the case that management accounts will tell you all you need to know. Traditional monthly management accounts are structured to provide a historical view of the performance of the business. Analysis of revenue and costs, and comparisons to budgets or plans, in monthly reports are only part of the picture. In our experience, management accounts are undoubtedly a vital part of the full picture of the MI for any business, but they are not the whole story and miss out on the 'balance' that arises from the non-financial measures that are vital for a good MI system.

In theory, a balanced scorecard should be subdivided into just four perspectives:

■ financial;
■ learning and growth;
■ customer;
■ internal business processes.

However, for SMEs we have found that it is better to be flexible in terms of the perspectives that are contained within the balanced scorecard. This means subdividing the broad perspectives into more focused areas. For example, for some businesses it is imperative that the scorecard contain an analysis of sales pipeline; for others the internal business process performance is divided into operational processes and back-office processes.

The behaviours that the scorecard drives are then critical to the success of the organization.

It already takes long enough to compile the management accounts!

Often the month-end reporting can take most of the month to sort out. It is not uncommon for the management accounts presented to the board to have been copied and pasted or, even worse, rekeyed multiple times before they reach the finished format. The inefficiencies in this monthly reporting have many implications for the management of the business – all of them bad!

Clearly the process is likely to be time-consuming, diverting (expensive) resource away from higher value added tasks. Manual operations introduce the risk of inconsistencies and errors in the reported numbers, decreasing the level of confidence that can be placed on them.

A significant contributor to successful MI is the design of a process that takes data from core systems in an automated way with minimal manual intervention. This approach should be applied not only to the financial systems but also to operational, HR and other business systems.

The key is then connecting the high-level measures that are identified on the balanced scorecard by linking them through to the source systems and data fields that are required to support them. Often this can be problematic, since the data can be seen as being 'trapped' in the system and will require specialist techniques to aid the data extraction and cleansing.

The aggregation of the source data must be totally automated to mitigate the risks of manual processes. This frees time for analysis of the numbers and for high-quality commentary to be added to explain the results. In addition, it also provides senior management with the confidence that the MI that they see on a monthly basis is created in a totally consistent, repeatable and accurate way.

MI should be compiled automatically and repeatably from core systems.

We have query tools that tell us all we need to know

There are some excellent query tools available to extract information from core systems. We tend to find that whilst these can be used to generate structured reports from systems, or for detailed analysis of specific problems or opportunities, they do not form a coordinated MI system.

In a true MI system much of the power of the information derives from the ability to cross-link information from different sources. This can require specialist resource, or may not even be possible within the query tools.

Query tools can form a vital part of the chain that leads to the full MI system, but they are a step along the way, rather than being the end of the story.

So what?

The final dimension in the MI picture is to take the KPIs and develop them to include forward-looking measures. When you are considering the requirements for MI, it is critical to ensure that adequate attention is devoted to extrapolating forwards. All too often a management information system misses the opportunity to provide senior management with the forward view of the business that can help them to make timely decisions.

Oh no, not another software system...

Developing management information should emphatically not be seen as a software system project. Hopefully you will have drawn, from the information here, the realization that at the core of an MI project is sound commercial and business analysis. This is supported by data extraction from core systems and a well-structured aggregation of these data. All of this should be drawn together in the balanced scorecard.

The end users of the information often do not want to review the outputs of queries, or use a new software tool to access MI. Consideration should be given to designing the reporting layers in software that is already in use within the business.

MI should be presented in a way that is familiar and intuitive for the main users to understand and use.

Conclusion

As you read through the many thought-provoking areas covered in this handbook, consider the implications of management information and the impact that it can have on the way that you manage your business. One way or another, you will be using some management information as you grow your business. The critical question is whether you can rely on its quality and accuracy.

Craig Goodwin leads the business process improvement team at Mazars. He has 20 years' experience as a business consultant in a wide variety of business sectors, specializing in delivering process improvement and management information projects. In all aspects of process improvement Craig has built a reputation for ensuring that the projects deliver pragmatic solutions that are right for the organizations.

Mazars acts for some of the fastest-growing entrepreneurial companies in the United Kingdom, offering a complete range of accountancy and business advisory services, including audit and assurance, tax advisory and compliance, corporate recovery and insolvency, consulting, forensic and investigations, corporate finance, and financial services for private individuals.

Tel: 01908 664466
e-mail: craig.goodwin@mazars.co.uk
www.mazars.co.uk

Breaking barriers

Businesses that use tightly integrated business applications are more agile and more efficient than their less integrated counterparts, says David Pinches at Sage

Business does not occur in silos. Most processes and transactions span several departments and can involve many people and a number of information systems. Problems can arise when departmental or functional barriers are crossed: data between systems may not be synchronized, or processes initiated in one department may not be properly understood, followed through or effectively automated by another. Integrated business applications can solve many of these problems, providing employees with clear interdepartmental processes and ensuring that they all have access to accurate and consistently structured information.

Over the past two decades, businesses of all sizes have invested heavily in information systems, and mostly to good effect. Companies have become more efficient and more productive, and are able to respond to their customers' needs more flexibly and quickly.

But many of these organizations are also, paradoxically, suffering from a kind of information disconnect. Typically, they have bought and installed their applications on a piecemeal basis, each time aiming to solve a particular business problem faced by a certain department or business unit. The finance department, for example, has accounting and forecasting software, manufacturing has production management, supply chain or distribution software, and the sales teams use forecasting, account management and lead tracking software. Each of these applications is effective, but there is a problem: improved efficiency and automation in one area often accelerates the pace of business and raises service expectations, showing up weaknesses, inconsistencies and poor

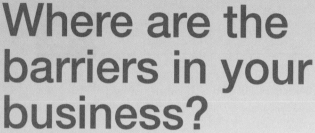

Where are the barriers in your business?

You may not be able to see them. But unless your departments share information, the barriers are there – hindering your efficiency, holding back your potential.

Sage 1000 is the new business management software that helps remove operational barriers within the company. By linking all aspects of the business, it enables departments to share information and work more effectively as a whole.

Visit **www.sage.co.uk/breakthrough** to take our barrier test: see how much you're being held back - and what you can do about it. Or call us on **0845 111 9988**.

Sage 1000: a breakthrough in business management

communications with systems elsewhere. And this is especially true when processes cross the so-called invisible barriers between departments.

Take a simple process, such as entering an order from a new customer. This might typically require new records to be created in the sales system, the accounting system and the production system. The order data might also be needed by those planning the allocation of resources, ordering parts, arranging for distribution or reporting on the success of a recent marketing campaign.

Clearly, a lot of information relating to the customer will be duplicated across several of these systems – but in each system the emphasis, details and even record numbers might be different. Unless systems are tightly linked, data entry mistakes will occur. And what happens if, later, the customer notifies the company of a change of address, or perhaps just the delivery address? What if only the salesperson is notified, but not the accounts department? Inevitably, where systems are not integrated, information held on one system may not accurately or immediately map on to another.

The problems multiply

Research into the effectiveness of business applications has repeatedly shown that the existence of these invisible barriers between application silos has a negative impact not only on productivity and customer service but on the responsiveness of the organization. Indeed, disjointed processes, inconsistent databases and the need for rekeying and retraining can all combine to frustrate and demoralize employees. Problems in the areas of sales and customer relations are often cited. A salesperson booking a new order, for example, may need to check that all the relevant parts are in stock, when the work can be scheduled and that the customer is creditworthy. Orders may have to be delayed while multiple systems are accessed.

A common approach to tackling these problems is to ask the staff to enter information into multiple applications – so-called 'swivel chair integration' or 'cut and paste integration'. But a 2005 survey by market researchers YouGov suggested that staff re-entering data using multiple applications often introduce errors and feel it is a waste of their time.

A tell-tale sign of a lack of integration is the overuse and proliferation of spreadsheets. This is because individuals either do not have access to data held outside their department or do not know how to use the application. As a result, managers ask for the data to be extracted into a spreadsheet format. If the underlying data then change, perhaps as a result of a new or amended order, or the data in the spreadsheet are themselves changed, this inevitably leads to inconsistencies and 'version control' problems.

Another symptom: the IT department struggles to deliver new applications, and to make existing systems work together. Each proposed new application must be assessed at length, frustrating those waiting for, say, a new customer relationship management (CRM) system. Interoperability with existing systems and the need to learn new systems create complexity and delays.

Real-time agility

One of the fashionable terms of modern business is the 'real-time enterprise'. Gartner, the analyst company, defines this as a business that 'competes by using up-to-date information to progressively remove delays to the management and execution of its critical business processes'. In the largest organizations, and especially those that trade heavily over the internet in real time, becoming 'real-time enterprises' can be an expensive and vast undertaking that involves an intensive programme of process improvement and a huge investment in integration technology.

But the 'real time' goal has relevance to all businesses. With or without electronic trading, competitive pressures mean that all companies should be able to quickly execute end-to-end processes in such a way that excessive bureaucracy, expensive and error-prone human involvement and processing delays are all reduced or eliminated.

Part of the challenge of 'real time business' is to ensure that once a transaction is initiated in one system, it can be completed with no more human involvement than is necessary. Some managers are attempting to provide their staff with the ability to initiate complete end-to-end processes (from order to payment, for example) and not to concern themselves with the underlying applications that make this possible.

Business intelligence and management reporting are also an essential part of this. A manager cannot anticipate and accurately respond to developments if he or she is not using the right tools, or does not have access to up-to-date information. This requires that barriers between applications are overcome.

Achieving integration

Some shining examples set by some of the world's largest companies, as well as some leading smaller ones, have sparked a realization by managers at many companies: any hope of achieving a high degree of business agility, or of even becoming a 'real time enterprise', will depend on their ability to execute business processes 'seamlessly' across multiple tightly integrated applications. 'When applications are tightly linked, and expensive and error-prone human involvement is reduced, processes can be completed more quickly, and information can be made instantly available to those who need it,' says Ken Vollmer, an analyst with IT market research company Forrester Research.

The problem of integration – or rather, a lack of it – can be overcome in one of two main ways. The first of these is to build or buy links between systems; the second is to buy a complete application suite that is 'pre-integrated'. Both approaches have their merits and the better course will usually depend on what technology is already installed, and on what processes and databases are involved.

Building the links

In the past, links between business applications (such as CRM and accounting) were expensive to buy, or difficult to build and maintain, and implementation usually required the help of outside consultants. But building links between systems is getting easier and less costly, largely because integrators increasingly make use of standard techniques and interfaces. This approach is most suitable where, for reasons of cost, function or preference, existing systems are left in place. At the base level (beyond rekeying the data), information can be moved around using file swapping or direct electronic data interchange (EDI) links. These low-level approaches, however, are mostly intended to overcome the problem of rekeying; they can be slow and expensive, and were not designed to support the web of interdependent cross-system links demanded by today's integrated business processes. And usually when one system at either end of a link is changed, the interfaces must be rewritten.

For that reason, most companies are more likely to aim a little higher, opting for the so-called loose coupling they can achieve using enterprise application integration (EAI) tools based on web services technologies and pre-built connectors. Web services are a set of standards for exchanging data and process information between systems, and while they were designed to work over the web, they work just as well internally. Developers can use these standards to 'expose' the programming interfaces of any piece of software, with the result that it can 'talk' to (or exchange data with) any other piece of software that has also had its interfaces exposed using those standards. Most leading software companies, including Sage, use these standards.

But web services are generic and basic, and don't deal with what the information means, and how it should be presented and used by each application. This is why pre-built adapters designed to link specific software packages are also available. These are typically based on an integration platform that can both understand and impose business rules and translate complex data schemata – along with providing other functions such as security, remote management and transaction auditing.

The integrated suite

Integration tools help to remove the barriers to information flow within an organization – but a more comprehensive approach is to implement a complete applications suite that effectively pre-integrates all of the major business applications in one tightly knit, business-wide software suite. These application suites were originally developed for the largest organizations by companies such as SAP and Oracle, but suites aimed specifically at mid-market and smaller companies are now available. Such suites can be regarded not only as a set of applications in their own right but as a platform into which new functions can also be plugged and integrated. Data from third-party and existing systems can be also be integrated with these suites if necessary.

'More customers want a single system, because a unified, more coherent view of the business naturally leads to a more coherent business strategy,' explains David Karlin, managing director of Sage's mid-market division.

Integration works

Until recently, effective integration was largely the preserve of large businesses. But tight, business-wide integration is now becoming easier and cheaper and, importantly, is now within the grasp of mid-sized organizations.

Ultimately, the decision of whether to invest in an all-in-one system or to stick with tried and tested systems that are separate or loosely linked will depend on a number of factors and preferences, such as the need to preserve investments, or for reasons of industry focus or business process complexity. Many will find that they can achieve the best improvements in terms of efficiency and productivity by investing in a single, integrated suite.

However the barriers to information flow are torn down, the benefits are immediately obvious: a much sharper and more flexible operation will emerge – one that is facilitated by instant access to accurate, up-to-date and timely information and is able to carry out its business free of unnecessary delays, errors and misunderstandings.

David Pinches is currently director of the accounts and ERP market unit within Sage. David has built up a wealth of experience in the business software industry, both in the United Kingdom and internationally, most recently with roles of general manager, marketing director and head of strategy.

Sage is the world's leading supplier of business management software, offering solutions for all sizes of business from start-ups to large corporate organizations. The only technology company in the FTSE 100, Sage has its headquarters in the North of England.

Enterprise risk management

Introduction

Reporting in annual accounts that your business has a risk management process in place and that risks are reviewed on a regular basis is meaningless. What really matters is how, where and when it was applied and by whom. In order to be effective, risk management needs to be a pro-active process, which is part of day-to-day activities and hence second nature to senior management. Companies that treat risk management as just a compliance issue expose themselves to a damaged balance sheet. It is now recognised that enterprise risk management can be used to identify and exploit opportunities and, as a result, make a significant contribution to bottom line performance. There are a series of emerging trends which can be capitalised on to provide competitive advantage and climate change is used here as a vehicle to discuss how opportunities might be explored and developed.

What is enterprise risk management?

Enterprises operating in today's environment are characterised by constant change and require a more integrated approach to manage their risk exposure. This has not always been the case, with risks being managed in "silos". Risks are, by their very nature, dynamic, fluid and highly interdependent. As such, they cannot be evaluated or managed independently. Enterprise risk management is aimed at providing this integrated approach.

Process composition

Enterprise risk management can be simply described as a process composed of six steps within two phases called Analysis and Management, as illustrated in Figure 1 below.

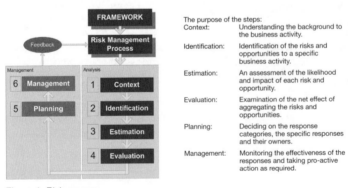

The purpose of the steps:

Context:	Understanding the background to the business activity.
Identification:	Identification of the risks and opportunities to a specific business activity.
Estimation:	An assessment of the likelihood and impact of each risk and opportunity.
Evaluation:	Examination of the net effect of aggregating the risks and opportunities.
Planning:	Deciding on the response categories, the specific responses and their owners.
Management:	Monitoring the effectiveness of the responses and taking pro-active action as required.

Figure 1: Risk process

Business growth through the application of risk management

While risk management can directly contribute to the economic use of resources, it can also be used to seek and analyse opportunities before your competitors do. Proactive 'horizon scanning' of emerging opportunities can provide competitive advantage through 'getting ahead of the game' and creating new markets or significantly increasing market share in existing markets (at the expense of competitors). There are a series of emerging issues which may be considered both a risk and an opportunity and are starting to affect us all now, but will grow in prominence in the years to come. They include climate change, energy sources, improvements in technology, social change, demographics and flu pandemics. Each issue is a significant subject in its own right, but all are interlinked. The key to unlocking their commercial potential is thinking through how these issues will manifest themselves and where the opportunities will lie.

Climate change

Looking at the first of these emerging issues, climate change is now widely recognised as the greatest long term challenge facing the world today. There is strong, indisputable evidence that climate change is happening and that man-made emissions are the main cause. The ten warmest years globally since formal records began in 1861 have all occurred since 1994. The Thames Barrier, once used every two years, is now used six times a year. The effects of climate change are clearly being felt now. However, the full effects are still being debated. Of interest here is that climate change will manifest itself in a number of ways, and that there are a number of opportunities for companies to increase shareholder value through the development of new products.

A model for identifying and evaluating emerging risks and opportunities

To seize commercial advantage from these emerging trends requires a systematic and methodical approach to understanding the issues, translating them into commercial opportunities and tracking their development to understand how the potential market is changing over time. It requires information that can be readily communicated and quickly assimilated. Hence a *model* is required of these emerging risks and opportunities, to map how they are going to manifest themselves and how they can be translated into market opportunities. Such a *model* should be incorporated into your business plan, for it is hard to imagine how any business will remain unaffected[1]. Without a plan (or business road map) how can any business know where it wants to get to and how it is going to get there? Businesses are not working in isolation and there are a number of government initiatives that are underway[2].

---

[1] As the Defra report entitled "Climate Change, The UK Programme 2006, Tomorrow's Climate, Today's Challenge" published this year states "failure to plan for a future in which environmental factors, such as climate change, are likely to be increasingly significant, may risk the long-term future of a business."

[2] The Government is planning to spend £80m in the next three years to support microgeneration technologies, with the aim of encouraging manufacture at higher scale leading to lower costs. In addition, it will provide £35m over the next 4 years for the development of carbon abatement technologies and consult on the barriers to wide-scale commercial development of carbon capture and storage (CCS).

Model composition

Due to limited space, the figure below describes a very high level, incomplete summary of the subject of climate change – one of the key emerging issues. Any development *model* needs to describe in detail: how, where and to what degree the emerging issue will manifest itself; what the results or characteristics of each manifestation will be; and what industries will be affected. It also needs to capture the products that might be produced to satisfy industry needs and the markets where these products might be sold. The *model* is subdivided into two parts, marked *External Event* and *Industry*. The first part, labelled *External Event* captures the issue, how it might manifest itself and the results of those manifestations. The second part, *Industry*, records the potential new products and their respective markets.

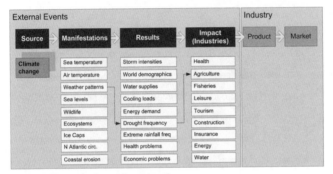

Figure 2: Example of model construction

Levels of sophistication of model construction

Larger SME's may wish to construct the model as a relational database, which incorporates the relationships between the manifestations, the results and the industries. It could, additionally, hold background information on each of the emerging risk areas to place each subject in context, a synopsis of every key publication, details of each organisation undertaking research and a description of each relevant piece of legislation. In the situation where there is a demand for multi users, the model could be Web enabled.

Conclusion

Enterprise risk management is an important tool to help businesses drive for growth. In particular, opportunities should be given at least the same attention as the potential risks identified. The outline of a model was described to structure an approach to exploitation of emerging trends. Such a model could be extended to address all of the key emerging issues described above, to strive for improvements in business performance.

Robert Chapman PhD
Principal Consultant with Siemens Insight Consulting

Growth and risk: two sides of the same coin

Alongside corporate growth comes the key challenge of identifying and neutralizing new sources of business risk, says Stephen Kelly of idRisk

Growth: managing the risk

Most organizations identify growth as being among their top business objectives. Achieving these growth objectives means staying in business to give your strategy the best chance of success. Of course, this means successfully managing risk (threats) to the business during this period.

As your organization grows, it inevitably becomes a more complex beast, and its risk profile will develop in parallel over the same time horizon to a similar level of complexity. Therefore, managing risk across the whole organization in a systematic fashion to give a true overview of your company's risk profile assumes greater importance as the business continues to grow. In addition, there is increasing exposure to regulation, legislation and compliance issues, which if addressed at face value can introduce inefficiencies into many growing businesses.

The issue

Investors seek out and reward good risk management when making investments: 82% are willing to pay more for companies that manage risk well. (E&Y, Investors on Risk: The Need for Transparency, *2005)*

Over 80% of institutional investors say they would pay 18% more for the shares of a well governed company. (McKinsey & Co. survey of fund managers, June 2000)

There is a huge opportunity for organizations to combine the work necessary to comply with new regulations and guidance with their drive to improve competitiveness through enterprise-wide risk management. The key benefit of effective risk management is an improved bottom line.

Growth and enterprise risk management

At each stage of an organization's maturity it is faced with choices (hurdles) that it must successfully overcome if it is to move to the next stage of its growth pattern. Prior identification (knowledge) of these barriers to success allows the formulation of structured responses to optimize the organization's chances of continued growth. There are two components to be considered: 1) your organization's size; and 2) the length of time that the organization has been in business (see Figure 9.3.1).

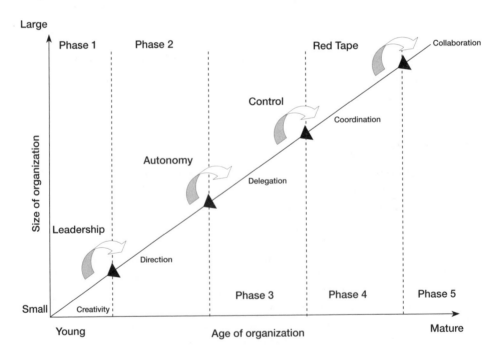

Figure 9.3.1 Growth-driven risk complexity of an organization

Factors to consider here are:

■ *The age of the organization.* Management principles and problems can be rooted in time, changing over the lifespan of the organization.

- *Size of the organization.* As organizations grow, increasing numbers of people and processes must interact efficiently and effectively. Levels of hierarchy tend to increase and coordination becomes more complex.
- *Stages of evolution.* Periods of continuous uninterrupted growth may occur and the organization may successfully rely on tried and tested techniques and behaviours.
- *Stages of revolution.* When these 'tried and tested' techniques no longer support the business effectively, a step change in approach is often required. Some companies may not survive these turbulent times. It is helpful to remember the words of Peter Drucker at this stage: 'The greatest danger in times of turbulence is to act with yesterday's logic.'
- *Industry growth rate.* This is a factor that influences how quickly a company goes through the various (r)evolutionary phases in the industry growth rate. Evolution tends to hold good while profits hold up – masking any underlying risk issues. In simple terms, a rapidly developing industry will 'age' an organization more quickly.

In summary, the systematic understanding of the growth-related problems and the impact of their solutions that your organization is faced with should be built into your organization's risk profile. In essence, a full risk workshop should be conducted, focusing exclusively on the issues of growth that confront your organization.

External factors

Additionally, there are a range of external factors that can either support or inhibit growth in the organization (see Figure 9.3.2).

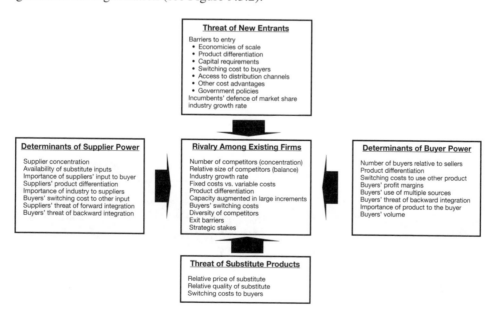

Figure 9.3.2   Porter's five forces model of competition

These external factors also need to be built into the growth risk profile of the organization.

The challenge

One of the main challenges for organizations is to enunciate their risk management information in terms that are meaningful and useful to senior management.

Relevance is key, and risk information must be presented in a style and format that support decision making and deliver business performance insights. To achieve this, organizations must be able to consolidate, calculate, analyse and distribute enterprise risk management information across the business. This challenge is fuelling interest and investment in business performance solutions. What is needed is the capability to report the effect of risks on your business performance metrics.

A business performance approach is the elusive key to unlocking the potential of an organization's enterprise risk management (ERM) initiative. It brings your organization's risk management information to life. This is vital because it is the usefulness of your risk management information that positions risk management as a decision-making tool in the minds of senior management.

The increasing complexity that the organization assumes as it grows should be mirrored by a step change in the maturity of the organization's risk management framework (see Figure 9.3.3).

Use existing business performance metrics to measure risk

Many organizations have the necessary foundations in place, together with strong risk management practices, but struggle to consolidate data from disparate sources across the organization. This situation is preventing the majority of organizations that have

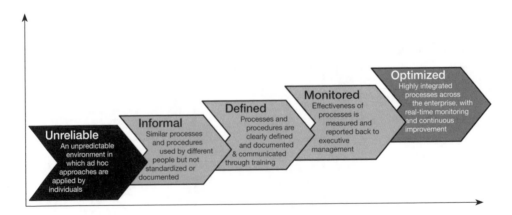

Figure 9.3.3 Growth-driven complexity of risk management framework

strong risk management frameworks and practices in place from achieving a single version of the corporate truth. Timely access to one comprehensive view of data goes to the root of providing effective risk management information for senior management decision making.

If you cannot achieve this comprehensive view quickly and consistently then you are prevented from taking appropriate action. Those companies that insist on keeping existing risk information silos will get considerably less benefit. Most organizations rely heavily on manual processes to consolidate multiple data sources when providing 'state-of-the-nation' reports to senior management and executive committees. This is inefficient, time-consuming and prone to human error. This is where reporting and communication of risk to internal management institutional investors and external regulators becomes an imperative. Reducing risk is a key business goal of every organization in today's dynamic, competitive economic climate.

In addition, your organization must focus on what 'we must do successfully' to provide greater assurance that you will meet your growth targets. The determination of critical success factors (what you must do well) is fundamental to ensuring that the organization is able to ultimately measure its progress towards the achievement of growth objectives (see Figure 9.3.4).

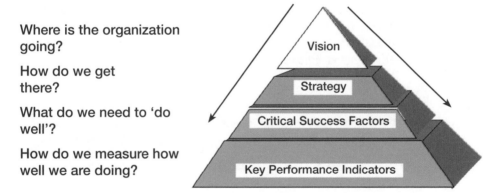

Where is the organization going?

How do we get there?

What do we need to 'do well'?

How do we measure how well we are doing?

Vision

Strategy

Critical Success Factors

Key Performance Indicators

Measure the factors that create value in the organization

Figure 9.3.4   Key performance indicators must be linked to strategy...

The threats to these critical success factors must also be incorporated into your organization's growth risk profile.

Risk management and performance reporting

So how do investors assess good risk management?

They consider board-level ownership, understanding and communication of risk issues as the keys to risk management success. Investors also see very clear benefits from getting it right, including fewer negative surprises, greater financial stability and opportunity for profitability.

■ Investors will reward or penalize companies on the basis of their perceptions of risk management:
  − 82% will reward good risk management by paying a premium;
  − 61% have avoided investments because of insufficient risk management;
  − 48% have de-invested because of it.
■ Investors believe responsibility for risk management starts at the top, with the CEO and the board.
■ Investors want more openness and face-to-face communication, beyond the reports and accounts, in order to understand risk management policies and practices.
■ Transparency was a top priority for 69% when making an investment, ahead of the business model and track record of the company.

A positive dialogue on your terms

The key is to have a complete and accurate picture of your organization's risk management position at any point in time so that information for decision making is available to senior management and the necessary reports are available for institutional investors, analysts and regulators. A positive ongoing dialogue is needed to ensure that investors and analysts do not get any surprises and that they have the necessary confidence in your risk management stewardship.

Stephen F Kelly, idRisk, working in partnership with Alexander Forbes Group. Alexander Forbes Risk Services Limited is authorized and regulated by the Financial Services Authority.

DO YOU KNOW THE SECRETS

Being able to identify and manage risk is increasingly recognised as a key leadership skill.

The Institute of Risk Management can equip you with the knowledge, tools and techniques fundamental to managing your organisation's risks.

OF GOOD RISK MANAGEMENT?

Courses for individuals

- professional qualification (MIRM)
- introductory qualification (CIRM)
- two-day training for directors
- a range of distance-learning modules

Enterprise-wide training

- two-day introductory risk management training
- adaptable to your organisation's needs
- choice of delivery – use your own in-house trainers, or IRM course providers

The Institute of Risk Management
Delivering high quality risk management education

For information on risk management qualifications, training, events, jobs, and membership, contact:

Aiden Watts
info@theirm.org
+44 (0) 20 7709 9808
www.theirm.org

A World at Risk

In many ways, life today is far less risky than in the past, yet great prominence is given to risk and its consequences. Despite technological advances and growing life expectancy we tend to perceive the world as increasingly uncertain and unpredictable.

This sense of uncertainty is all pervasive. It's there every time we open a newspaper, turn on a TV or surf the web: we are inundated with images of risk. Yet we cannot avoid risk, nor should we. Just imagine a world without it – in the absence of risk, there would be no innovation, no reward and no responsibility. Businesses face risk every day. In fact, without risk a business or organisation would not grow and thrive. Risk is a positive force for growth and success, turning uncertainty and discovery to every individual's and organisation's advantage.

Risk management, meaning on the one hand the avoidance of shocks and uncertainty in the areas where we have no control, and on the other the successful implementation of change where we can control the outcome, is coming of age as a discipline.

Organisations that manage risk effectively and efficiently, are more likely to achieve their goals and at lower overall cost
Today, risk management is no longer just a job role. It is also an essential management skill alongside more established areas such as HR, IT and marketing. In other words it's something that all business leaders do. Despite this, there are aspects of risk management that do require specific technical skills.

Introducing IRM

IRM promotes excellence in risk management through delivery of relevant practical education and training.

Established as a not-for-profit company, and governed and led by its members, IRM is independent of any one university, sector or specialism. It is an 'educational hub' for risk management, bringing together people interested in risk from every sector.

Training and qualifications

IRM offers a range of courses, from on-line risk awareness training through to internationally-recognised professional qualifications.

The two-day introductory training course *Management of Risk and Uncertainty* offers business leaders the opportunity to learn the fundamental risk management tools and techniques.

For those who want to learn more, IRM offers a six-month Certificate qualification (CIRM) and a three year professional Diploma programme (MIRM).

The Institute can also provide a programme suitable for adoption as your organisation's own in-house training, which is fully adaptable to suit any sector or business area.

Want to know more?

For information on risk management education, training and events, contact IRM on **info@theirm.org** call **+44 (0)20 7709 9808** or see **www.theirm.org**

'The policy of being too cautious is the greatest risk of all'
– Jawahardal Nehru (1889-1964)

Steve Fowler
Chief Executive Officer
The Institute of Risk Management

Project success in dynamic enterprises

Cut the leeches sucking your resources dry and make your projects nimble 'dolphins', says Ky Nichol, Senior Principal Consultant at Pcubed

Fast-growing, dynamic enterprises have a unique set of opportunities and challenges. Often launched with the aim of reaping sizeable returns from newly forming high growth sectors, they play a high-stakes game to come out on top.

Beyond the competition and rewards, there are two further characteristics of this environment that these organizations are required to address if they are to survive. First, high potential returns and growth opportunities are rarely in existing sectors, or sectors adjacent to the enterprise's existing skill sets. Organizations are challenged with building capabilities from scratch without a clear framework or boundaries. The other side of the coin is the opportunity to do things right from the beginning.

Second, high-growth business sectors are found at the emergent cutting edge of marketplaces. Their entrants balance the risk of unfavourable market collapse against high potential rewards. It's an environment fraught with uncertainty, yet it is also one riddled with opportunity, which energizes an execution culture.

These vanguard companies that operate in this arena have the challenge to build the right capabilities and manage the right risks to forge the best path through this unknown territory. Composed of equal helpings of opportunity and uncertainty, the best path can never be a case of crafting a master strategy, then hounding delivery to hunt it down. This is a domain where iterative learning practices win out and organizational agility combined with light but firm process is the best practice.

From our experience at Pcubed of delivering over £30bn worth of business change programmes, we have worked with our clients to develop effective approaches to this challenge. Focused upon how we invest in projects, how we tend them during execution and how we have set them up in the first place, this approach builds on pragmatic project management best practice together with hard-won experience.

Where it all tends to go wrong

Fast-growing, dynamic enterprises have limited resources with which to make their venture a success and must invest well to attain market leadership. Consequently, the approach taken to launching and managing the projects is critical. In this area there are common mistakes to be avoided, mistakes that result in hampering the organization if not destroying its competitiveness.

The first common error is concerned with how enterprises launch their projects. The nature of the competitive marketplace requires rapid reaction times to outmanoeuvre the competition. Although often taken as an excellent driver for motivating the organization into action, it also drives a perception of planning as an obstacle, because 'we just want to get things done'. Organizational nosedives take place here, ranging from avoiding categorizing anything as a project and allowing a chaotic environment of pet project mayhem, to very little project definition, resulting in projects that either crash and burn or do not deliver against business requirements.

The second failure mode relates to poor herding of the project portfolio. Assuming that projects have passed the first hurdle and have been objectively evaluated by the organization prior to investing in them, the next challenge is farming them effectively so that they deliver their benefits. Here organizations need to be able to cull poorly performing projects and foster the star projects. Without the capability to weed out problem child ventures, the organization is brought down by too many projects over-indulging at the resource trough.

The third failure mode results from betting the portfolio on 'whale' projects. It seems to be in our nature to match the huge challenges in our marketplaces with huge integrated projects. With all of our eggs in few baskets, it becomes difficult to steer these behemoths within our portfolios. As a result, they either continue for far longer than they are useful, as we cannot bear to cull them, or we kill them before they deliver, as we cannot steer their bulk.

Lessons learned

In working with our clients to avoid these pitfalls we have collectively developed a number of lessons learned. In overcoming the first challenge of scrutinizing the entry of a fledging project into our portfolio, there are a number of critical points. These are focused upon getting objective comparable information on the proposed project and being able to evaluate new projects against current commitments (Table 9.4.1).

Against the challenge of quickly eliminating the leech projects that suck scarce resource out of the portfolio for poor return, it is vital to evaluate the portfolio

Pcubed®

Pcubed is the global leader in program management, helping organisations to deliver successful change. With unmatched expertise in the discipline of program management, **Pcubed** has successfully delivered more than 2,500 individual engagements across industries and the public sector.

Our global resource pool of more than 350 professional consultants helps optimise the performance of our clients' program portfolios, shapes and drives key program initiatives and improves our clients' underlying project management capability. Results matter and our pragmatic approach means that we:

Deliver the desired results on programs by providing teams of experienced program management professionals to shape, manage and drive them to successful completion

Improve your capability to deliver programs and projects through practical, sustainable processes and tool solutions

Get the job done by providing experienced and focused resources whose objective is the success of your program

Complex Program Delivery

Programs and large, complex or critical projects cost organisations a great deal – in money, effort and reputation. Actually ensuring that they ultimately deliver what the organisation needs is a difficult task and there are no 'silver bullets' to ensure success.

Pcubed's solution to this is to assist clients in creating effective program delivery structures – shaping the program itself – and to ensure that the delivery processes are robust enough for the task in hand. This pragmatic approach is combined with 'hands-on' delivery and coaching or mentoring staff to ensure success.

Project Portfolio Management

Whilst the large and complex programs claim much of the attention, the reality is that, at any one time, organisations have many projects to manage. Managing such a portfolio of projects is always a challenge.

Pcubed's solution to this challenge is to apply standard and consistent project management tools and processes in a practical and sustainable way to improve delivery performance, reduce costs, manage resources more effectively and gain better management control at all levels. This builds capability into your organisation for both immediate and long term benefits.

So, whether your issues with your current projects are to do with getting the most out of IT, collaborating and using resources more efficiently across your organisation, financial control or deciding which projects are worthwhile, managing your portfolio effectively is essential.

Project & Program Staffing

Mobilising your organisation to meet the demands of a large program or a number of projects is a time-consuming and costly affair. Competition for key skills is fierce and you need people that are capable, experienced and committed to achieving your objectives. Permanent staff increases your cost base and contractors are of variable quality and commitment.

Pcubed's solution to this problem is simple. We provide staff with the key skills that you need backed not only by their own experience but also by the **Pcubed** organisation. Our staff are rigorously selected and come with the assurance that they are employed and managed by Pcubed, supported by all of the resources within **Pcubed** and dedicated to making your project a success. Whatever your needs, you always need the assurance that your resources can rise to the challenge of your project. **Pcubed** delivers this.

Solutions That Deliver

Pcubed offers solutions to your most pressing problems through the right combination of people, processes and tools with an emphasis on the practical and realistic – delivering results, not theory or dogma. Our approach has been forged out of working with more than 500 of the world's most successful organisations across industries and the public sectors.

Your success lies in our experience.

Programme Management – It's not what you've got it's how you use it.

How do hundreds of organisations get the right mix of processes, tools and competencies to deliver success?

Pcubed is the world's leading provider of Programme and Portfolio Management solutions to governments and Global 500 companies. Pcubed provides consulting and delivery services, and software solutions that measurably improve the outcomes of our client's strategic projects

Enabling Organisations to Deliver:

- Benefits realisation driven programme and project management

- Portfolio investment assurance to ensure confidence in spend

- Programme assurance to ensure confidence in delivery

- Vision, insight and control of programme and project information

Pcubed Solutions

Investment Assurance
– the ability to see which projects you should deliver in what order and to make sure the benefits are achieved.

Programme Assurance
– defining and delivering programmes using identified best practice processes and experienced and qualified Pcubed people.

Pcubed Programme Server
– the process and technology to properly manage the requirements for clear compliance, governance, gateway readiness and clear fact based reporting.

Contact us to find out more.

Pcubed, making success happen

www.pcubed.com
+44 20 74 62 01 00
ukinfo@pcubed.com

Pcubed
every project successful

continually. For fast-growing, dynamic enterprises, the challenge is often one of making the tough calls early. To make this happen the focus must be upon collecting a consistent set of key information on progress, together with achievability reviews. On that foundation, limited resources can be prioritized to the areas of highest likely return (Table 9.4.2).

Table 9.4.1   Evaluation of new projects

Promising Practices	*Danger Signals*
Objective business cases for projects and programmes	Lack of understanding of organization's capabilities
Live understanding of organization's capacity	Organization's desired strategic benefits unknown
Common evaluation framework for all projects and programmes	Programme and project contribution to strategic benefits unknown

Table 9.4.2   Prioritizing of proposed new projects

Promising Practices	*Danger Signals*
Programme and project assurance processes act as funding gateways between project and programme phases	Unusable programme and project information, collected on infrequent basis
Resourcing process driven by active programme and project prioritization	Lack of recognition of the impact of changes in the wider business context on the portfolio
Active management of delivery risk at an aggregate level	Business cases rarely updated if at all during life of projects or programmes

In tackling our inclination to create big projects to tackle big challenges, it is a question of scope engineering. Far better results come from the launching of more numerous and nimble 'dolphins' under the oversight of a programme with appropriate ownership and sponsorship (Table 9.4.3).

Implementing the above practices requires effort in amending organizational project management approaches, with a particular focus on governance. It is important to note, however, that none of them requires an onerous overly rigid system to make them work at the cost of organizational agility.

Table 9.4.3 Scope engineering of proposed new projects

Promising Practices	Danger Signals
Optimize the attractiveness and achievability of the desired goal through risk and benefits workshops	No distinction between programme and project management
Programmes focused on 'big goal' with series of modular projects to be culled or modified as needed	Lack of sponsors and owners responsible for the delivery of the overall scope
Active management of delivery risk at an aggregate level	Project management culture of making do with existing skills despite 'stretching' project scope

Conclusion

To a fast-moving, dynamic enterprise there are enough challenges resulting from the volatility of the marketplace without having to deal with projects that don't deliver. Whilst nobody could say that delivering projects is easy, there are a number of practices you can put in place to significantly increase your chances of success without hindering your organization's agility:

■ Set out to fund projects that are set up to deliver strategic benefits to the organization and that fit with current portfolio obligations.
■ Herd the projects within the portfolio effectively through the reviewing of consistent progress information and the staggering of funding by project phase rather than having whole-life budgets.
■ Set up your projects as modular, nimble 'dolphins' that you can steer, cull and initiate as necessary to deliver a programme responsible for the market-killing big goals.

To learn more about how to deliver value from portfolios and programmes, please contact Pcubed, 10 Bloomsbury Street, London WC1B 3SR (tel: +44 (0)20 7462 0100; e-mail: ukinfo@pcubed.com; website: www.pcubed.com).

Managing transition and change

Change is too complex to allow room for any assumptions about outcomes, say Peter McInnes, Nic Beech and Robert MacIntosh at Strathclyde Business School

Change, and how to manage it, remains one of the most enduring challenges in modern organizations. Many people regard the pace and complexity of change as ever-increasing. This is due to a range of factors, not least the impact of globalization, changes in technology, and the increasing demands and expectations of customers. As a result, there are few organizations for which 'standing still' is a serious option. Change and transition are the subjects of considerable volumes of research. However, there is no one best way to manage change that researchers and experienced practitioners can agree upon. This is because of the complexity of the subject matter, and the fact that each organizational situation will differ from previous ones. Hence, the lessons of change management cannot be transferred easily from one context to another, or from one successful leader to another, as what worked once in one situation will not necessarily work a second time in new circumstances.

However, this is not to say that it is impossible to learn from experience and research. We can develop better ways of approaching change, but we should not expect a one-size-fits-all, mechanical solution. The solutions are not mechanical; they are human, and as such the 'solution' is about improving human judgement and the ability to act and react effectively when leading and managing change. When one is managing change, effective communication is fundamental to success. Indeed, many failures of change initiatives are attributed, in whole or in part, to communication failures. In this chapter we will explore some of the complexities of change and their implications for management and communication.

Difficulties of managing change in growing firms

The size of a firm bestows upon it certain advantages and disadvantages with regard to the context in which leaders have to communicate and lead change. In small and entrepreneurial enterprises there are advantages in that it is often possible for the leader or entrepreneur to communicate directly with the staff. Normally, bureaucracy and 'red tape' can be avoided, and staff's reactions to communications can be recognized and resolved in face-to-face interactions. In larger firms there are the potential advantages of greater resource to apply to a particular change initiative, perhaps a higher degree of professional managerial support to analyse and implement a change, and a depth of experience that can help a senior team to predict and avoid some of the problems of change.

On the other hand, small and large organizations typically have the corresponding weaknesses. In small organizations there may be a lack of resources, and the leader can accidentally form a bottleneck in communication if he or she is overwhelmed with the everyday activities of keeping the business going. Communication might be relatively unsystematic, and there are fewer experiences to draw on in managing the change. Conversely, in larger organizations the leaders might be relatively remote from the staff, despite the best of intentions. Red tape can self-generate and grow rapidly, and the time required for fully effective face-to-face interactions might be prohibitive.

For the growing organization the skill is in maintaining the advantages of the small, whilst developing the advantages of the large. This entails knowing the staff sufficiently to be able to communicate effectively, being able to recognize when communication and change are working and when they are not, and adopting an inquiry-based approach to the management of change.

The multiple nature of organizational change

Change can be a radical transformation, for example when there is a merger, when a completely new product is launched or when a new market is entered in a remote part of the world. Alternatively, change can be more transitional or incremental – for example, when modifications are made to products or when there is an expansion into a market segment that is related to the company's current market. In either case it is vital that the staff affected by the change have a clear understanding of *why* the change has to happen, *what* is expected of them in the new way of being, and *how* the transition between the current practices and the future will be managed.

When the change is radical, there are often compelling reasons for it (such as dramatic loss of market share or dramatic opportunities for growth), and hence the emphasis of communication should be on the 'what' and the 'how'. When the change is transitional or incremental, it may be that staff do not immediately see the justification

www.strath.ac.uk/business

University of
Strathclyd
Business
School

STRATHCLYDE BUSINESS SCHOOL:
THE FIRST CHOICE FOR BUSINESS PROFESSIONALS

Strathclyde Business School, the longest established business school in Scotland and one of the largest of its kind in Europe, is committed to combining excellence with relevance in its teaching and research within an environment of continuing quality improvement.

The School is accredited by the three leading international bodies: EQUIS (the European Quality Improvement System), AACSB International (the Association to Advance Collegiate Schools of Business) and AMBA (the Association of MBAs), placing it in the top 1% of business schools worldwide.

The School offers one of the most modern, integrated MBA programs in the world. The Strathclyde MBA uniquely brings a holistic and integrative perspective to management education, with Strategic Management and Change being an available area of focus.

Strathclyde Business School offers an extensive choice of courses at undergraduate and postgraduate level, as well as opportunities for research, consultancy and executive education in the following subject areas:

Accounting	Hospitality Management
Business	Human Resource Management
Business Enterprise	International Business
Business Technology	Management
Business Law	Marketing
Economics	Operational Research
Finance	Tourism

EFMD
EQUIS
ACCREDITED

Accredited by
**Association
of MBAs**

E-mail:
business-school@strath.ac.uk

for the disruption to their normal way of working, and hence there needs to be a focus on the 'why' before the 'what' and the 'how' can be dealt with.

We should note, however, that change is 'in the eye of the beholder'. That is, what might be a transitional change to some might feel like a revolution to others. It is easy to underestimate the impact of a change on staff who have become used to a particular way of working, and the approach to communication needs to take this into account.

The multiple nature of organizational life

As firms grow, they typically employ staff who have different skill sets, attitudes and functions. This is important, as a company of clones may not have sufficient diversity to be creative and to effectively fulfil the requirements of specialized functional areas, such as design, marketing, production and so on. There may be staff of different ages, and staff focused on different parts of the product or market. Hence, we should expect there to be differences in opinion and perception. People perceive things as they impact upon themselves, and hence what might be a revolutionary change for some might be unimportant for others. To see most firms as simple and unambiguous would be a false vision. Rather, we are arguing that firms can be seen as multiple and contested. As a result, the process of change should be seen as one in which different versions of the firm are negotiated between different stakeholder groups, where the processes and mechanisms of continuity provide something of a common language through which this negotiation might be conducted; and where a central task of leadership is to manage the negotiated understanding of the *why*, the *what* and the *how* of change.

Communication and identity issues

Thus far we have drawn attention to the multiplicity of organization in three senses: first, the difficulties of bringing about change in growing firms; second, the multiple nature of change in organizations; and third, the potential multiplicity of perspectives on the future. These multiplicities have a profound effect on the way that change might be managed. For example, the common-sense notion that resistance often amounts to 'parochial self-interest' is made more problematic, as these interests represent a different idea of the organization and how it might progress. Whilst we do not wish to argue that *all* interests and views have an equal place in all circumstances, it is clear that one-directional high-level communication processes are insufficient, as they do not always help people understand the future state and their place within it.

The fact that there are different groups of interest and understanding, or different *identity groups*, underlies many of the problems that arise in managing change. Identity encapsulates the issues of who we are, what we do and how we relate to others. People often secure some sense of identity from their context as it currently exists, and change can disrupt their sense of self and 'place' in the organization. This generates ambiguity and confusion for individuals struggling to understand what the organization is and does, and how they, and the groups they belong to, contribute to this. Crucially, people often ask what place they will have in the future organization. The challenge for communication, then, is to explain to people the change in a way that allows them to see, or construct, a place for themselves in terms of the activities they will be carrying out and how they fit with those of others.

An inquiry-based approach to managing change

We are not suggesting that it is possible to give a one-best-way 'solution' to managing change, transition and communication. Rather, we believe that a stronger approach is to enter change management armed with a set of questions, the answer to which can inform managerial judgement. It is this judgement that is fundamental to the management of change. On the basis of the foregoing, we would suggest that the following areas for inquiry could be helpful to those managing change:

■ Don't assume complete unity in the organization. Rather, work out who the main sub-groups are and what their attitude to change might be.
■ Don't assume that others will understand your words as you intend them. Rather, consider the meanings others will read into your words.
■ Don't assume that leaders' intentions normally work out in practice. Rather, treat change activities as a series of mini-experiments in which you carefully monitor the results and check for unintended consequences.

Robert MacIntosh holds a chair in Strategic Management at the University of Glasgow. He began his academic career as a researcher at Strathclyde and completed his PhD in engineering there before moving into the area of business and management. He was recently Director of the MBA Programme at the University of Strathclyde and his main research interests lie in the area of strategic change. He has researched change processes with a variety of organizations from the public, private and voluntary sectors. Further details: robert@gsb. strath.ac.uk.

Mentoring for growth

A mentor can help you to work on your business, not in it, says Philip de Lisle

> *MENTOR n: 'a person who offers support and guidance to another; an experienced and trusted counsellor or friend'*

I'm always surprised at the number of times I've heard people say, 'why on earth do I need a mentor?', particularly at the SME end of the corporate space. Yet if you ask, most company owners and/or directors will admit to feeling lost and lonely at some point in their business lives. More importantly, they probably don't feel they can share these feelings with colleagues for fear of looking weak. This is where a mentor can help by bringing objectivity and focus to bear in an environment of total confidentiality and discretion. One can have a mentor at any point in one's career (and more than one, come to that), but I'm going to concentrate on board-level mentoring as this is the area that I know best. But before a mentor can help you grow your business, you've got to find one.

What is a mentor?

Let's start by getting one thing clear at the outset. A mentor is not a coach. And a coach is not a mentor. At the risk of oversimplification, the role of a coach is to encourage and question in order to get you, the individual, to be the best that you can be. A mentor is solely concerned with challenging you to get the best out of you and your business. Clearly, mentoring has an element of coaching within it and vice versa, but the focus of the role is very different. Unfortunately, the press seem to interchange the words 'mentor' and 'coach' at will – witness the *Sunday Times* Special Report in April 2005 ('Coaches can make you a real superhero') – which does neither role any favours.

'OK', I hear you say. 'So what?' Well, focus on the word 'challenge'. Running a business is a challenge in every sense of the word, from gaining sales orders to motivating/encouraging/directing your team through to keeping the bank manager happy (especially the last one). But ask yourself this: when was the last time that you were able to have a dispassionate discussion about your business and, more importantly, be really listened to by someone who genuinely wanted to help? Or had someone you could turn to, to bounce ideas off without feeling exposed to ridicule?

A good mentor will not tell you what you need to do even if it is blindingly obvious to him or her (you won't 'buy in' to the answers if they do). But the mentor will pose questions so that you find your own solutions. He or she certainly won't tell you what you want to hear.

Choosing a mentor

So, you've decided that getting a mentor is a good idea. How do you go about choosing one? Obviously there are no hard and fast rules on this, but here are some things to consider:

■ You must like each other, otherwise you won't feel comfortable baring yourself and the experience will be an unhappy one.
■ Look for someone who will stand up to you and challenge you. You will be asked a lot of questions, some of which may seem trivial or stupid, but might very well unlock the problem issue.
■ Be prepared for a bumpy ride in some of your sessions (I've had clients cry during a session – things can get emotional).
■ Do you want a mentor with experience of your industry? A disadvantage of this is that their vision might be as clouded as yours.
■ Be very clear what outcome(s) you want or need in order to achieve a good match. Never forget that you control the relationship – the mentor can only work with what you choose to share.
■ Be wary of those claiming to have a defined process (ie a formula) for mentoring. In my experience, mentoring needs to be very flexible if the mentored person is to get the most value from it; the mentor should have no preconceived ideas about the issue(s) under discussion, otherwise he or she may miss a vital nugget of information that can unlock the problem.

Finding your ideal mentor may take time, but the best way is usually by way of personal recommendation through your own network.

Should you pay for mentoring? A thorny question. If you can find someone who is prepared to devote a considerable amount of time to helping you for free, then you won't need to. The United Kingdom seems to have a traditional view of mentors as being white-haired (semi)-retired businesspeople (some of you may remember the BBC series *Troubleshooter* starring Sir John Harvey-Jones in the early 1990s). This view is not generally shared by the rest of the world. The downside of not paying for a mentor is that you are reliant on the mentor's generosity – and his or her schedule might not coincide with yours. Paying a mentor immediately puts your relationship on a professional footing and allows you to agree your expectations at the outset. As you will be dealing with a fellow professional with time management issues similar to your own, it will force you to set aside time to prepare for and conduct your sessions together – very much a case of working on your business rather than in it. My view, admittedly biased, is that professional mentors are more likely to make a real difference to your business because they are being paid to do so and can (and should) be judged accordingly.

Using your mentor

Now that you've chosen your mentor, what are you going to do with him or her? It's a good idea to use the first session to create a road map of what you want to achieve in the next month, six months, year and three years. Then decide what areas of that plan you want to work on with your mentor. Use your mentor during this planning session to critique everything, as the mentor's diverse experience should add considerably to what you can expect to achieve. In fact, plan a key area to work on with your mentor, because he or she can help you understand situations as they are and as they might be in the future. (I find role understanding, as in 'what do you think X will be thinking if you do that?', to be really helpful to clients.)

We all understand that to grow a business, you've got to increase sales either by landing new business (the 'sexy' end of sales) or by selling more to your existing client base (also known as 'farming', and very unglamorous but hugely profitable). Your mentor can help you to really understand your sales process and therefore improve it because he or she isn't 'doing' it but just observing. The mentor can help you see where cracks in your process are appearing (why do customers only order a maximum of three times?) and repair them (is it because the sales team sound bored on the phone?)

And what about your team? If your company is growing, do they have the necessary skills to grow with it? Would they benefit from a session or two with your mentor? Would you? (It may be useful to have another's insight into their capabilities and what might help them be more successful.)

Growing a business is never easy. But exiting one is even harder; I know – I've done it once or twice. If you are growing a business to exit it, then a mentor is a key part of your arsenal, as he or she can be an extra pair of eyes and ears to watch over what you are doing. One of the key benefits you will find is that you start to view your world in a different way – a bit like Zeus looking down from Mount Olympus.

Bringing down the curtain

As your working relationship continues, you might start to feel that you are getting less value from your mentor. Don't be alarmed or surprised by this. Like any relationship, it can begin with fireworks as the ideas you come up with can have dramatic and quick results (or returns on investment), but as time goes on it settles down to mutual respect and understanding. That doesn't mean the mentor is not valuable, but more that you are gaining in experience and expertise, so that the changes you make together are more subtle. But there is likely to come a point when a change of mentor will be beneficial. If you are paying a professional mentor, he or she will expect and understand this, but it can be tricky to end a 'no-cost' mentoring relationship.

So what is the key benefit of mentoring for growth? It forces you to work on your business, not in it. Which is what you've always wanted to do, isn't it?

Philip de Lisle is a veteran troubleshooter and mentor whose skills have been honed in challenging industries such as IT, telecoms, advertising and PR, and management consultancy. He is a mentor to many well-known business leaders and has more than 20 years' experience as a company director, during which time he has bought and sold numerous businesses, the most successful of which was Business Online Group plc. Further information:

Tel: 08456 44 22 98
e-mail: philip@philipdelisle.com.

10

International expansion

Are you ready to export?

The export market presents some unique challenges, says Jim Sherlock of the Institute of Export, but the potential rewards can make a major contribution to your company's overall success

Whoever said 'exporting is fun' had obviously never actually done any. There are many words that might describe exporting, but 'fun' would not be the most obvious one. 'Frustrating' would be in there somewhere, as would 'complicated', 'confusing', 'unpredictable' – even 'infuriating'.

But talk to experienced exporters and you will also hear words like 'fascinating', 'absorbing', 'exciting' and, most importantly, 'rewarding'. The fact is that exporting provides an incredible diversity of functions and environments, which balances the good with the bad and makes it an incredibly worthwhile experience for all those involved.

However, the unfortunate fact is that many companies entering into the export trade are not properly prepared and will only ever experience the bad side. Add to this the more typical situation in modern trade, which is that most exporters are also importers and, therefore, international traders rather than simply exporters, and the result can be even more problems.

If we are to get to the rewarding parts, in a personal as well as in a commercial sense, then we have to accept that there is an enormous range of pitfalls for the unwary, and our job is to prepare ourselves and our companies so that we enter overseas markets in full knowledge of what to expect – and ready to handle it.

First, we have to accept that overseas markets will inevitably be different from our home market – and it is not just that they speak a foreign language. Good research can reveal a myriad of political, legal, economic, technological, social and cultural differences. These have to be considered when we are deciding what we are going to sell and how we will sell it.

Then, when we are successful in getting the orders, we are faced with the complex and detailed procedures concerned with getting the goods or services delivered and, most importantly, getting paid.

So what sort of questions would an exporter have to answer before entering an overseas market?

- Do I have the commitment of the whole company to a long-term development of overseas markets?
- Do I have the administrative and financial resources to conduct an efficient operation?
- Do the current staff have the expertise to market our goods and services successfully overseas and collect payment?
- Can I find appropriate support from my bank, government services and freight forwarders?
- Which markets offer me the greatest potential at the minimum risk?
- What modifications will be needed to make my product/service saleable there?
- What price is the buyer prepared to pay and on what basis – ex-works or delivered?
- Do I need an agent or a distributor and, if so, how do I find one?
- How do I promote my products effectively?
- Are there any Customs barriers that I need to consider?
- How do I cover the risks of theft and damage to my goods in transit?
- How do I make sure that I get my money?

The answers are not always so obvious and will be different from one market to another. However, good research and the use of the many sources of information and advice available both in the United Kingdom and overseas will provide many answers.

Specifically, you should first contact your Local Business Link and talk to an international trade adviser (ITA), who can offer help in almost every aspect of your export planning and direct you to other sources of help and information. Foremost in providing that help is the employer of the ITAs, UK Trade and Investment, which is the export trade development section of the Department of Trade and Industry (DTI). It has an excellent website (www.uktradeinvest.gov.uk) full of vital information and links to your local ITAs and other useful sites.

Register for free and gain access to a wide range of information and support. In particular, go to 'Our Services' – 'Preparing to Trade' and try the 'Are you ready to export?' online questionnaire covering all the questions listed above and many more. The short time it takes you to complete the questionnaire will be time well spent when you print out the subsequent report which is generated from your responses. It will also allow you to make a direct contact with your local Business Link and an ITA who can follow up the preliminary report.

It is often the case that such a report will highlight the need for specialized training for new exporters in export marketing and the technical processes involved in distribution and payment. A number of organizations offer relevant short courses, notably the Institute of Export, which offers a comprehensive short-course training programme (details on www.export.org.uk).

Finally, it may be that as new exporters you are eligible to participate in a UK Trade and Investment programme called 'Your Passport to Export Success', which offers hands-on help, essential staff training and subsidized overseas visits.

There is a lot of information and help out there. Just make sure that you are not sharing the fate of the exporter who lost money because:

■ Its bone china dinner services specially designed for the Italian market failed to sell at all because they lacked a pickle bowl.
■ The Libyan flags in the left paws of the promotional teddy-bears were seen as an insult to the flag and were destroyed. (In most Muslim countries the left hand is for toilet purposes only!)
■ The sole distributor they appointed was actually already contracted to sell a direct competitor's products – which it continued to do with great success.
■ The 'before' and 'after' photographs that had worked so well for the sale of depilatory creams in English-speaking countries did not work so well when translated into Arabic, which reads from right to left. The firm forgot to reverse the pictures!

And how about the loss of £155,000 worth of goods because a comma instead of a full stop on an invoice presented against a letter of credit meant the bank rejected the documents? The buyer, quite legitimately, refused to pay, and, because the exporter did nothing, the original buyer then picked them up at the auction in the port of destination some 10 weeks later at a quarter of the original price. All could have been avoided with some basic research and good advice.

Exporting offers huge rewards both to the companies and the people involved, but the ill-prepared 'amateur abroad' will not survive in this fascinating but dangerous jungle.

Following experience in the UK export manufacturing sector and 20 years as Senior Lecturer in International Trade at Central Manchester College, Jim Sherlock, FIEx, MCIM, CertEd, is now a full-time trainer and consultant in international trade. He is the Director – Educational Projects of the Institute of Export, currently leading a number of projects in the United Kingdom and overseas in partnership with UKTI, the European Commission and a number of major manufacturing and service-sector corporates.

He is the co-author of *The Handbook of International Trade* (Kogan Page), author of *Principles of International Physical Distribution* (Blackwells) and a contributor to *Directions in International Marketing* (Routledge), *Financial Management Handbook* (FT Law and Tax), *Your Business Your Bank* (Institute of Directors), etc.

Dilemmas in international trade

Like music hall jokes, a number of the dilemmas faced in international trade are all too familiar, says Martin Allison at The Royal Bank of Scotland. The difference is that you don't have to sit and wait for the inevitable punchline

There are benefits commonly claimed for extending the range of countries you operate in. From a sales perspective it can:

■ open up new sources of income;
■ reduce exposure to downturns in the 'home' economy;
■ address vulnerability to increased competition in core markets.

From a purchasing perspective it offers:

■ access to new or enhanced product or services;
■ a means to reduce costs.

But everything in life comes at a price:

■ There will be a diversion of people and energy, potentially at lower returns, whilst a market presence or relationship is established.

■ International trade involves potentially greater uncertainty and risk: commercial, financial, economic, market related.

■ Strains on cash flow as physical and cultural distance translate into extended time frames between paying and being paid.

As we all know from painful experience, spotting an opportunity does not equate to realizing it! In this chapter I seek to illustrate some of these dilemmas that arise when you engage in international trade, but also to share some tips learned from customers who have managed them successfully. As I do so, you may see the similarities with a music hall joke!

Some common dilemmas

Got the sale, but where is the money?

Perhaps the oldest one of all! In a world where so much trade is on open account, it is particularly easy to be distracted by the big prize and lose sight of whether a buyer is ultimately good for the money.

Great sale, but how did it make a loss?

A common variation of the above. There can be quite a range of unfamiliar direct and indirect costs that arise when dealing in a new environment. And how often do the goalposts move during the course of a negotiation (after initial price indications have been given)?

Safe, but no one will buy!

I have come across exporters whose terms are cash in advance, payment in sterling. If you are in a powerful position it might be possible to get away with these terms, but they may not be a general recipe for sales success.

Why haven't I got what I paid for?

Trust is often crucial to commercial relationships. But this scenario begs the question about what steps have been taken in advance to ensure that promise equates to fulfilment.

Got the order, but how do I meet it?

Problems meeting an order are very visible to finance providers. Sometimes a business has committed to a significant order before the means to fund the supply, manufacturing, warehousing and credit terms have been fully explored.

Some tips

Do your groundwork before the event

The message that you should do your groundwork before the event will be reinforced more specifically below. But a range of potential issues can be identified, and addressed, up front with careful preparation.

Smart questions = smart answers

A surprising percentage of smart questions begin with 'what'? So, when considering new markets and trading relationships, examples might be:

- What can I afford to lose? This helps define your appetite for risk and even deals you may have to walk away from.
- What are the market norms? In some markets, open account is an absolute requirement; in others, secured terms such as letters of credit may be available.
- What is the nature of the relationship? There may be a level of mutual dependency that fosters trust and cooperation. Power may rest with the buyer or seller. Both can inform the appropriate response.
- What can I best manage now? Often there are alternative ways of managing risk. Each will carry with it performance obligations. For example, letters of credit are secure, but you need to present correct documentation to ensure prompt payment. Credit insurance requires you to comply with policy conditions if you wish to be certain of a successful claim.

Smart answers that fall out are likely to include:

- A clear view of the acceptable range of terms you can safely negotiate.
- Similarly, the areas of risk you are exposed to and need to actively manage. For example, if the target market has a norm of open account, then solutions such as credit insurance or factoring, that can help manage risk, could come into play.
- The need to be brutally honest about capabilities within your organization and those you need to acquire.
- Areas where you need to access expertise available externally. At one extreme it may mean using third-party skills (for example, to manage documentation); at another, just getting appropriate advice. In between may be simple training needs.

Have a clearly defined approach for each market

The commercial environment does vary. China is different from Hong Kong. Despite the considerable reform in China, the track record for enforcement of commercial rights will be stronger in Hong Kong. Within Europe there can be significant differences between North and South in the way business is conducted.

Address all elements of your approach in parallel

Some readers may have come across the old 'buy, ship, pay' framework. A number of activities in international trade can be divided into market development, transport and customs, and the financial elements (not least, making or receiving payment). An appropriate response involves building a response to each in an integrated way. You don't buy without thinking about how goods will be delivered and customs cleared. Payment and delivery risk can be managed better if there is good control of the logistics.

Similarly, careful structuring that takes account of the whole 'trade cycle' from initial order through to ultimate repayment by an end buyer can sometimes enable businesses to raise much higher levels of working capital finance than might otherwise be available. (This is particularly relevant for cash-hungry small businesses and has been a strong area of development in trade finance in recent years.)

Make the salesperson and the credit manager close allies

The premise here is that a salesperson will only negotiate an inappropriate contract out of ignorance (for example, of suitable credit terms to ask for). Similarly, credit managers need intelligence on the workings in particular markets. Effective functional responses cannot be developed in isolation.

Summary

A number of the common dilemmas faced in international trade can be as depressingly familiar as a music hall joke. Careful forethought and simple, practical approaches can help ensure you avoid the resulting groan of pain! I have suggested some practical tips. You may have some favourites of your own.

Martin Allison is the Head of International Banking Systems (IBS) at The Royal Bank of Scotland (RBS). IBS is a business that provides a full range of financial solutions and expertise to the bank's customers across all segments. It is a major force in the provision of trade-related financial services and recognizes how important international trade is to its customers.

Appointed as Head of IBS in January 2006, Martin has worked for NatWest and RBS for the majority of his career and started the Graduate Management Trainee programme 20 years ago in Leeds. He has held positions in Business Development, Corporate Finance, Change Management and General Management in the mid-market sector in many parts of the UK, most recently as Managing Director, Commercial Banking in London and the South East of England.

Contact details:
Tel: 020 7427 9054
e-mail: martin.allison@rbs.co.uk

Global expansion

Determine a structure for working overseas, says David Sayers at Mazars, otherwise one is likely to be imposed by the local authorities

One of the most difficult decisions for any growing business to make is when and if to start trading overseas.

In the first instance, simply selling goods to an overseas customer might create significant issues in terms of increased credit risk, possible duties and tariffs, and adherence to local laws. Nevertheless, a UK business with a sound product or service would be neglecting its true potential if it did not look overseas for different markets.

Often such things happen completely by chance, by word of mouth, without the need for an aggressive sales pitch. On the other hand, many businesses will be dependent upon third-party sales agents in the first instance, where a high degree of trust may need to be established before an effective working relationship is created. If adequate market research has already shown potential sufficient to justify you in creating your own overseas office, the business will be brought into a web of local labour laws and commercial and real estate issues. In tax terms alone, compliance costs can easily add on 30 per cent to overseas tax bills for owner-managed businesses.

The purpose of this chapter is to examine some of the potential pitfalls and opportunities inherent in overseas expansion and to provide some guidance through what can be something of a minefield.

Small acorns

In the first instance it is important, in tax terms at least, to draw a line between trading *with* and trading *in* a country. In direct tax terms it is only the latter scenario that will normally create a taxable presence. However, for VAT purposes it is often the case that an obligation to register will come about well in advance of direct tax reporting – for example, under the distance selling regulations. This is particularly the case with US sales tax, where even the presence of an itinerant salesperson can create a liability in every state he or she visits. Failure to register at the correct time can lead to significant indirect tax penalties in certain countries.

In theory, in direct tax terms a taxable presence can be created by the same travelling salesperson with no fixed base, if the salesperson can conclude contracts on behalf of his or her employer. In the same way, if a third-party agent acts exclusively for the home state business, although the agent may be part of a completely distinct enterprise, he or she can unwittingly create a tax charge for the customer.

Corporate structures

Once a decision is taken to set up a more permanent presence, then you need to decide on your choice of vehicle. Often this is tax driven, but it also depends very heavily on how the entity concerned will be perceived in the local market by the end consumer of the product or service. In most countries, customers will feel more comfortable dealing with a locally established, recognized entity rather than a nebulous branch of an overseas parent whose identity they can't confirm.

Even choosing a company can create unexpected tax and commercial consequences. In France, for example, there are many different kinds of corporate form – for example, non-trading companies designed specifically to hold real estate, vineyards and agricultural operations. Each entity needs to be scrutinized to determine its tax and legal status, both locally and in the home state, as often mismatches arise.

Setting up a company too can sometimes take months. Minimum share capital of 25,000 euros is not unusual – a far cry from the UK shelf company industry, which provides a £2 company in 24 hours.

Beware also of allocating too much power to local directors; they can often find themselves in conflict with shareholders' wishes and be extremely difficult and expensive to remove.

Code contradiction

For Anglo-Saxon businesses setting up abroad, one of the biggest differences to come to terms with is contradictory local codes. Much of continental Europe is founded on a civil law system based on written legal codes, rather than the Anglo-Saxon common law system, which is based much more on precedents created by judicial decisions over time. Whilst the impact of EU law has diluted this difference to some extent, certain entities such as trusts, and ideas such as the separation of legal and beneficial ownership, are often alien concepts to our continental colleagues. In addition, many UK businesses are quite unprepared for the accounting and legal complexities they may face.

As has been widely documented in the press in recent years, such systems are often highly protective of their workforce, offering a wonderful comfort blanket for employees, but a heavy social cost in terms of payroll taxes and redundancy packages.

In certain countries it is not uncommon for employers' national insurance to be almost 50 per cent on top of basic salary and for compensation for loss of office to be a year's salary or more.

Financing the expansion

Building a business in a new market is likely to have a significant impact on working capital. Local banks will often be wary of new start-ups from overseas asking for credit facilities, even with a parent company guarantee, and are invariably less flexible than UK banks. It will therefore usually fall to the parent company to fund the new overseas business through an inter-company account.

If the loan is to exist for any length of time, the UK tax authorities will usually ask for interest to be charged or make a corresponding adjustment to the parent company's tax computation. Moreover, if the subsidiary is inadequately capitalized, the local tax authority may seek to recharacterize some of the loan as equity and thereby deny a tax deduction for part of the interest. Therefore, whilst loan finance is often the first port of call, businesses will often find that they are called upon to inject a significant proportion of equity in order to create a third-party lending scenario. Unlike a loan, this equity is often rather difficult to recover if funds are needed in the United Kingdom.

The same third-party test applies to inter-company pricing. Most tax authorities around the world will insist that prices charged between parents and subsidiaries are demonstrably arm's length, with often onerous documentation requirements and draconian penalty regimes.

Making it more permanent

Prospective users of commercial property will also find that leases and acquisitions are subject to higher taxes than in the United Kingdom. A comparative analysis of stamp duty rates across Europe makes the oft-complained-about UK rate of 4 per cent seem relatively modest. Most countries, unlike the United Kingdom, impose a capital gains tax on non-resident landlords holding investment property. Others will impose a penal tax rate on property held in a tax haven, some even taxing the sale of shares in foreign real estate companies rather than the sale of the asset itself.

Bringing the cash home

Let us assume that your overseas business ventures have been successful and that you now have subsidiaries in a dozen countries. The key issue for any outward investor is successful repatriation of cash for use in the next venture. In order to do this, however, our successful entrepreneur may have to negotiate a myriad of exchange controls and withholding taxes, each of which is a potential cost of capital. In recent years China has attracted an immense amount of inward investment, not least because of low labour rates and attractive tax incentives. Nevertheless, it still has a restrictive exchange control environment and many of the tax incentives are geared around local reinvestment rather than repatriation of profits.

With some planning, a holding company jurisdiction will have been chosen at the outset that permits a free flow of funds back to the ultimate parent without withholding taxes. Such funds may then be recycled, perhaps without even having to go back to the ultimate parent (therefore escaping tax) and used to reinvest in the next venture.

Conclusion

Investing time in planning and research early on is likely to produce significant savings further down the line. Following these golden rules should facilitate your expansion overseas:

- Draw a line and establish your modus operandi overseas in advance, before the local authorities do it for you.
- Don't just accept the first corporate form that is offered to you. Make sure it meets your requirements both in the United Kingdom and in the local jurisdiction. Take heed of what the tax authorities and your customers will think.
- Plan for culture changes and carefully calculate the on-costs of both setting up and closing down if it all goes awry.
- Look at your financing plans in advance. Don't be fearful of injecting too much equity; many countries will expect a much higher minimum than in the United Kingdom. Expect banks to be more complex and burdensome.
- Look out for onerous lease commitments and a higher overall tax burden on commercial property. Always add on at least 10 per cent to the purchase price to allow for on-costs.
- Think about your outward investment structure at the earliest possible stage. It may seem expensive early on, but the investment is usually worthwhile in order to avoid future tax costs that might impact on profits at a later date.

David Sayers is Head of International Tax for Mazars in the United Kingdom. He has extensive experience in advising businesses on setting up new ventures all over the world through Mazars' international offices. His primary expertise lies in tax planning, but he is often involved in bridging the cultural and linguistic gaps that may arise. David is a regular presenter on international taxation issues both in the United Kingdom and abroad.

Mazars' clients include a wide range of owner-managed businesses (including some of the United Kingdom's fastest-growing entrepreneurial businesses) as well as international corporate groups and listed companies (17 per cent of the FTSEurofirst 100), public-sector bodies and numerous private individuals.

Tel: 01582 700704
e-mail: david.sayers@mazars.co.uk
www.mazars.co.uk

Doing business in China

China is a growth phenomenon, but whether you are sourcing production there or exporting your goods, the rules of engagement might not be what you expect, says Joanna Lavan of Connect China

Chinese economic growth has averaged 10 per cent per annum over the past 20 years and the statistics for its manufacturing are staggering. For example, over 50 per cent of the world's cameras and 90 per cent of the world's toys are produced in China. China is the world's fourth largest exporter, with a 6 per cent market share of global exports, and 50–60 per cent of China's imports are materials used to produce exports. Companies simply cannot afford *not* to look at the opportunities in China.

There are real opportunities both ways. Many British companies are taking advantage of the cheaper labour, skilled workforce and large markets to produce high-volume, low-value and labour-intensive products in China and keeping the higher-value, higher-tech products for manufacture at home. The rapid development of the service sector in China has presented immense opportunities for British companies too. And add on to that the potential for selling your products to the Chinese domestic market, with a population of 1.3bn.

Take a medium- to long-term view

You need to be committed to the China market as regards both financial and time resources. Remember that China is a medium- to long-term market and it is important to stay focused on your goals, even if you encounter problems. It is also important to be patient.

Be selective in choosing the right partner

1. Draw up a detailed brief of the product/service/company you are seeking.
2. Ask the agencies to draw up a list of potential partners with *verified* contact details. The information you receive should include a brief overview of each Chinese company, with full contact details, including a name who can communicate in English. The Chinese companies should all have been contacted by the agency and have shown interest in your enquiry.
3. Once you have received the research information, contact each of the potential partners immediately whilst it is still fresh in the Chinese mind. Leave any amount of time before you make contact and you may have been forgotten, and the leads will go cold.
4. From initial communications you will be able to draw up a shortlist of the most suitable suppliers. Try at this stage to plan a visit to China to meet them. Planning before you visit the market will be necessary.

Translate your business materials

1. Exchanging business cards is one of the first things you do when meeting potential Chinese partners. It is essential to have your business cards printed in Chinese on the reverse side of your English cards. Make sure you put the appropriate title on. China is a hierarchical society; the right 'title' can affect whether you get to meet the decision makers.
2. Also have an A4 profile of your company translated to leave with the Chinese. Remember, the majority of Chinese managers don't speak English.
3. Any technical documentation/specifications should also be translated to make sure that everything is understood.
4. Take samples or drawings with you to show the manufacturers, *but* at the same time take necessary precautions to protect your intellectual property rights.
5. Use a credible agency with Chinese nationals for your translations.

Visiting China

1. At this stage it is ideal to visit each of the potential partners to get to know them and look over their facilities. 'Ninety-nine per cent of success is showing up.' China is a huge market and each region has its own consumer preferences and business needs. No one is better suited than you, or a representative of your business, to investigate and determine whether you can build up a good relationship with any of the potential partners. By visiting China, you can better understand the Chinese business.
2. Even if the potential partners speak English, use an *interpreter*. Because there are more than 700 strong dialects spoken in China, try to select an interpreter from the region you are visiting. The interpreter can then understand what is going on behind the scenes!

3. Make sure you visit with a full meeting schedule already arranged (it may not be confirmed fully until the day before you leave) and book your interpreter.
4. It is a good idea at this stage to have an understanding of Chinese business culture.

Pay attention to *guanxi*

The Chinese business mentality is very much 'You scratch my back, I'll scratch yours.' Frequent contact fosters friendship, and the Chinese feel obligated to do business with their friends first. Developing and nurturing guanxi (*not what you know, but who you know!*) requires time and resources.

For large and long-term orders, building *guanxi* is particularly important. You will need to visit your partners regularly to consolidate the orders and to strengthen and extend the relationships.

Do your due diligence

Preparation is the key to success. Some firms have assumed that China is too different and too opaque, so they enter the market with less information than they would normally require. Once you have selected potential partners, it's important to carry out due diligence on each of them. Due diligence reports on a company can be bought in modular form from £30 to £450 from agencies specializing in providing credit information or through legal firms located in the province where the Chinese partner is registered. You will, however, need to bear in mind that Chinese companies keep at least two sets of books!

Chinese negotiation tactics

Observing Chinese business etiquette is important for successful negotiations. Try to give the Chinese 'face' and not to embarrass them.

In China, negative replies are perceived as impolite. Instead of saying 'No', they will say 'Maybe', 'I'll think about it'. 'No big problems' may mean 'We still have problems'. When they say 'Yes', it does not necessarily mean that they agree with you; it means 'I hear what you say'.

The Chinese can be gracious hosts but tough negotiators. It is common for them to 'promise' future orders to negotiate for discounts from the seller. Don't be fooled by this tactic and keep in mind your bottom profit margin.

Other tactics deployed include making reference to their competitor's quote, playing a delaying tactic if they know you have a tight time schedule, breaking for a banquet (which often means plenty of alcohol) and change of personnel for 'good cop, bad cop' techniques. *Remember, time has a different value in China!*

It is a common practice that the top management do not get involved in direct negotiations, to avoid any awkward situations. They will emerge when the negotiations reach a sticky point to add extra weight and/or to offer a 'mutually' beneficial compromise – although it generally leans to their favour.

During the negotiations, you need to clarify:

■ scope of supply;
■ payment terms (beware of retentions) and secure payment: cash with order, L/C, etc;
■ delivery terms;
■ other commercial terms – eg guarantees;
■ price.

Leave the price until last during negotiations!

Using a good interpreter not only aids the negotiations by conveying accurate messages to both parties, but he or she can also pick up the 'small talk' that may influence the decision making.

Intellectual property rights

If your intellectual property is critical, think twice about taking it to China. Everything is copied, down to the 'smallest manufacturing fault'. Registering your trademark or patent is recommended and does provide some protection, particularly since China's entry into the World Trade Organization. If you are sourcing from China, try to spread the manufacture of components across several manufacturers. Don't put all your eggs into one basket!

Contracts

It is worth noting that when you are dealing with the Chinese, all contracts are 'China type', with terms and conditions in favour of the Chinese. The Chinese and Westerners tend to 'interpret' contract conditions in different ways. Zhou Enlai, first Premier of China, once said, 'We Chinese mean what we say.' The difficulty is to work out what they are really saying.

For Westerners, signing the contract marks the end of the negotiation; whilst to the Chinese, the contract signifies only the beginning of your business relationship. There is always room for further negotiation!

The contract needs to be prepared in *both* languages, English and Chinese, so that both parties know what is contained in the contract.

Always keep your contractual promises – even if the other party 'appears' not to.

When the going gets tough…

The Chinese will push you as far as they think you are prepared to go but they always like the last word.

To avoid an embarrassing situation or to soften the atmosphere, suggest a break or invite the Chinese to a banquet. Talk about their favourite subjects such as food, family and Premier League football. This is a 'relationship-building' process and hopefully will lead to their regarding you as a friend – and everything can be sorted out between friends.

Remember, goodwill, friendship and a handshake can often mean more than a contract.

Payment terms

Ask the Chinese supplier to quote fob Chinese port for the goods. This enables you to compare prices without the shipping element. Some Chinese factories will have long-established relationships with shipping companies, which may have an impact on the final price.

It is quite common for the Chinese to require a payment upfront for the goods you order. This normally covers the cost of the raw materials and labour. The balance of the payment is very commonly made via a letter of credit.

It is in your interest to negotiate and retain a small percentage (eg 10 per cent), which will be paid once you have sight of the goods in satisfactory quantity and condition as per the contract.

Ganbei!

One of the most important ways of building and developing your business relationship with your potential Chinese partner is through eating and drinking. From the first meeting, you are likely to be invited to a banquet with plenty of food (lots of courses, usually selected by your host!) and plenty of toasting with the Chinese spirit Maotai, wine or beer. *Ganbei* literally means 'Empty your glass!' Each of the Chinese representatives will take their turn in toasting you. Beware... you may empty your glass several times against their one. But it's part of the fun!

Just one final word when doing business in China... I Ching (the oldest book in China) says, 'The only thing that does not change is that everything changes.'

ConnectChina is a private independent consultancy that helps companies and organizations develop business in China through trade and investment. Services include project management, feasibility studies, research, identification of partners, business communications, business events, specialist training.

For further information, contact:

Joanna Lavan, FIEx
Director
ConnectChina Ltd
Unit 33, Batley Business and Technology Centre
Batley

West Yorkshire WF17 6ER
Tel: +44 1924 420780
e-mail: joanna@connectchina.co.uk
www.connectchina.co.uk

Hong Kong – gateway to China

The Pearl River Delta is the world's factory and Hong Kong is its hub, says Dora Kay, head of international marketing, Airport Authority Hong Kong

Trading has been key to Hong Kong's economic growth. While we have traditionally matched buyer and seller for consumer goods which are exported from Asia to the major markets in Europe and the United States, we have now extended our scope to manage the entire supply chain, integrating the whole process end to end from the earliest stages of production all the way to the consumer.

Leveraging trading strengths

There are some 380,000 small and medium enterprises (SMEs) in Hong Kong, forming the backbone of our economy. The majority of SMEs are engaged in business with two or more economies, leveraging Hong Kong's traditional strengths as a trader into being a logistics hub and supply chain management centre in the region. With the opening of China in 1978, in particular the establishment of special economic zones in southern China, together with foreign direct investment, the Pearl River Delta (PRD) has seen a phenomenal development of its manufacturing industry.

Integrating with the Pearl River Delta

Hong Kong and the PRD have been closely linked with each other in many ways. Culturally, a large proportion of Hong Kong's residents have their roots in the PRD. Thus, many of the dialects spoken by people in the PRD are also spoken in Hong Kong. Economically, there has been a perfect blend of our respective strengths. Hong Kong is rich in capital, business experience, market knowledge, international contacts and management expertise. On the other hand, the PRD has an abundant supply of land and labour at a much lower cost. As a result, based on a perfect blend of our respective strengths, there has been a massive relocation of Hong Kong's labour-intensive production lines to the PRD, thus creating one of the world's biggest economic booms. The PRD is now undisputedly 'the world's factory', while Hong Kong is a fully fledged service economy, with 87 per cent of our gross domestic product coming from services.

Acting as China's supply chain manager

Now that China is a member of the World Trade Organization its economy will grow further and it will play a more prominent role in world trade. In addition to enhancing its export capabilities, China, with its vast population, will become one of the fastest-growing importers of goods and services from around the world. Hong Kong's extensive knowledge and experience in global trade will play an important role by adding value to this development process.

For many years, Hong Kong has been a major trading post in the region. We are endowed with an excellent natural harbour and the world's busiest container port, as well as one of the world's busiest airports for both passenger and cargo flow. We also possess an excellent communications infrastructure and an efficient and well-educated workforce. All these advantages, together with our wealth of experience in international trade accumulated through the years, have enabled Hong Kong to position itself as the supply chain management centre of the region, where a myriad of supply chains criss-cross and are controlled from Hong Kong. Our position as a global and regional business centre is also underpinned by the rule of law, economic freedom, a business-friendly environment, free trade and entrepreneurship.

All roads converge on Hong Kong

In terms of land transport, Hong Kong is at the centre of China's national highway system. This network comprises expressways running up the coast from Hong Kong to Shanghai and Beijing; from Beijing to Zhuhai in the PRD; from Chengdu, Sichuan, to the PRD; and from Kunming, Yunnan, to the PRD. All these routes converge on Hong Kong and significantly expand our catchment area. The planned Hong Kong–Zhuhai–Macao bridge will further enhance our accessibility in the region.

Hong Kong International Airport: gateway to China

As the movement of goods becomes increasingly dependent on air to meet time-sensitive delivery requirements, Hong Kong International Airport (HKIA) plays a pivotal role in the economic integration between Hong Kong and the PRD, acting as the natural gateway of the region. Located strategically at the mouth of the PRD, and on the international time zone between Asia and the West, HKIA is within five hours' flying time to 50 per cent of the world's population. Over 80 airlines operate some 5,500 flights a week from HKIA to more than 146 destinations worldwide, including 43 in mainland China. In 2005, HKIA's passenger and cargo volumes reached record highs of 41 million and 3.4 million tonnes respectively. Furthermore, air cargo now accounts for 34 per cent of Hong Kong's trade value at a whopping US $201bn.

Multi-modal transport hub

Maximizing our airport island location, special facilities and services have been developed and are continuously being upgraded, to enhance accessibility to our PRD catchment area, which has a population of 50 million. On land, 200 luxury coach trips link HKIA with 50 cities in the PRD every day, with 1.5 million passengers taking advantage of this service in 2005.

Passengers travelling between HKIA and the PRD can also make use of SkyPier's high-speed ferry services. In 2005 this sea–air transport service enabled over 1.3 million passengers to be transferred directly from SkyPier to their aircraft boarding gates via bonded coaches, thereby bypassing Hong Kong border entry formalities. The world's first cross-boundary luggage check-in service was also introduced recently at the Shekou SkyPier terminal in Shenzhen to enable passengers to fully enjoy their travel while flying via HKIA.

An on-airport Marine Cargo Terminal provides one-stop service, including round-the-clock customs clearance and truck delivery services to and from the air cargo handling facilities at HKIA. Linking some 20 ports in the PRD and HKIA, the Marine Cargo Terminal is strategically important to Hong Kong as the premier gateway of southern China.

Meeting future demand

A new multi-purpose development, SkyPlaza, will be opened at HKIA in the latter half of 2006. In addition to office, retail and catering facilities, SkyPlaza is a building complex where rail, air, road and sea transport will seamlessly converge. SkyPlaza will also serve as HKIA's second terminal, with airline check-in counters and customs and immigration facilities to meet future demand.

Mindful of the need to maintain and enhance its position as the superhub of Asia and gateway to China, HKIA is developing Master Plan 2025 to review and revise its long-term vision and strategies, and plan the infrastructure necessary to meet future demand.

For further details, contact kayd@hkairport.com.

Information by market

HM Revenue & Customs holds a wealth of free information on flows of business into and out of the United Kingdom. Stephen Browning gives direction on how to check the performance of particular types of product

It is widely accepted that information is a highly valued commodity. It is vital to industry and to politicians, and is even used extensively by the criminal fraternity. The trick with information is the ability to rationalize the quantity of data to the ultimate in quality.

Information overload is as potentially damaging as a lack of material facts. The ability to extrapolate essential figures from a plethora of data with relative ease, therefore, is a crucial aspect to anyone relying upon the resulting outcome. Just as crucial is the capacity to access data requirements, at times to suit, with minimal corporate expense.

The creation of www.uktradeinfo.com has taken all of these factors into consideration and forms the basis for the ongoing website development. This website is a government site run by the Statistical Analysis of Trade Unit (SATU), which is part of HM Revenue & Customs (HMRC). The information contained within the site is centred around the statistics involved in all UK imports and exports of physical goods.

So, what benefits may existing or potential international trading businesses expect from the use of this website?

The Trade Data section has provision for the manipulation of trade data tables ranging from 1997 to now. This includes the ability to 'drill' down to an eight-digit (commodity code) level. Access requires a simple registration process. The service is free of charge.

Figure 10.5.1 is a simple trade data table showing some tailored data. The figure shows data that have been extracted, and manipulated, from the UK world trade for 2005. The result shows the UK imports and exports of two different type categories of books to and from the Irish Republic, Australia and the United States. The quantity shown equates to the net mass in kilograms.

Completed tables may be downloaded to an Excel spreadsheet or converted into a variety of graphs.

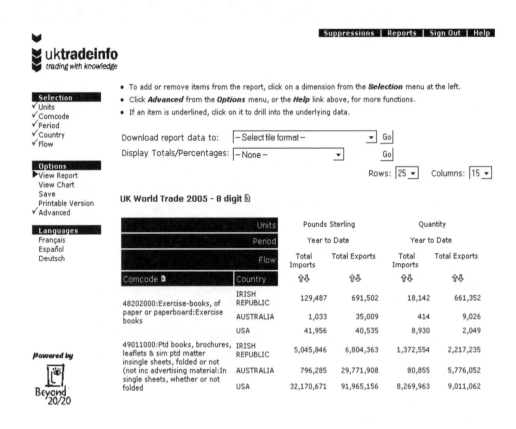

Figure 10.5.1 Trade data table from www.uktradeinfo.com

Note: Listed under the 'Selection' options is 'Comcode'. This features a searchable function to help find the correct commodity code.

A table for UK Regional trade data may be created using a similar process. Figure 10.5.2 gives regional data for the North East of England. The figure illustrates, in pounds sterling, the amount of import and export trade in the North East for Inorganic Chemicals, Textile, Yarn, Fabrics, Made Up articles etc and Iron and Steel. The commodities have been selected by using the Standard International Trade Classification (SITC) codes.

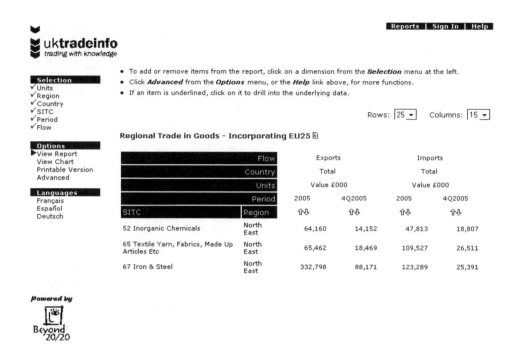

Figure 10.5.2   UK regional trade data from www.uktradeinfo.com

In addition to trade data tables, www.uktradeinfo.com features other useful areas such as Importers' Details and information on exchange rates relative to pounds sterling.

Figure 10.5.3 demonstrates the type of information available from the Importers' Details section. There are different search options, such as a commodity code, a named commodity, a postcode or even a company name. In the example, the names and addresses have been obscured. The frequency of import activity is shown by the periods (Jan 2005 etc).

The figure shows the companies that have registered imports of books for 2005. Also listed are the commodity codes and the periods that the imports were declared.

The final illustration, Figure 10.5.4, relates to exchange rate data. The exchange rates shown are those that apply to the accepted rates applicable to HM Revenue & Customs documentation. These are set on a monthly basis. The graph on the right will highlight any trends (large fluctuations etc). The example given is the exchange rates between pounds sterling and the US dollar.

As well as demonstrating exchange rate trends, the information available could be highly instrumental in any decisions about developing into new countries or, indeed, expanding business in existing countries that a company may be dealing with.

As well as all that has been demonstrated, www.uktradeinfo.com has a lot more to offer. For example, each of the 25 countries in the European Union (EU) has a Country Profile. There is also a profile on the 3 countries that are likely to be joining the EU: Bulgaria, Romania and Turkey.

| Close Window | Print Window | Save File |

IMPORT DETAILS SEARCH: Results returned for search on : Comcode / Commodity : books	
1196 Records found.	
COMPANY NAME	**COMCODE**
	•48202000 Exercise books (KG) Dec 2005 •59019000 Tex fab coated with gum or similar-o/t that used for the outer covers of books (KG SQM) jan 2005, May 2005, Jun 2005, Jul 2005, Aug 2005, Sep 2005 Oct 2005, Nov 2005, Dec 2005
	•49030000 Children's picture, drawing or colouring books (KG) *Jul 2005 , Oct 2005* •59019000 Tex fab coated with gum or similar-o/t that Used for the outer covers of books (KG SQM) *Aug 2005 , Nov 2005*
	•48201010 Registers, account books, order books & receipt books (KG) *Jun 2005*
	•48201010 Registers, account books, order books & receipt books (KG) *May 2005*
	•49030000 Children's picture, drawing or colouring books (KG) *Apr 2005, Aug 2005, Nov 2005*
	•49030000 Children's picture, drawing or colouring books (KG) *Jul 2005*
	•48201010 Registers, account books, order books & receipt books (KG) *Aug 2005*

Figure 10.5.3   Information available from the Importers' Details section of www. uktradeinfo.com

There is a free e-mail alert service. This facility provides cross-governmental informa-tion direct to a nominated e-mail address. Free registration for the e-mail alert is easy, and there are many subjects and areas available. It is also very simple to change the original profile or to unsubscribe altogether.

The World Links section has proved to be quite a useful tool for locating contacts abroad, eg embassies or the local British Chambers of Commerce.

Staying with links, there are many links to other government departments that are useful to the world of international trade.

Another important area is the Codes and Guides section. This gives Airport, Seaport and Country codes. It also includes details of classification guides/rulings and, particularly for traders dealing within the EU, the online version of the Intrastat Classification Nomenclature (ICN). This is mainly used to find the appropriate commodity code for products. The online ICN has a search facility for locating appropriate commodity codes.

Also, www.uktradeinfo.com facilitates the Internet submission of the Intrastat Documentation for traders dealing within the EU. There are two methods of submitting Intrastat Supplementary Declarations via the internet. One option is ideal for any

Country USA ▾

Date	Rate = UK £
01 Apr 2006	1.7469
01 Mar 2006	1.7438
01 Feb 2006	1.7628
01 Jan 2006	1.7391
01 Dec 2005	1.715
01 Nov 2005	1.7614
01 Oct 2005	1.8126
01 Sep 2005	1.8098
01 Aug 2005	1.7294
01 Jul 2005	1.8225
01 Jun 2005	1.8344
01 May 2005	1.9168
01 Apr 2005	1.8738
01 Mar 2005	1.8788
01 Feb 2005	1.8766
01 Jan 2005	1.9129
01 Dec 2004	1.8562

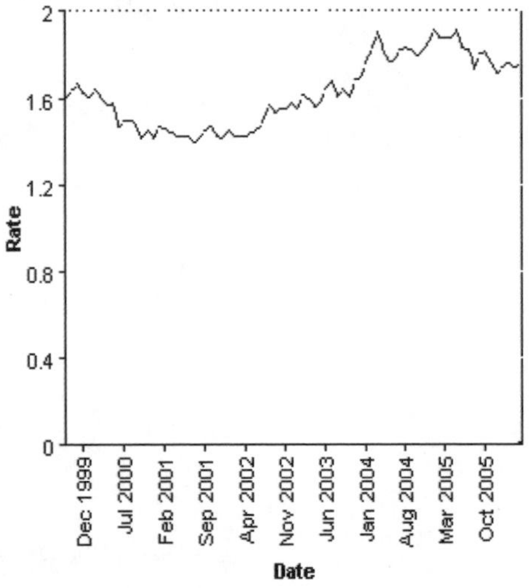

If you need a weekly figure for Customs documentation please use the HM Revenue and Customs site found here ▶

Figure 10.5.4   Exchange rate data from www.uktradeinfo.com

company that only submits a few lines of trade per month. This method involves online completion of a Supplementary Declaration, and is subject to a time limit, for completion and submission, of 30 minutes.

The second option caters for traders with large monthly declarations. This method is a Comma Separated Variant (CSV) file. Completion is offline. Once the file is complete, it is uploaded to www.uktradeinfo.com and then submitted. The CSV option sounds very complicated but it is, essentially, an Excel spreadsheet. This file is downloadable from www.uktradeinfo.com as a CSV Generator Tool.

Both options, once submitted and confirmed, are issued a unique reference number for that transmission. There is a notification issued for errors. This facilitates savings in time and enables quicker submission of the declarations. Postage costs are also reduced.

For information, call 01702 367485 or e-mail uktradeinfo@hmrc.gsi.gov.uk

Every world-class business needs a world-class location

Taking care of your business
www.nfia.co.uk

Netherlands
Foreign Investment
Agency

Taxation and international expansion

Liesbeth Staps gives a Dutch perspective on how tax affects any choice of international location

Introduction

As your business grows and you are expanding abroad, thinking long-term is even more important to your business than it is in your home base. Important aspects are proximity to your customer base, availability of quality, affordable labour force and office space, and cost and delivery times for your products, but these can all change with business growth. Taxation is a significant factor for international companies in the choice of locations where to establish their business. Your fiscal structure should allow international expansion for your business as well.

The European Union: a competitive market

The fiscal regimes in Europe are under continuous development with the access of the Eastern European countries and the open marketplace. Many countries are reviewing their fiscal regime to be able to be more competitive in the European market. The aim is to create better tax conditions for foreign investors, which could benefit your company in expanding abroad. The Dutch government has created a competitive fiscal regime that stimulates entrepreneurship and foreign investment in the Netherlands.

Dutch government plans

The Dutch 2006 corporate tax income rate is 29.6 per cent, ranking in the middle of the European scale. The government plans to further reduce this rate to 29.1 per cent in 2007 and 26.9 per cent thereafter. As an incentive to small and medium-sized enterprises the government has lowered the starting rate from 29 per cent to 25.5 per cent for the first bracket (profits up to 22,689 euros). The plans include a reduction of this rate to 20 per cent and the introduction of a second step-up rate of 23.5 per cent for profits between 25,000 and 60,000 euros in 2007. These new statutory tax rates put the Netherlands on a very competitive footing with other EU locations. A corporate taxpayer can use available allowances and deductions to achieve an effective tax rate that is even lower than the statutory tax rates.

Tax treaties

For internationally operating companies, avoidance of double taxation is essential. For this reason, countries have concluded bilateral tax treaties with other jurisdictions. The Netherlands has one of the most extensive tax treaty networks in the European Union. The treaties generally provide substantial reductions of withholding tax on dividends, interest and royalties, and the Netherlands does not withhold any tax on interest and royalty payments leaving the Netherlands.

When you are assessing your international company structure, the taxation of shareholding is imperative to acknowledge. For example, it could be beneficial for the UK company not to be the principal shareholder of future subsidiaries, but rather the subsidiary's subsidiary in a country with a good participation facility. One of the most important provisions of Dutch corporate income tax legislation is 'participation exemption', which makes all benefits related to a qualifying shareholding exempt from Dutch corporate income tax.

Tax planning

For your business planning with a long-term perspective, you need to know how any changes in your foreign company will affect taxation. One of the specific features of the Dutch tax system is the possibility of discussing in advance the tax treatment of certain operations or transactions. This has been accomplished through advance pricing agreements (APA) with, and advance tax rulings (ATR) by, the Dutch tax authorities.

Naturally, your tax planning largely depends on the kind of activities you conduct. For your distribution activities, a VAT deferment scheme and bonded warehousing are important for your cash flow planning. For R&D activities, the situation on intellectual property and patents is of utmost importance. In the Netherlands it is proposed that companies will have the opportunity to allocate royalties or other eligible income derived from the intellectual property or patents to an R&D box, with a tax rate of 10 per cent.

Advantages

With the globalization of business the demand for financial reporting standards has increased. The International Financial Reporting Standards (IFRS) accomplish international standardization and help to facilitate and improve the quality of financial reporting. Additionally, the Netherlands has practical provisions that may imply – in particular for Dutch subsidiaries of UK multinationals – a considerable reduction of their administrative burden. In the Netherlands it is possible for a company to compute its taxable profit in the functional currency (other than the euro) of the multinational group it is a part of. The annual tax return must be filed, usually within five months after the closing of the preceding financial year. The standard tax year is the calendar year, but a company may have a different year, such as its parent's fiscal year, as its tax year. Both tax reporting in a foreign currency and tax reporting in a different tax year will be subject to approval by the tax inspector in advance.

By thinking ahead, you can create not only a good first step on the Continent, but even better stepping stones for further European expansion.

Liesbeth Staps is deputy director of the Netherlands Foreign Investment Agency in the United Kingdom and Ireland, which provides companies with assistance regarding establishing, expanding or reorganizing their pan-European operations in the Netherlands. The NFIA can assist you at every stage of your strategic decision making with information, advice and practical help in strict confidence, without obligation and free of charge.

Netherlands Foreign Investment Agency
38 Hyde Park Gate
London SW7 5DP
Tel: +44 20 7225 1074
e-mail: info@nfia.co.uk
www.nfia.co.uk

11

Corporate finance

Optimizing the deal structure

In corporate finance, complexities almost inevitably arise during the course of negotiations, says Andrew Millington at Mazars

At the outset of most corporate finance transactions both sides are optimistic that the terms and the financing behind the deal can be kept simple and straightforward. It is during the, sometimes heated, negotiations that the laudable objective of 'keeping it simple' often goes out of the window as complications emerge, respective stances are taken and both the vendor and purchaser endeavour to improve their positions.

Consistently, the level of complexity increases as a deal progresses and more creative and complex provisions are introduced to mitigate identified risks, deal with an issue or alter 'value' in light of new information. The resultant signed deal can often be considerably different from that originally envisaged and can be highly complex.

Why the keep it simple approach fails

The complications in structure or financing generally emerge as a result of:

- meeting price expectations;
- business-specific problems or uncertainties that emerge;
- financing issues; or
- other shareholder concerns.

In any adviser's kitbag are a range of tools that can be creatively adapted to overcome price gaps and transaction issues. These can be a mixture of innovative deal structures or novel financing structure.

In the majority of cases you would hope not to employ too many. It complicates the transaction process and the documentation, and may have unforeseen post-transaction consequences or complications. If there are too many in a deal, you know you are straying into dangerous territory.

Structuring options

In some situations these provisions can extend for a number of years and stem from a need to meet a price level that the purchaser and/or financier is unwilling or unable to afford at the outset: for example, a disagreement on future performance or the outcome of key contract negotiations. Examples of the more usual tools used in structuring include:

■ realization of surplus assets or sale of non-core entities;
■ property removal and leaseback;
■ deferred consideration – such as loan notes or consultancy arrangements;
■ contingent consideration – additional payments dependent upon future events or financial performance;
■ working capital adjustments.

In such situations, structuring options can only be effective if the problem is understood and it is possible to tailor a structure to meet the particular issue or gap that exists. More innovative options that are available – and are usually a sign that the structure is being pushed to the limits – include:

■ residual equity interest for a vendor;
■ clawbacks – eg future surplus asset realizations;
■ use of loan notes with rolled-up interest or a premium on redemption, perhaps linked to the outcome of certain specified events;
■ put and call option arrangements.

Financing options

The adviser also has at his or her disposal a range of financing structures to solve the problem. Usually there are more limitations on creativity with this kind of structure since, at some point, banking or equity limits will be reached or breached.

From a vendor's perspective, if there is an ongoing involvement or equity participation, understanding the structure is hugely important. Even if there is a clean break, appreciating the financing structure should allow the consideration to be protected or enhanced if circumstances or events permit. However, there can be advantages in considering different financing options from both a seller's and a buyer's perspective.

In considering the optimal structure for a transaction, the approach is to use the cheapest source of funds first and work up the pyramid of more expensive borrowing, with external equity investment as a last resort if required. In between, there are a number of options that may be available, such as the use of mezzanine debt or vendor finance.

The cheapest form of finance is existing surplus cash resources (although this is unlikely to be a significant portion of consideration). It may be enhanced, though, with any surplus assets that are able to be realized by the completion of the deal: investments or property.

Traditional bank and asset borrowing continues to be available across the market with little apparent shortage of appetite to lend.

In the majority of transactions it is rare, unless the business is asset rich or has significant unused borrowing potential, for the combination of these two sources (free cash and asset lending) to be sufficient to fund a deal.

The next option, assuming the business is of sufficient size and profitability, is mezzanine funding. This stretched slice of additional debt carries a significant premium cost but is cheaper than raising external equity investment.

It is now common in transactions to see vendors accept deferred consideration, perhaps in the form of loan notes that can be settled over a period of, say, two to three years. In many situations this can meet the requirements of the seller in terms of price and payment timescales, and for the purchaser it is cheaper and more flexible than introducing external equity.

This funding route can also provide some comfort to a purchaser of the seller's continued confidence in the business. If the vendor has an ongoing role in the business, the combination of deferred consideration and equity is a powerful driver to continuing contribution.

In addition to the standard elements of financing structures there are further options that can help bridge a gap:

■ over-lending, including from asset-based lenders;
■ deferred consideration insurance;
■ additional standby or occasional use facilities;
■ sale and leaseback of property.

Watch out

The further the structure is pushed and the more creative it becomes, the more you can expect the parties to the deal to:

■ pay great attention to due diligence;
■ have a greater focus on reported performance;
■ seek tighter covenants and powers in documentation.

Above all, the transaction will take longer to complete.

Conclusion

In any financing structure there is usually an optimum that generates the maximum amount of fundraising from appropriate sources without pushing each element to the very limit. Ideally, keep each financier just inside their comfort zone. If one or more elements have gone too far, there is no slack or room for change, either pre-deal or soon thereafter.

Andrew Millington is a Corporate Finance Partner with Mazars, the international accountancy and advisory firm. He has more than 15 years' experience and has led a large number of M&A and MBO transactions for companies of varying size in a wide range of industry sectors. Andrew is in charge of UK Corporate Finance. Prior to joining Mazars, he was an investment director at Barclays Private Equity. Before that, he was a senior manager in Corporate Finance at Coopers & Lybrand.

Mazars acts for some of the fastest-growing entrepreneurial companies in the United Kingdom, offering a complete range of accountancy and business advisory services, including audit and assurance, tax advisory and compliance, corporate recovery and insolvency, consulting, forensic and investigations, corporate finance and financial services for private individuals. Contact details are as follows:

Tel: 0121 212 4579
e-mail: Andrew.millington@mazars.co.uk
www.mazars.co.uk

Business grooming

Selling equity? Refinancing? Trade partnering? Stephen Harris of Mazars highlights the specific considerations involved in different types of transaction

The steps that should be looked at for grooming a business are no different in principle from those for an individual. Whilst first impressions undoubtedly create a lasting memory, you want to ensure that the whole experience will be consistent.

Where are you going?

Before looking at how to groom a business, we need first to establish where the business is looking to go. Whilst there are generic housekeeping issues that need to be considered in all instances, there are specific areas that will have greater importance depending on the intended transaction. For example, is the business grooming itself for:

- an outright sale?
- a part sale to allow for a change in control?
- an approach for financing (debt or equity)?
- trade partnering?

Outright sale

In an outright sale you will be selling, along with your other shareholders, the ownership of the company. It is highly likely that you will not be carrying on with your day-to-day responsibilities and duties after a sale of this nature. Indeed, you may not have a job at all!

Therefore, some immediate and very specific considerations are:

- Is this the right option? Are you ready to let go of that part of your life?
- Is it the right time? Is the business performance going to attract the right interest and valuation from a purchaser? Is the purchaser likely to understand the dynamics of the market and the performance of your business as well as you do?
- Can your financial performance be improved? Over time, businesses become cluttered, just like houses. Consider whether you need to reorganize and/or declutter.
- Is the business operating effectively? Is the business model an attractive one, using up-to-date practices and procedures?
- Who would your business be most attractive to? You probably know already who would most like to buy it...
- Is it enough? After you have looked at the performance, effectiveness and potential purchaser, do the sums add up? Will you get what you want from the sale?
- What message will you send out? Staff, suppliers, customers and the local community will probably be interested if you sell up; what message do you want to give them?

One other thing is often a cause for concern if the potential purchaser is a competitor. What can you do to protect the intellectual capital and confidential trade arrangements that exist, especially if, having investigated your company, the potential purchaser then does not complete the sale? Grooming should address these areas and give you the best chance of success.

Change in control

Changes in control need to encompass the areas in an outright sale, although there will be greater flexibility in the messaging and the valuation, as you will be around to ensure a smooth handover.

However, there is still a need to look at improving the position. Any business valuation will take account of performance; can it be improved? The valuation is often based on a multiple of the profits. Improve those and the value you receive will increase.

One area that you will have less flexibility in is the party that will be most likely to acquire your shareholding. In a staged change in control, either your management or potentially a new team will be the prime purchasers and you will need to ensure they are equipped to handle it.

Grooming your management team is also important; they will have to make a good impression on the backers of the transaction.

Financing

Grooming for financing will depend to a certain extent whether you are looking at straightforward refinance or whether you are looking for increased finance to grow and develop.

Refinancing

If refinancing, you may be looking to replace existing facilities or restructure the overall level of finance that you have. This may involve switching between different debt products or involve equity providers.

Development finance

Finance for development may again involve a mix of debt and equity products. In this instance, though, there will be an increase in the level of financing.

In both these scenarios the business will need to have a very clear financial plan covering how the changes in financing structure will be serviced, in terms of both the increased financing costs and the capital repayment strategy. Again it is important to consider various aspects:

- Is this the right option? Money is only the starting point; what are you going to do with the money to improve your business performance?
- Is it the right time? Is the business performance going to attract the right level of finance? Potential investors will want to understand how the business performance going forward will differ from your performance to date. You will need to understand the dynamics of the market, and the financier will expect you to articulate your plans and how they relate to the market.
- Can your financial performance be improved? Equity providers will expect a far higher return than the bank. Venture capitalists will put much greater pressure on you to ensure you meet the exit timetable. Your own performance will be under increased scrutiny.
- Is the business operating efficiently? Is the business using up-to-date practices and procedures and is there the financing to help this? Is this built into the model?
- Who would your business be most attractive to? You may not be selling it now, but an equity provider will expect you to understand who is most likely to be interested.
- Is it enough? The very worst thing you can do is have to ask for more! Likewise, asking for too much shows that you may not have confidence in the business plan you are putting forward.

In addition, if equity participation is involved, you must be able to answer the question: how will I get my money out and how much will it be?

Trade partnering

Another way in which your business could be developed and therefore require grooming is through trade partnering (where another business, sometimes a much larger one, has something that you want and need, for example distribution capability). Also, you have something that they would like, but for whatever reason (perhaps valuation expectations or geographic issues) you are not ready to sell.

Trade partnering requires you to be very clear what you want out of a relationship and how your product/know-how/intellectual property can be properly protected so that you preserve the value of the business. These relationships can be very rewarding but need to be handled with considerable planning to ensure that the business stands up to the scrutiny of another party whilst at the same time the business's assets are protected.

Generic areas

When you are looking at any potential transaction there are many other areas that need to be considered. These are of varying importance dependent on the business, but should be ignored at your peril:

■ service agreements for directors;
■ option arrangements to ensure appropriate incentives for managers and staff;
■ employment contracts and up-to-date employment practices;
■ Environmental Protection Act considerations;
■ health and safety at work regulations;
■ intellectual property and capital – whether formal patent protection or well-documented procedures for the latter, including intellectual property ownership waivers. If you cannot prove it is yours, the value will diminish rapidly.

Further areas that often affect businesses looking at transactions are as follows:

■ Make sure the business continues as if there is not going to be a transaction. Plan for it by all means, but don't take your eye off the ball.
■ Ensure regular communication with key parties. No communication means there is likely to be a problem somewhere.
■ Manage the timetable. If you have an end date in mind, start early. The vast majority of businesses are sold to people who are already known to the vendor.
■ Use advisers. Most businesses will undertake a major business transaction just once. Specialist corporate finance advisers have a wealth of experience and will know where the pitfalls are (and how to avoid them).

Whatever direction you are taking your business in, make sure you plan well in advance and groom it with the final outcome in mind. If you don't, you may find you end up with less than you bargained for on all fronts!

Stephen Harris has spent more than 20 years in the business advisory sector helping owner-managed businesses, covering equity and debt raises as well as advising on acquisitions and disposals, including those from recovery positions. He is a Director of Corporate Finance in Mazars' Milton Keynes office.

Mazars acts for some of the fastest-growing entrepreneurial companies in the United Kingdom, offering a complete range of accountancy and business advisory services, including audit and assurance, tax advisory and compliance, corporate recovery and insolvency, consulting, forensic and investigations, corporate finance and financial services for private individuals. Contact details are as follows:

Tel: 01908 664466
e-mail: stephen.harris@mazars.co.uk
www.mazars.co.uk

thecapitalfund
Business Venture Finance
just for London

About The Capital Fund

The Capital Fund is a £50 million venture capital fund which backs fast-growing, small and medium-sized enterprises (SMEs) in Greater London. Initial investments can be up to £250,000 and the Fund has the ability to invest a further £250,000 after six months or more. In some circumstances, alongside other new investors, The Capital Fund can follow on its investments with up to £5 million in any one company.

The Capital Fund was launched in 2002 and will be invested over a period of up to 6 years. The Fund is the largest of the nine Regional Venture Capital Funds and has both public and private sector investors. The primary objective of the Fund is to maximise returns to our investors by investing in SMEs with high growth potential and management teams capable of delivering that growth.

We have a streamlined investment process with an initial web-based application which ensures that companies provide the essential information we need for prompt decision-making. For more information or to apply for funding, please visit our website, **www.thecapitalfund.co.uk**

The Fund can invest in:

- SMEs based in Greater London (the 32 boroughs of London and the City of London)
- Most industry sectors (with a few restrictions)
- All stages of development, from early stage through expansion to MBOs

We are looking for these SMEs to have:

- Financial requirements consistent with The Capital Fund's ability to invest
- Experienced management teams that are personally and financially committed to the company
- Good potential for growth in sales, profits and shareholder value
- Clear customer need for the products/services offered, ideally demonstrated by a sales track record
- Convincing strategy for marketing, selling and delivering products in the face of competition
- Exit possibilities for The Capital Fund in 3 to 5 years' time
- Effective financial systems and cost controls

We normally invest in companies by way of:

- Equity capital (for a minority of shareholding) and
- Unsecured loan

Prior to investing, we will undertake commercial and financial due diligence into a company. After investing, we usually appoint a Non-Executive Director to the board of an investee company who is an industry expert or a person with specific skills from which the management team can benefit.

*For more information or to apply please visit **www.thecapitalfund.co.uk***

Twenty-one tips for raising venture capital

What happens when entrepreneurs have exhausted all the obvious sources of finance for their young, fast-growing businesses, and turn to institutional venture capital investors? Geoff Sankey, Managing Director of The Capital Fund, London's £50 million Regional Venture Capital Fund, offers some tips for improving your success

Getting your hands on finance

You're an entrepreneur who has spotted a gap in the market. You are absolutely certain you know exactly what it will take to fill the gap, but you'll need to spend a lot of money you don't have to turn your brilliant concept into reality. You might even have already developed your great idea into a functioning product or service but have exhausted all your personal cash reserves before you can launch it properly on to the market. Perhaps you have already started a business and it is proving to take longer than expected to generate sales, but in the meantime those essential overheads *are* growing and somehow have to be paid for. Maybe your business is doing really well, thank you very much, growing much faster than expected in fact, but the additional staff, equipment or working capital you need to fuel this growth is way beyond the level that can comfortably be funded from internally generated cash flow. What are you going to do? Exactly: like the vast majority of entrepreneurs, you will probably go to the bank and ask for a loan, or at least an overdraft.

The bank says 'yes'

And the bank might say 'yes', in which case you need look no further. And if it does say 'yes', you can be pretty sure that, as well as liking the look of your business, it has calculated that the amount of capital you are borrowing is more than covered by the net disposal value of your company's assets. To put it another way, the bank must feel secure in the knowledge that in the unlikely event that your business should fail, it would stand a good chance of getting all or most of its money back through the sale of assets. That's why it's called 'fully secured' debt, and this principle is fundamental to the bank's business model. Banks are simply not geared up to lose money; they are not 'risk' investors. Also, if the bank says 'yes, you can reasonably assume that, having scrutinized your history, current position and projections, it is as sure as it can be that your business can generate enough internal cash flow to comfortably cover the necessary regular interest charges and to pay back the debt as and when agreed.

The bank says 'no'

However, if the bank says 'no', as is probably more likely in the case of a young business, this may in fact have a lot more to do with your lack of asset and income cover than its perceptions of the quality of your ideas and achievements to date. A solution to this problem might be for you to agree to personally guarantee the bank debt, even to the extent of allowing the bank to have a formal charge – like a second mortgage – over your property if you are a homeowner. But what if you are not willing or able to take this courageous step? Who do you turn to then?

Friends, family and angels

Increasingly these days, entrepreneurs are turning to their friends and family for relatively small amounts of risk capital. This means of financing your business can be quick and can require only the simplest of documentation. However, it can come with strings attached: emotional pressures and well-meaning but disruptive interference in day-to-day management can be a problem, particularly if things start to go wrong. Also, the cash resources of your friends and family are likely to be limited, and this means that your loved ones will be far less likely than institutions to be in a position to make further investments if the need arises.

In recent years there has been a significant growth in private equity investment by high net worth individuals – that is, the same idea as friends and family investment but from 'strangers' – and this type of capital is increasingly available via formal 'angel' networks. The angel networks operate in many respects like venture capital (VC) institutions, attracting, reviewing and selecting the better-quality opportunities for presentation to their members.

Venture capital institutions

In the United Kingdom the market for finance aimed at young, growing businesses has come a long way over the past 25 years. Venture capital is now a very definite and expanding segment within the financial services sector and is referred to as an 'industry' in its own right. Take a look at the British Venture Capital Association's website – www.bvca.co.uk – for listings of some of the principal institutions active in the United Kingdom today. These are generally professional fund management companies that make their living managing other people's money, often raised from pension funds.

So once you have reached the limit of your secured bank finance, signed all the personal guarantees you're prepared to give, and exhausted the patience and the pockets of your nearest and dearest, you might find yourself preparing to present to some VC institutions. If so, here are some tips designed to make this process a little less daunting and a lot more productive. Good luck.

Twenty-one tips

1. Plan to devote time and effort to the process – it's worth it. It might help to think of how much product you'd have to sell to generate an equivalent boost to your net assets. You will need to be able to develop your business and sell your products whilst the fundraising process progresses.
2. Don't wait until the last minute. The process of raising venture capital will typically take three to six months, and VCs don't respond well to time pressure, unless of course they think they are in competition!
3. Bear in mind that venture capital investment is a highly selective process. VCs typically invest in only 2–5 per cent of the opportunities they see – and they see a lot of proposals. The proposals selected will have potential for high growth in sales, profits and shareholder value and have the management team to achieve that growth.
4. Remember that venture capital investment is a highly subjective business – it's got a lot to do with assessing future performance – so be prepared to hear some fairly subjective reasons if a VC declines your proposal.
5. VCs take a portfolio approach. Some companies will fail, so the valuation and rate of return they seek on all investments will take this into account – that is, the successes must pay for the failures.
6. Know your investors: before you approach them, find out if they have any industry-sector preferences or experience, and the stage and size of investment they go for. Look on their website for details of businesses they have invested in.
7. Consider using a reputable and knowledgeable fund-raising professional if you are new to the game. As a starting point, look at the 'Associate Professional' listing on the BVCA's website. A professional will help to focus your efforts and should know the preferences and criteria of likely investors – but you will have to pay them.
8. Personalize your approach: try to avoid making your initial contact look like a mailshot.

9. Keep your information memorandum and presentation short, clear, balanced and up to date. Make sure you cover background, current position, products, markets, management, strategy, financials and the shape of the deal you are looking for. Also, increasingly these days VCs accept – and even prefer – initial applications via their websites.

10. In an uncertain world, VCs like facts and figures – rather than just projections, guesses and speculations – so do your best to give them as much quantitative information as you can in support of your proposal.

11. Don't be afraid to include a SWOT (strengths, weaknesses, opportunities and threats) analysis in your proposal; the VCs will need it. Don't pull any punches on the weaknesses and threats. All businesses have them, and VCs will expect you to know exactly what they are so that you can plan and execute appropriate countermeasures.

12. Always keep in mind that VCs want to back complete, balanced teams, rather than individuals, so make sure you cover all the key management functions relevant to your business, eg general management, marketing, sales, finance, development, production, fulfilment, etc. VCs also will be looking for both breadth and depth of experience, financial and personal commitment.

13. You will no doubt be projecting a very rapid increase in sales, so a comprehensive sales plan is *absolutely essential*. You should regard this as the heart of your proposal. Be prepared to answer very detailed questions about what you will need to do – and the resources you will need to do it – in order to achieve your sales projections. And I mean detailed questions: routes to market, channel partners, lead generation, prospect qualification, sales call rates and conversion, target customers, sales cycles, market drivers, customer needs, product benefits and advantages, pricing policies, marketing strategy, the competition, etc. Be ready to talk about your sales pipeline, sales contracts, recurring revenues and prospects.

14. Don't assume that VCs know your products, sector or industry, so keep things simple to begin with and avoid – or at least be prepared to explain – any technical complexities and jargon. Don't be afraid to go right back to first principles if necessary. In the latter stages of the investment process the VCs will probably enlist the services of sector experts if a detailed assessment is required.

15. If you get to make a presentation to VCs, be professional and try to look like a team. Work out in advance who will say what and when, and don't bicker, argue or fight in front of your VCs – yes, it does happen!

16. Remember that you are selling a stake in your company, so treat VCs the same way you'd treat any potential major customer or commercial partner.

17. Be direct, open and honest. If you don't have the answer to a question, say so.

18. Know what you'll do if you can't raise the funding you are looking for; it will do wonders for your credibility.

19. It may help you to keep in mind that VCs are investing other people's money and that they are highly regulated. To do their job properly (and meet their Financial Services Authority obligations) they will need to have a detailed understanding of you and your business before they invest. This takes time, so you may need a lot of patience.

20. Get legal advice from a firm that understands venture capital. In the long run, it could save time, money and heartache. Yes, the BVCA website is a good place to start your search.

21. At the end of the day, venture capital is all about buying and selling shares, so be prepared to make a commitment to sell your company – most likely to a trade acquirer in three to five years.

Geoff Sankey is the Managing Director of The Capital Fund, London's Regional Venture Capital Fund.

The Capital Fund is a £50 million venture capital fund that will be invested over a period of up to six years. The Fund is focused on the equity gap and can make initial investments of up to £250,000 in London-based SMEs. After six months or more, the Fund can invest up to a further £250,000. Under certain circumstances, alongside other new investors, the Fund can invest up to £5m in a single company. The Fund invests in businesses at all stages of development – ie start-ups, early stage, development, management buy-outs and management buy-ins. In all cases the investment management team looks for businesses that are able to demonstrate the potential for rapid sustainable growth.

The Capital Fund is managed by YFM Venture Finance Limited. YFM Venture Finance is authorized and regulated by the Financial Services Authority and is part of the YFM Group.

Further information:

Tel: 020 7812 6772
e-mail: info@thecapitalfund.co.uk
thecapitalfund.co.uk

menzies | corporate finance

Menzies Corporate Finance specialises in buying and selling owner-managed businesses. With expertise in managing transactions up to £100m, we provide a complete service to ensure satisfactory deal completion.

Menzies Corporate Finance is a specialist division of Menzies Chartered Accountants. Our specialist team deals with all aspects of corporate finance transactions including disposals, acquisitions, MBOs, MBIs, flotations on AIM and Ofex. We can also advise on a range of fundraising options including bank or working capital finance, loan stock and third-party non-equity investors. We specialise in all types of mid-range corporate transactions and can help with: preparing an information memorandum; discreet inquiries; preparing a business plan; price negotiations; business valuations; raising finance; terms and conditions of transactions; due diligence; compliance with financial assistance regulations and preparing completion accounts.

Please contact Mike Grayer, Head of Corporate Finance, for further information.

Our team

Mike Grayer
Head of Corporate Finance
mgrayer@menzies.co.uk

Alan Skinner
askinner@menzies.co.uk

Jeremy Rayment
jrayment@menzies.co.uk

Ralph Mitchison
rmitchison@menzies.co.uk

Mike Dawe
mdawe@menzies.co.uk

Simon Massey
smassey@menzies.co.uk

Address: Heathrow Business Centre, 65 High Street, Egham, Surrey, TW20 9EY
Tel: 01784 497100   **Fax:** 01784 497101
Website: www.menzies.co.uk
Other offices: Kingston upon Thames, Portsmouth, Walton-on-Thames, Woking, Blackwater Valley, Leatherhead

INTERNATIONAL ASSOCIATION
Moores Rowland International
is an association of independent
accounting firms throughout the world

AIM or Ofex

Mike Grayer of Menzies Corporate Finance looks at flotation on AIM or Ofex as a means of raising capital for your business and the factors the business owner or director needs to consider before making such a move

'Why float?' and 'What is the difference between AIM and Ofex?' are two questions often asked when considering a stock market flotation. Floating your company can provide you with access to capital, an opportunity to cash in on your investment and a positive rise in your business's profile. Here I focus on the advantages and disadvantages of floating on both the Alternative Investment Market (AIM) and Ofex, setting out key features offered by each, along with the benefits and issues involved.

Why float?

Raising capital, despite being the obvious answer, is not the only one. Typical funds raised on Ofex lie in the region of £0.5m–£3m; for AIM the figure tends to be £3m-plus. Companies may also consider an 'Introduction'. This is where a company will join the market without an initial fundraising, enabling it to:

- ascertain the value of its shares in order to assist in the making of future acquisitions;
- create a market-driven value for the company's share employee scheme;
- introduce a regulated market for the shares.

Many companies use this route to 'introduce' themselves to a market with a view to raising cash at a later date. Institutions like to see a public market track record before investing, so for a small, growing company the 'introduction' route is often the most cost-efficient step. It also creates higher 'visibility', giving profile to customers, suppliers and staff.

Difference between AIM and Ofex

AIM

AIM is the London Stock Exchange's unlisted market. Introduced in 1995 to encourage a wider range of companies to go public, it reduces the associated costs and obligations when making a comparison to the 'Official List'. AIM also provides companies with the opportunity to widen their shareholder base and allow shareholders the potential to unlock capital.

Whilst admission to the Official List requires the fulfilment of a detailed set of conditions, the requirements for admission to AIM are limited. There are no minimum conditions relating to the size of companies, market capitalization, the price per share or the length of trading, as entry to AIM is based on disclosure. AIM applicants do not have to comply with pre-set criteria but are required to disclose an accurate and comprehensive description of their businesses in order to allow investors to make informed assessments of the risks and rewards of the proposed investment.

AIM tends to cater for companies with a turnover range of £10m–£150m. Entry costs, whether fund-raising or not, tend to be at the £350,000-plus level, with ongoing costs of around £75,000 a year. Fund-raisings tend to be in the £3m–£20m range, averaging around £5m. Investors are largely institutional; however, there is a higher percentage of retail investment than on the Official List. Substantial investor tax benefits may also be applicable, as AIM stocks are deemed 'unlisted' and 'unquoted'.

Ofex

Ofex is a private market that specializes in small and medium-sized enterprises, providing an efficient mechanism to raise new equity, a higher profile amongst new investors, customers and existing shareholders with an opportunity to realize value. Shares are bought and sold on a 'matched' basis through a market maker.

Ofex may be cost-effective for companies of the size of anything up to £20m. Entry costs, with no fund-raising, may be as little as £30,000. In our experience, fund-raisings tend to be in the range of £500,000–£3m, averaging around £1.5m, with costs of fund-raising likely to be in the £150,000 range. Investors tend to be predominantly high net worth individuals and retail investors, with an increasing number of institutions.

Ofex is authorized and regulated by the Financial Services Authority (FSA). As with AIM, substantial investor tax benefits may be applicable, as Ofex stocks are also deemed 'unlisted' and 'unquoted'.

Choosing the right market

As we have seen, cost is a key difference between the two markets. AIM has greater liquidity for the sale and purchase of shares, whereas Ofex shares are traded on a matched basis. As for regulation and reporting, Ofex is seen as a 'lighter touch' and may be considered a good training ground for relatively inexperienced directors in the ways of the City.

Both markets should be seen as a ladder; you can step up and step down according to your funding needs. Ofex is the single biggest feeder for AIM, and AIM is seen as the bridge between Ofex and the heady heights of the Official List. In terms of profile, you will enjoy more coverage the higher up the ladder you are, but the costs increase accordingly. It is important to consider whether you'd rather be a larger fish in a smaller pond until you are truly ready to step up.

There are subtle differences between the markets in terms of regulation and market infrastructure, but it basically boils down to the size of your company, the size of your fund-raising and the profile level you wish your company to enjoy in a way that is economically viable and acceptable to your shareholders.

It is essential to understand how to use the funding ladder in a way that suits your company. There are opportunities available to companies of all sizes, ages and aspirations. AIM has been extremely successful in attracting companies since its formation and, in particular, over the past three years. In part, this has been due to a very effective marketing effort by AIM. However, the growth also reflects the fact that it has become easier to raise £1m–£3m from institutions (particularly venture capital trusts) for a new AIM admission than for a private company via the traditional private equity route. In our opinion there is, however, a risk of AIM becoming a victim of its own success. With AIM becoming larger and more diverse, a smaller company may benefit from a higher profile on Ofex.

The significant growth in the size of AIM, and the discernible trend for Nomads (nominated advisers) to seek initial public offerings (IPOs) of £5m-plus, would appear to leave a significant opportunity for Ofex to become the natural source of public equity in the sub-£5m range, provided that institutions and private investors can be encouraged to support the market through IPOs and secondary offerings.

Seeking a quotation for a company's shares is one of the most important steps that directors and shareholders can take. All the issues should be carefully considered before a decision is taken. Many of the issues are complex and often interrelated, so it is essential that professional advice be taken at an early stage.

Where should you go?

The Official List has the highest profile but also the highest cost, and also there are rules which state that you must have at least 25 per cent of the shares in public hands. AIM does not have the same level of restriction, but would cost you £350,000-plus, whether you are doing a fund-raising or not. The Ofex option provides significant cost saving for an introduction (approx £40,000) and a fund-raising (approx £150,000).

One approach would be to step on to Ofex first, and then at a later date do the fund-raising timed with a move to AIM, so that it would be possible to benefit from the institutional support of that market. Timing is an important consideration. On all markets an introduction can take as little as three to six weeks, but an IPO will take three to six months.

With thorough planning, together with careful selection of a team of professionals who have the necessary expertise and experience, the route to flotation can be relatively smooth.

Mike Grayer (FCA) is head of Menzies' Corporate Finance team and has extensive experience of corporate transactions. He is the firm's lead partner dealing with Aim- and Ofex-related transactions.

Menzies is one of the leading accountancy practices in the South East, with 38 partners based in eight offices across London and the Home Counties.

For further information, please contact Mike Grayer (tel: +44 (0)1784 497100; e-mail: mgrayer@menzies.co.uk; website: www.menzies.co.uk).

Structured finance

Structuring the most efficient, cost-effective financing package can make all the difference between success and failure for a company, says Kevin Smith of AWS

It is all too easy for the owners or management of smaller businesses to think that funding for their growing operations comes only in the form of equity or debt, and that debt can only be in the form of a term loan or an overdraft. This perception is often caused by the unimaginative approach of many banks, and, sadly, many of the banks' small business advisers don't seem to know terribly much more than the businesses that they are meant to be advising.

The reality is, of course, rather different, with a whole range of different products available from banks and other, more specialized providers of funding. What is the perfect solution for one company may not work at all for a very similar company, and structuring the most efficient, cost-effective financing package can make all the difference between success and failure for the company. This is particularly true for growing businesses, and, at the very least, the wrong financing package can hamper growth.

Equity

There are many different types of equity. As well as 'normal' equity there can be different classes of shares with different voting rights, preference shares (which rank ahead of 'normal' equity in the payment of dividends) and many other variations on the theme.

It is also worth remembering that ownership of shares in a company and control of the company can easily be varied by using a shareholders' agreement, so that ownership of the majority of shares does not necessarily translate into control. This structure is often used when equity is injected by a venture capital firm that only seeks to own a minority stake but needs to be able to exercise control in order to limit the risks on its investment.

Senior debt

All banks offer senior debt, and many branches, in practice, only offer senior debt. This is debt that is backed by some form of security (often a first fixed and floating charge on the assets of the company), and the funder ranks before almost every other creditor. The standard term loans and working capital or overdraft facilities invariably fall into this category.

Subordinated debt

Subordinated debt, as the name implies, ranks behind senior debt. This type of debt is often only available to larger companies and, strange as it may seem, is often part of a package of debt that includes senior debt. Larger syndicated loans may offer both types of debt, with the subordinated debt tranche paying a higher interest rate to reflect the higher risks being taken by the funder. Despite the fact that subordinated debt ranks behind senior debt, it often has some form of security attached to it and so the funder still ranks ahead of unsecured creditors.

Mezzanine finance

Mezzanine finance is a form of subordinated debt but is actually midway between debt and equity (hence the name 'mezzanine'). It would typically be structured as debt but would have options, warrants, equity kickers or some similar structure to provide some of the potential upside normally enjoyed only by holders of equity. These may be linked to various performance criteria or events such as flotation or takeover of the company. As with subordinated debt, the risks for the funder are higher, so the cost of this type of finance is higher. Nevertheless, providers of mezzanine finance are prepared to accept levels of risk not acceptable with standard bank facilities.

Asset finance

Leasing is the most common form of asset finance. The major difference with asset finance is that it looks primarily to the value of the asset as security rather than to the strength of the balance sheet. This can be particularly useful for smaller companies with only limited balance sheets or for companies that operate in asset-intensive sectors. Leases can be either on balance sheet (finance leases) or off balance sheet (operating leases) and, depending on the equipment being leased, 100 per cent of the cost can be financed.

Factoring or invoice discounting is another form of asset finance, as the lender looks towards the quality of the trade debtors and outstanding invoices as security, rather than the balance sheet. Again this can be useful for smaller companies, especially during periods of rapid growth, as the facility advances a percentage of outstanding invoices (typically up to 80 per cent of eligible invoices) and as such is more flexible. The funding is also available more quickly than a bank overdraft facility, which looks back in time rather than forward and is far more reliant on the balance sheet. Because it is trade related, with predetermined repayments of advances, higher gearing is possible than with a working capital overdraft facility.

Trade finance

The term 'trade finance' is normally applied to companies that are exporting, as financing trade within the same country can easily be achieved using general bank facilities. There are many different forms of trade finance (letters of credit, bills of exchange, forfeiting, tolling, pre-export, countertrade, project finance... to name just a few), and many of these can either be with or without recourse to the company seeking the facility.

Trade finance can be just as useful to small and large companies alike, as not only is it a way of passing a lot of the risks on to a bank, but again it can often be done without particular reference to the size or strength of the company's own balance sheet.

Many foreign banks specialize in this type of finance and are more than happy to provide facilities alongside a company's other bank relationships.

Structured finance

Structured finance as a term is normally applied to large, complicated transactions where a whole range of different financing techniques are employed in order to put together a package that provides a workable solution that would not be possible using more conventional lending methods. However, the principle is just as valid for smaller companies.

By using a little more imagination and identifying the strengths of the growing business's financial structure it is possible to mitigate risks more effectively, and by playing to these strengths it is possible to structure a financing package that is larger, more flexible and more cost-effective than traditional lending. Remember that as a company grows, its funding requirements will increase and change over time, and a good relationship with flexible, enlightened funders will help to ensure that suitable funding keeps pace with the growing company. Finding such a funder (or indeed a combination of funders) is not necessarily easy but it will always be worth the effort.

Kevin R Smith
Managing Director
AWS Structured Finance Ltd
Tel: 01892 667891
Fax: 01892 610891
e-mail: kevin.r.smith@awsconsult.co.uk
www.awsconsult.co.uk

and:

Chairman,
Aspen Waite Chartered Accountants
www.aspenwaite.co.uk

Tax planning

Don't fall into the trap of tainting your investments for tax relief, warns Colin Copeland at Mazars

You can't think about tax too early

It happens so often. A deal is struck for the sale of a business and the question is then raised, 'How do we do this in the most tax-efficient manner?' The answer, unfortunately, is that the most efficient planning is often not available just before the sale. In some cases it should have been undertaken several years earlier.

The relief

One of the most effective forms of tax relief for owner-managers, assuming capital losses are not available, is business asset taper relief (BATR). If the assets qualify throughout the holding period and have been held for more than two years, then only 25 per cent of the gain is chargeable to tax. At the higher income tax rate of 40 per cent this gives an effective rate of 10 per cent of the gain (25 per cent × 40 per cent).

For companies selling trading subsidiaries, the substantial shareholdings relief provides for an exemption from capital gains tax where the relevant criteria are met. Similar rules and issues to those set out below for BATR apply if the exemption for substantial shareholdings is to be effective. In that case, the investee company must be a trading company or the holding company of a trading group.

Getting dressed for the right party

BATR is available in respect of the sale of business assets or certain shares. If the business is held in a company, the vendor may prefer to sell the shares. However, the availability of tax relief for intangibles, notably goodwill, may mean that the purchaser wants to buy the trade and assets, not the shares. If this happens, the company may have a corporation tax charge on the gain (subject to the availability of losses), and the owner will have the issue of getting the cash out of the company in a tax-efficient way.

If a trade and asset sale is the likely exit route, then the use of a partnership rather than a company may be an alternative strategy, but this brings with it a great many other issues (including tax and risk) that need to be looked at and carefully considered. It is also something that needs to be considered when the business is set up, and at that point the potential exit is probably not at the top of the agenda.

BATR: the investment trap

A relatively common circumstance is that a company carrying on a successful trading business may, at some point, have some investment activity. This could arise from letting surplus property, diversifying the company's activities or acquiring investment assets. Commercially, these will often represent sound business planning. Putting surplus cash into lower-risk investments, possibly held in another group company, is often a commercially sound thing for the directors to do. However, if the non-trade activities amount to a substantial extent of the company's activities, the shares may no longer qualify for BATR. On a group basis, the whole group may be tainted. Although taper relief may be available, this will be at the much lower non-business rate.

How is 'substantial' measured?

The Revenue regards 'substantial' in this context as 20 per cent or more. In measuring this, the Revenue looks at a number of indicators, including the company's income, the asset base of the company, expenses incurred or time spent by officers or employees and the company's history.

The timing issue

The maximum BATR is achieved after two complete years of ownership. However, a point sometimes overlooked is that the gain is initially divided by reference to whether it was a business asset or non-business asset throughout the relevant period of ownership. So if, for example, shares are acquired in January 2000 and sold in February 2010, but they did not qualify as business assets until January 2007, the first seven-tenths of any gain would be non-business and the remaining three-tenths would be business. The business part would qualify for the full BATR, a 75 per cent reduction in the gain, whereas the non-business part would qualify, at today's rates, for a reduction of only 40 per cent, leaving 60 per cent of that part of the gain chargeable.

In short, removing the non-business element two years before disposal might not provide the complete answer.

Demerger

The key to maximizing tax efficiency of a group may be to keep trading activities and investment activities completely separate – in different groups. Where they currently sit under the same holding company, the separation may be achieved tax-efficiently by a demerger if the relevant tests are met. For owner-managers this is often a sensible way of keeping the family investments away from the riskier trading activities. The availability of business property relief (BPR), which would effectively exclude the value of the business from the estate for inheritance tax purposes, and how that might affect succession planning, is something else that might be considered for family businesses where a sale is not contemplated. The principles (BPR does not apply to investment business) are similar to the above, although some of the detail is different.

All of the above is, of course, subject to detailed rules, and it will be necessary to look at the particular aspects and characteristics in every case. In overview, it is wise to check the trade/investment mix of your business periodically and to consider carefully the structuring of any investment decisions. At the end of the day, the tax saved could be a very significant amount.

Colin Copeland is a Tax Director at Mazars. Over many years, Colin has built up extensive experience of advising businesses on a wide range of tax-related issues, with particular emphasis on tax planning and transactions advice. Prior to joining Mazars, Colin spent 17 years working in the London offices of one of the Big Four practices and has worked for clients of all sizes and in numerous industry sectors.

Mazars acts for some of the fastest-growing entrepreneurial companies in the United Kingdom, offering a complete range of accountancy and business advisory services, including audit and assurance, tax advisory and compliance, corporate recovery and insolvency, consulting, forensic and investigations, corporate finance and financial services for private individuals.

Tel: 01234 402000
e-mail: colin.copeland@mazars.co.uk
www.mazars.co.uk

12

Succession and exits

www.strath.ac.uk/business

University of
Strathclyd
Business
School

STRATHCLYDE BUSINESS SCHOOL:
THE FIRST CHOICE FOR BUSINESS PROFESSIONALS

Strathclyde Business School, the longest established business school in Scotland and one of the largest of its kind in Europe, is committed to combining excellence with relevance in its teaching and research within an environment of continuing quality improvement.

The School is accredited by the three leading international bodies: EQUIS (the European Quality Improvement System), AACSB International (the Association to Advance Collegiate Schools of Business) and AMBA (the Association of MBAs), placing it in the top 1% of business schools worldwide.

The School includes the Hunter Centre for Entrepreneurship, a world-class player in the teaching of entrepreneurship and enterprise, which is dedicated to nurturing the entrepreneurial capabilities and intentions of all Strathclyde students, staff and alumni.

Strathclyde Business School offers an extensive choice of courses at undergraduate and postgraduate level, as well as opportunities for research, consultancy and executive education in the following subject areas:

Accounting
Business
Business Enterprise
Business Technology
Business Law
Economics
Finance

Hospitality Management
Human Resource Management
International Business
Management
Marketing
Technology Entrepreneurship
Tourism

E-mail:
business-school@strath.ac.uk

Preparing for the ultimate customer

What are the hallmarks of serial entrepreneurs selling their third or fourth business? Jonathan Levie and Sharon Eaton at the Hunter Centre for Entrepreneurship at the University of Strathclyde report

Selling your first business can be the most traumatic business experience of your life. As part of a global research project on entrepreneurial exit, we have interviewed dozens of exited entrepreneurs. We found that entrepreneurs selling their business for the first time are often intimidated by the enormousness of the transaction. It means so much to them, psychologically and financially, and buyers do their best to take advantage of this. The second time around, entrepreneurs have learned a lot about exiting and tend to be more confident, but they can still make mistakes. We found that entrepreneurs on their third or more business prepare for their exit in remarkably similar ways. In this chapter we'll show you how these experienced exiters do it, and the lessons that a first-time exiter can take from their experience.

Preparing for exit: getting the 'product' ready

We found that serial entrepreneurs are able to detach themselves emotionally from their current business and view it as if it were a product to be marketed to a customer. Some high-technology, venture capital-backed entrepreneurs did this too with their first business. Experienced exiters try to build a business of value to potential buyers, even if they have no current plans to sell it. As one entrepreneur put it: 'Focus on where people perceive the value to be in the organization and then, understanding where the value is, organize around the value. When [potential acquirers] come in, in the future, they will be attracted to the fact that the business is orientated in a value-friendly way.'

Experienced exiters use the process of due diligence, where buyers inspect before they buy, to their advantage. Buyers expect that they will find skeletons in cupboards and that this will enable them to reduce the price. Serial entrepreneurs begin preparing the business for the customer's due diligence at an early stage. They anticipate issues that are likely to come up during due diligence, and resolve them, removing any reasons for price slippage. In many ways this is just good business practice, and helps the business whether it is sold or not. Here is how one experienced exiter thought about due diligence: 'Preparing for due diligence is all about housekeeping, not fundamental change about how you run your business. It's like selling your house, giving it a tidy and hoover before [prospective buyers] come round. You get a better price for it even though it's the same house.'

Market intelligence: know your ultimate customer

Experienced exiters are sensitive to market dynamics and stress the importance of timing. They are very aware of their potential buyers and are always alert to selling opportunities. They think about who would have the most to lose if they were not around, and who would have most to gain by acquiring them. They look for buyers who believe they can extract strategic value, not just financial value. Here's what they told us:

> You really need to understand how valuable you are to the acquiring business. All the traditional benchmarks about private company valuations go out the window if you are – and it's a big if – the final piece of the jigsaw. That piece is gold-plated or even diamond encrusted.

> I would say you would definitely, definitely get more value if you can align your business with one of their strategic goals.

> You need to negotiate with people who understand strategic value.

> You have got to sell your business – it's not just financial numbers. If someone just wants to buy your business based purely on an accountant's view of the world, then you will never get anything for it. Any of the businesses I have been involved in, the accounts have always valued the business a lot, lot less, so I don't sell businesses based on financial results. I sell businesses based on the sizzle, the future, where you can take this business.

Attracting potential buyers

Experienced exiters have learned to get themselves noticed by the acquirer by creating an impact on the acquirer's business, and drawing the acquirer to approach them rather than the other way around. They meet the decision-makers of potential acquirers at business-related social events and become known by them. They find out how their business might create further value for potential acquirers, perhaps in ways the acquirers themselves might not have spotted. They try to have several potential acquirers in the frame, at least implicitly, although in some sectors, experienced acquirers would rather walk from a prospective deal than get involved in an open auction. They learn about potential acquirers' previous deals, their styles of negotiating and price-chipping tricks. They learn what life is like in a business that has been acquired by their target buyer. This is particularly important if they care about their staff and the culture they have forged for their business. This is all time-consuming but is well worth it. As a twice-exited entrepreneur told us:

> I think the first time I did it I really didn't get to know the buyers very well at all. I think my accountant probably did more of the work than I did and the lawyers came in towards the end. But this time, I would say I spent 5..., 10 times as much time on it as the lawyers and accountants combined – a completely different scenario. This was much better for fully understanding what was going on, much better.

Using advisers to best effect

Getting the best advisers – meaning those who have done deals like this before successfully – and making sure the people you want are on the team, and not junior staff, are crucial for first-time exiters. Advisers are much more important for first-time exiters than they are for serial exiters. This is because for first-time exiters, most of their financial and psychological capital is bound up in the business being sold, and if the exit fails, the entrepreneur may lose the best chance of selling well. A strong, experienced negotiator who is not emotionally connected to the business and who can stand up to the power plays of large acquirers can earn his or her fees many times over. Many of the entrepreneurs we interviewed reflected on how much more confident they were in negotiations the second time around. However, they also noted that you cannot let your advisers control the process:

> One of the things I learned the first time around was that if you don't control your lawyers there is a great danger that the lawyers will end up fighting over points that vendor and purchaser really wouldn't fight over.

You have got to manage your advisers... at the end of the day they need guidance, they need to be told, [you have to] work with them. Don't let them run the show otherwise you will... see the bill at the end of it.

Conclusion

Typically, our experienced exiters sketch out the basics of the deal with the acquirer, based on a detailed knowledge of the value their business would bring to the acquirer, and then instruct advisers to make sure the deal is legal. First-time exiters often lack the information and confidence to do this. They therefore might gain from retaining an adviser who could negotiate for them – but only if the business is well positioned and the adviser is well informed. Most of the information on which the negotiator can base his or her strategy can be gathered by the entrepreneur well in advance. The entrepreneur also has responsibility for positioning the business both strategically (for strategic value) and operationally (for due diligence), again well in advance. One entrepreneur summed it up this way: 'I think that the biggest lessons were about getting to know the acquirer, the understanding of the fit with the acquirer, and getting to know the advisers.'

Selling your first business is, in more ways than one, a big deal. It pays to prepare, and lack of experience can be offset by buying in experienced advice. The combination of positioning, information and experienced advice is the key to a successful first-time exit.

Dr Jonathan Levie is based at the Hunter Centre for Entrepreneurship at the University of Strathclyde. His research interests range from nascent entrepreneurship to early corporate growth to exit.

Sharon Eaton was formerly a research assistant at the Hunter Centre for Entrepreneurship and is the founder of Biochannel Partners, a business that turns distributors into channel partners.

Succession planning and partial exits

You have started, built and managed a business that is providing you with a certain lifestyle and is still demanding a lot of your time. You enjoy it and still get a buzz out of the cut and thrust of being in business, and remain a major stakeholder in it. However, you can't take it with you, so make sure you enjoy at least some of it while you can, says Stephen Harris at Mazars

Succession planning for businesses is about planning and implementing a managed process that will allow you to obtain real value from your business at the right time. This may be through realizing all of the value in a clean exit or through a sale of a minority stake.

There is also a middle ground: realizing a significant but not a controlling stake can often be effective, as it may allow you to realize elements of value whilst retaining control. At the same time, it gives a clear indication to likely successors of your intent and probable timescale of your aims.

So it's easy to effect?

In theory, yes... Succession planning should start early, with a clear understanding of the steps required and likely timescales. Parties that may be affected by the transaction include:

- major customers and suppliers who have, over the years, grown used to dealing with you;
- providers of finance, who trust in your management and judgement;
- other stakeholders, who trust you to enhance their value in the business.

As part of succession planning, you need to consider the effect that any changes will have on the business, as well as any additional burdens that will need to be met and the resources required to meet them.

What will I need to do to achieve this?

Assuming that you would like to assess the potential of freeing up an element of equity value in your business, the first issues to consider are:

- the people you want to be your successors and how to approach them;
- how much value can be obtained;
- what you can expect afterwards.

Successors

There are often key people in your business whom you rely on but who have little or no direct stake in the ownership of the business. They may already be formal directors or people you have identified as being crucial to the future.

What is important is being able to approach them and to discuss and listen to their interest levels without committing yourself or the business to anything that cannot ultimately be delivered. Your discussions also need to be carried out in a way that will ensure that their enthusiasm and commitment are maintained even if the plans do not come to fruition.

Younger family members may be the obvious successors, but care should be taken to ensure that the dynamics of the business are not affected. The key here is succession for the business, not just share ownership changes between generations.

If there is no direct successor within the business, the options may include introducing an outside candidate, perhaps through recruitment or a formal management buy-in. In many cases, management buy-ins are funded by new debt from a bank, and selling shareholders retaining a significant stake, replacing the need for a private equity investor.

Value

The value that you can expect to receive may vary according to:

- The intrinsic value of the business you have created and its prospects. Whilst the value that the business might achieve on the open market will have a bearing on the transaction, often in succession situations the dynamics between the parties can be different and the price may reflect this.

- The ability of successors to participate in the ownership. This is not just their financial capacity but personal preference. The fact that you identify them as a candidate does not mean they will necessarily want to accept the challenge or will gain the confidence of financial backers.
- Your expectations of what you want now! A realistic assessment of the 'like', 'want', and 'need' levels at the outset will help set expectations for later in the process.
- The ability of the business and the new management team to find the right blend of finance and financing partners.
- Any business-specific issues such as pension deficits, existing debt levels or reliance on key customers.

The amount of flexibility shareholders have in terms of immediate cash requirement and timing of any further payments can help to improve the overall terms significantly.

Post-transaction

After the transaction you may still be a major stakeholder in the business but you should have received an amount of capital that will allow you to change aspects of your personal life – maybe not needing to work a seven-day week, or being able to take the long holiday you have always promised yourself.

Unless it is your absolute goal to carry on doing the same thing, we strongly recommend that any succession planning that gives you an element of value should also enable controlling management to have the freedom to make changes to the way in which the business is run.

Ultimate exit?

In any partial exit, clearly you will retain an equity interest. You will have therefore a more than healthy interest in the new team's business plan, performance and their exit horizons. This should be compatible with your overall plan for a complete exit, and, hopefully, a second significant realization of value.

What should I do now?

It's never too early to start planning. If you are interested in exploring ways in which a managed succession plan could benefit you and your business, ensuring a compelling future and realizing value, start planning now. The earlier you start the process, the greater the range of options available to you.

Stephen Harris has spent more than 20 years in the business advisory sector helping owner-managed businesses, covering equity and debt raises as well as advising on acquisitions and disposals, including those from recovery positions. He is a Director of Corporate Finance in Mazars' Milton Keynes office.

Mazars acts for some of the fastest-growing entrepreneurial companies in the United Kingdom, offering a complete range of accountancy and business advisory services, including audit and assurance, tax advisory and compliance, corporate recovery and insolvency, consulting, forensic and investigations, corporate finance and financial services for private individuals. Contact details are as follows:

Tel: 01908 664466
e-mail: stephen.harris@mazars.co.uk
www.mazars.co.uk

Tax target: 10 per cent

It pays to think well in advance about how you will be taxed on the disposal of any assets, says Nigel Landsman at haysmacintyre

Paying tax at more than 10 per cent on the sale of your business? Why? With careful planning you should be able to ensure that the ownership of your business qualifies for capital gains tax business asset taper relief (BATR), resulting in an effective rate of tax of 10 per cent.

Taper relief

Taper relief was introduced for disposals of capital assets after 5 April 1998. The rates and qualifying conditions for BATR have changed a number of times before we arrived at today's relief. The relief currently reduces the taxable gain by 50 per cent (an effective rate of tax of 20 per cent for a 40 per cent taxpayer) after one whole year of ownership and 75 per cent (an effective rate of tax of 10 per cent for a 40 per cent taxpayer) after two whole years of ownership.

Business asset taper relief

In order to achieve the 10 per cent tax charge, the asset must be a business asset qualifying for BATR throughout the period of ownership (which is the period after 5 April 1998). Currently, business assets must fall within one of the following categories:

- shares in an unquoted (including AIM) trading company or the holding company of a trading group;

haysmacintyre

vision through partnership

Nurturing your business

- Like you, we will nurture your business to help it grow

- Yet we understand that our job is to make it easy for you to devote as much energy as possible to the business – not the accounts or the tax man

- At a moment's notice you can call on our team of Chartered Accountants, tax advisors and other specialists for the full range of compliance, advisory and transaction support services

- To avoid the pitfalls, you can rely on our many years' experience working successfully with new and growing businesses in all types of areas both here and overseas

- You'll get straightforward explanations of the options for raising finance and guidance – whether with banks, private finance or the public markets

- You'll get help balancing the long term with the day-to-day issues and how they interact with your personal wealth and objectives

- As you would expect, we provide the usual services efficiently yet we try to look at things differently to provide ideas that have real value

- Our partners are friendly, accessible and keen to get to know you and your business

- And you won't have to pay the earth

So nurture your business, call haysmacintyre today for an informal, confidential and entirely without obligation discussion.

Graham Elliott
gelliott@haysmacintyre.com
020 7969 5610

Andrew Broome
abroome@haysmacintyre.com
020 7969 5519

Neil Simpson
nsimpson@haysmacintyre.com
020 7969 5512

haysmacintyre
Fairfax House
15 Fulwood Place
London
WC1V 6AY

T 020 7969 5500
F 020 7969 5600
E marketing@haysmacintyre.com
W www.haysmacintyre.com

- shares in a listed trading company that employs the individual owning the business asset;
- shares in a company in which the individual is able to exercise at least 5 per cent of the voting rights;
- an asset used for the purposes of a trade carried on by an individual, a partnership of which the individual is a partner, an individual's qualifying company or by a person carrying on a trade who employs the individual.

If the asset does not qualify for BATR for the whole period, then it is 'tainted'. Where there is tainting of the asset, the period of ownership is time-apportioned between periods qualifying for BATR and tainted periods that do not qualify for BATR but instead qualify for ordinary taper relief, with the appropriate taper relief being given for the gain attributable to each period.

Tax planning

A lot of assets will have a tainted period of ownership arising from previous periods of non-qualification as a business asset (whether due to the earlier, stricter BATR qualification rules or to an earlier period of non-trading) or as a result of the trading activities diminishing or ceasing, so planning is required to try to eliminate or minimize the tainted periods. Most often the tainting will occur as a result of non-trading activities becoming substantial (which Her Majesty's Revenue & Customs (HMRC) defines as more than 20 per cent). This will happen where, for example, a trading company reduces its trading activity, perhaps because it is winding down the trade, or has merely taken the decision to invest in property or let former trading property.

When looking at the substantial test, HMRC will consider the following features:

- the amount of investment income as a proportion of total income;
- the value of assets used in non-trading activities compared to the value of those used in trading ones;
- time spent on the non-qualifying part of the business as opposed to the business as a whole;
- the business in its entirety.

It is possible to obtain HMRC's view of whether a company qualified as a qualifying company for BATR purposes during its previous accounting period.

Where an asset is transferred between spouses 'living together', the transferee will take over the transferor's period of ownership. However, where the transferor is entitled to BATR and the transferee is not, then the entitlement to BATR will be tainted. If this is the case, then a transfer back to the transferee, prior to sale of the asset, should be considered.

The activities the business asset is used for should therefore be reviewed to ensure that the non-trading activities are not allowed to become sufficiently large to be substantial, thereby tainting the BATR available.

When considering the disposal of an asset, it is advisable to consider the availability of the full rate of business asset taper relief well in advance of any disposal so as to ensure there is sufficient time to action any planning necessary.

Nigel started his career with HM Revenue and Customs giving him a knowledge and understanding of how it operates.

Nigel specializes in partnerships and private clients, where he advises on all areas of personal tax and trusts including inheritance tax planning, capital gains, tax planning and tax issues relating to non UK residents.

Nigel contributes to both external and internal publications, in particular to technical updates produced by the firm and he speaks at internal seminars. His specialist knowledge in personal taxation advice, and personable attitude, means he is able to translate complex technical matters into basic English.

haysmacintyre, Chartered Accountants and tax advisers, comprises 23 partners and 130 staff based in Holborn, London. It provides high quality auditing and assurance, business and personal taxation, corporate finance, financial planning and other business support services.

Around 40% of the firm's business is within the corporate sector – small and medium sized enterprises many of which are within the property, media and entertainment, sports, motor trade and manufacturing sectors, 25% is for charitable and not for profit organizations and the remainder is for professional practices and private individuals.

haysmacintyre is a founding member of MSI, an international network of accountants and lawyers with over 200 firms in 90 countries.

haysmacintyre
Fairfax House
15 Fulwood Place
London
WC1V 6AY

Tel: 020 7969 5500
Fax: 020 7969 5600
E-mail: marketing@haysmacintyre.com
www.haysmacintyre.com

Index of advertisers